Aunt Eleanor's Men

Aunt Eleanor's Men

A True Story of
One Woman's
Pursuit of Grandeur

V.E. Palm

with Cynthia Teal

Published 2017
Printed in the United States of America
Print ISBN: 978-0-9990060-0-9
E-ISBN: 978-0-9990060-1-6
Library of Congress Control Number: 2017914035

Cover design by Tabitha Lahr
Interior design by Tabitha Lahr
Front cover photo courtesy of the author
Back cover photo © Sunshine Special near Forney, Texas, 1929, University of North Texas Libraries, the Portal to Texas History, texashistory.unt.edu, courtesy Museum of the American Railroad.

For information, address: vepalm3@gmail.com

To my grandmother Florence McKinnie Elsner, 1885–1971

Contents

Book One: The Family

Book Two: Cynthia Tells Her Story

Aunt Eleanor's Timeline

(1875–1941)

1874: Eleanor McKinney is born in Ohio. Her mother is Genevieve Hastings. No certificate of birth has been found.

1882, June 27: Eleanor's father, Albert McKinnie, marries Ida Gilman in Portland, Oregon.

1886: Eleanor resides with her father in Portland, Oregon, as Miss Christina McIntire, age eleven.

1899, April 19: Eleanor marries William Charles Toomey in St. Paul, Minnesota.

1904, September 18: Eleanor and William Toomey are divorced.

1905, January: Eleanor moves to New York and becomes a stage showgirl, Margaret Busby.

1906, October 10: Eleanor marries Ben Teal, theater stage manager, in Boston.

1907, January: The Teals live at Fifty-Ninth Street West, New York.

1907, October 6: Ben Teal Jr. is born in New York City.

1908, July 20: Eleanor Teal is arrested and held for subornation of perjury in the Frank and Helen Gould divorce case.

1909, February 23–26: Eleanor is tried and convicted in the Gould case.

1909, March 10: Eleanor is sentenced to one year on Blackwell's Island, New York.

1909, December: Eleanor is released from Blackwell's Island Prison.

1913: The Teals adopt Agnes Fitzgerald (Cynthia Marie Teal), age nine.

1917, April 20: Ben Teal dies in New York at the age of sixty-two.

1917, summer: Eleanor and her two children leave New York for Texas. She meets Dr. George Edgar Paddleford in Galveston.

1917, December 18: Eleanor marries George Paddleford in Houston, Texas.

1918–21: The Paddlefords live in Los Angeles, California. George Paddleford is an executive of the Mexican Petroleum Company. He spends most of his time in Mexico as superintendent of the Tampico oil fields.

1921, September–October: George Paddleford confirms Eleanor's real identity. Eleanor, Cynthia, and Ben Jr. return to New York. They reside at the Plaza Hotel.

1921, November 15: Eleanor and George Paddleford separate.

1921, November 15: Cynthia Marie Teal marries Edward Jeffries Naughton in New York.

1921–22: Eleanor and partners Naughton and Brownlow run a gambling den, known as Brownies, on Fifty-Fifth Street, off Fifth Avenue, in New York.

1922, January: Paddleford divorce court depositions take place in Los Angeles.

1922, March: Police raid and close Brownies gambling den. Eleanor, Cynthia, and Ben Jr. leave New York by ship for Europe.

1922, April: Eleanor, Cynthia, and Ben Jr. arrive at the Crillon Hotel in Paris.

1922, June 11: Eleanor is arrested and jailed in Vienna, Austria, for obtaining goods by fraud. Charges against her come from merchants in Lucerne, Paris, and Vienna. Eleanor is extradited to Lucerne, Switzerland.

1922, November: Cynthia publishes her story which is syndicated in newspapers.

1922, December 12: Eleanor is acquitted by the criminal court of Lucerne.

1923, January 6: Eleanor is reported ill in a Switzerland prison.

1923, February 15: Eleanor returns to Los Angeles. Eleanor seeks to defend herself in George Paddleford's divorce decree.

1923, March 23: Eleanor resides at 6864 Bonita Terrace, Los Angeles. Pasadena police raid the house for the return of furniture and goods delivered by Pasadena merchants. Eleanor is jailed for grand larceny.

1923, May 19: Eleanor fails to appear in court. A bench warrant is issued. Her lawyer tells the court that she is in Portland, Oregon, looking for her fifteen-year-old son.

1923, June 23: A second bench warrant is issued for Eleanor's arrest in the Pasadena grand larceny charge. Eleanor's lawyer presents a letter of an apology from Eleanor mailed from Mexico City.

1923, July 20: George Paddleford is given a decree of divorce in California. Ben Teal Jr., age fifteen, is a witness. Eleanor remains a fugitive from justice.

1924, November 20: Eleanor and Cynthia are arrested in Zurich, Switzerland, on suspicion of swindling. Eleanor is charged with defrauding a hotel clerk of 150 francs.

1926, May 29: Eleanor and Cynthia are arrested at the border in Innsbruck, Austria, for fraudulent possession of goods from a Berlin shop. Eleanor claims to be the wife of W. G. Howells, a wealthy Egyptian shipbuilder, later referred to as Wilson Howells Roberts.

1926, December 19: Cynthia is recorded as a passenger on a ship from Glasgow, Scotland, to New York. It was the last time her name appeared in the public record.

1927, March 23: Eleanor arrives in New York from Glasgow, Scotland.

1927, October 28: Eleanor is found in Salinas, California. She has been held for six weeks, under the name of Grace Potter, on charges of swindling goods from a shopkeeper in Carmel.

1927, November 21: Eleanor is tried and found guilty of defrauding a Carmel shopkeeper.

1927, November 28: Eleanor is sentenced to serve one to fourteen years in San Quentin prison.

1928, January 26: Eleanor is visited in San Quentin Prison by Dr. F. L. R. Silvey, a former associate of George Paddleford. He proposes marriage.

1928, March 8: Dr. Silvey pursues his intentions to marry Eleanor. The San Quentin warden denies the request.

1928, May 21: Eleanor is paroled and released from San Quentin and faces a new trial in Salinas. The judge grants her parole, thanks to the efforts of Dr. Silvey.

1929, April: Eleanor is arrested for passing bad checks in Santa Barbara. She is tried and again imprisoned at San Quentin.

1930, October 16: Eleanor is paroled from San Quentin after serving eighteen months.

1931, January 30: Eleanor marries John Chauncey Fawcett of Brooklyn, New York, in Nassau, Bahamas. They live at the Hotel Ambassador in New York City.

1931, March: Eleanor and Fawcett separate after an argument. Eleanor goes to Europe.

1931, March: San Quentin parole officer Ed Whyte seeks information on Eleanor's whereabouts.

1931, April: Eleanor claims to have been dining with Benito Mussolini in Rome when she received a telegram from John C. Fawcett stating, "Genevieve Paddleford, unmasked."

1931, May 23: Eleanor is arrested in Carlsbad, Austria, for attempted fraud.

1931, September: Ed Whyte receives a letter from Eleanor, postmarked Kingston, Canada.

1931, December 19: John Fawcett is granted an annulment of marriage.

1931, December 20: Eleanor gives a news interview in San Francisco. Ed Whyte orders her to stay in San Francisco, per the terms of her parole.

1932, spring: Eleanor is on the run. The Fawcett family reports that they have seen her in Havana, Cuba.

1932, summer: Eleanor stops to visit Florence McKinnie in Havre, Montana.

1932, November 6: Eleanor is back in Los Angeles, where police initiate a widespread search for her on suspicion of unpaid bills.

1933, July: In a letter to Florence McKinnie mailed from Switzerland, Eleanor claims her marriage to J. R. Thompson.

1934: Eleanor is imprisoned at Chambery, France.

1935, late summer: Eleanor is deported to the United States from Switzerland.

1936, September 28: Eleanor is arrested in Pueblo, Colorado, and charged with grand larceny in Seattle. She is sentenced with ten to fifteen years in Washington State Prison.

1938, November 28: Eleanor is credited with helping to solve the notorious Bassett murder case while in prison. She appeals for release but is denied.

1941, September 19: Eleanor dies of nephritis in Washington State Prison at 1:30 p.m. She is buried at Washington State Prison.

Prologue

Sequestered in the folds of family histories in small frontier towns are early stories often forgotten or just not allowed out from hidden places. My great-aunt Eleanor's story was one of those. It was found in Chinook, Montana. Oddly, it had never been included along with the many other stories told and retold at family gatherings. Then, in time, as one family generation succeeded another and questions of family history became more persistent, Aunt Eleanor's story emerged. It was revealed in newspaper clippings stuffed into a manila envelope by my grandmother Florence McKinnie Elsner, one of the early residents of the pioneer town of Chinook. The clippings uncovered episodes in the life of Aunt Eleanor McKinney, my grandmother's sister-in-law, a notorious con woman, who was active across the United States and Europe at the turn of the twentieth century. Over the years, Florence received these clippings from a contact in Chicago. Her name was Alice Moline, referred to only once as Aunt Alice in a found letter written to Florence from Aunt Eleanor. No public record of Alice Moline has been discovered. The mysterious manila envelope, closeted for so many years, was given to me by my mother, Laura McKinnie Palm, before she passed away at the age of 104. It was the first I'd known of it.

Aunt Eleanor was born somewhere near Columbus, Ohio, in 1874. She died in Washington State Prison in 1941. A newspaper at the time of her passing called her "the queen of the gold diggers." Documents show that she married four times, though there are hints that she may have briefly clinched another two. Her story is populated both by the men she married and by others who encountered her wit, beauty, charm, and demons.

This is also the story of Eleanor's daughter, Cynthia Teal, who, in 1913, at the age of nine, was adopted from the New York Foundling Home by Eleanor and her second husband, Ben Teal, a celebrated Broadway theater director. Cynthia went on to become an accomplished singer, but she also became an unwilling confidant in Eleanor's unrestrained extravagance and fraudulent masquerades.

In her own published memoir about her life with Eleanor, Cynthia wrote:

> *I was captivated by the beauty of her in the photographs, and the thought comes to me now of what an amazing career that beauty gave her, what a patchwork of triumphs and downfalls and marriages and millions and fraud she made of her life; what a mean and sordid Fate had claimed her at the end of her pyrotechnic path—arrested for petty swindling, accused of flimflamming shopkeepers, and charged with shoplifting a few yards of lace!*

Aunt Eleanor never settled in one place long enough to call it home. She resided in the finest houses, hotels, and apartments in the United States and Europe, and at times in those countries' most infamous prisons as well.

My curiosity over an envelope stuffed with news clippings led me on a cross-country road trip, in search of clues to Aunt Eleanor's past, starting at the New York Public Library for the Performing Arts and ending at the Oregon Historical Society in Portland, with stops along the way in small Ohio towns, and a visit to the James J. Hill Library in St. Paul, Minnesota. That trip, plus a lot of online research, helped me put together the story you are about to read. My greatest surprise came when I found the published writings of Cynthia Teal, my long-deceased coauthor, who provided startling firsthand accounts and in-depth character descriptions of my infamous aunt.

—V.E. Palm

BOOK ONE:

The Family

Chapter 1:

Albert

Albert McKinney, a smart, gregarious young man eager to leave a disreputable past and seek a fortune elsewhere, pulled up stakes from his home near Columbus, Ohio, in1876, and drifted west, leaving behind his baby daughter, Eleanor, and her unwed mother, Genevieve Hastings.

He arrived in San Francisco and, having learned the shoemaking business from his father, found a job selling boots for a custom-boot maker. There he picked up the art of salesmanship. Three years later, he changed the spelling of his name from McKinney to McKinnie and signed on as a sales agent for the Pacific Mutual Life Insurance Company, founded by the highly regarded California governor, Leland Stanford in 1868.

Albert's history suggests a man motivated by deals and angles, and his success as a salesman was almost immediate. In July 1880, the *Morning Oregonian* announced in its business section, "Mr. A. McKinnie, manager for the Pacific Mutual Life Ins. Co. for Oregon, Washington, and Idaho, is doing a large business for his company. He will call especial attention to the list of policy holders in Portland in a few days, who are comprised of Portland's best businessmen."[1]

Albert resided at Portland's most elegant hotel, the Esmond. During that period, he became acquainted with James Madison Gilman, one of Portland's leading capitalists. He learned that Captain Gilman, as he was known, had an unmarried daughter, Ida Gilman, the only surviving child of the captain and his wife, Laura Frances Gilman. Early in the Gilman marriage, two infants had succumbed to congenital heart failure. The heartbreaking loss of these little ones must have swelled their devotion to Ida.

Albert charmed Ida Gilman, and they were married in the Gilman home on June 26, 1882. The wedding was opulent. The *Portland Oregonian* gave it a full column. Many dignitaries and business leaders were in attendance. The paper noted:

> *Telegrams received from San Francisco and elsewhere were numerous. The bride was elegantly attired in cream-colored brocade satin trimmed with Spanish lace, and veil of illusion. The ornaments were diamonds. Among the presents were a set of elegant and valuable diamonds presented by the bride's father, and, last and most highly prized, a silver set of six pieces from the Oregon Board of Directors of the company which Mr. McKinnie represents.[2]*

The couple spent their honeymoon in Victoria and on the Sound. Albert was thirty-one. Ida was twenty-three.

Back in Ohio, in March 1880, around the time Albert had begun making a name for himself in Portland, a coroner in Fayette County, Dr. E. B. Pratt, signed a death certificate. The deceased was Eleanor's mother, Genevieve Hastings, of Madison Township. The cause of death was reported as "unknown."[3]

Eleanor was born in December 1874 and would have been six years old when Genevieve died. Her formative years in Ohio are a mystery. When the baby was born, Albert's parents—James and Clara McKinney, who lived in Cardington Village, near Columbus—took in the mother and infant. Also living in the household were Albert's younger brother, Rudolph, and younger half sister, Clara. It is interesting to note that sometime after Albert's departure in 1876, records reveal that the McKinney

Ida Gilman McKinnie, 1882

family relocated seventy miles north to Fremont, Ohio. Albert's brother, Rudolph, also a shoemaker, went on to Chicago, where he married shortly thereafter. The Chicago relatives will appear briefly later in Eleanor's story.

Folks in the 1800s were always picking up and seeking new opportunities. However, the James McKinney family had lived in Cardington Village for a number of years, and it seems odd that they would all have left there at about the time baby Eleanor and her mother were taken into their home. Perhaps there was an aura of suspicion, relentless gossip, or shame surrounding the unwed mother and child. In any event, the family never returned to Cardington.

It is unknown whether Genevieve and Eleanor joined the family from Cardington to Fremont. It seems likely that Genevieve, instead, took her child to Madison Township in Fayette County, where they may have lived until Genevieve died about four years later in March 1880. What happened to Eleanor after her mother's death is anyone's guess. The logical and most likely answer is that she was placed in an orphanage. Did Albert make these arrangements for Eleanor from Portland, Oregon, and did he make any promises? Apparently so. Two years after her mother's death, Eleanor was found living with her father in Portland under an assumed name.[4]

Eleanor appears to have been present at the wedding of Albert and Ida. Ida gave birth to a son a year later. They named him Gilman after his grandfather, Captain James Madison Gilman. Six years later, a daughter was born, named Laura after her grandmother, Laura Frances Gilman.

Eleanor's arrival in Portland points to Albert's having made the journey back to Ohio, with Eleanor then accompanying him on the return. Travel at this time would have employed both river steamship and passenger trains. The Northern Pacific transcontinental train did not yet reach all the way to Portland.[5]

Shortly after Eleanor's arrival in Portland, a new name, Christina McIntire became associated with the name Albert McKinnie. It first appeared among the list of Albert and Ida's wedding guests. Christina McIntire was subsequently listed frequently in the Portland directories from 1885 to 1891 as living in the same residences as Albert McKinnie. And, most telling, Christina McIntire was named a beneficiary in the James Madison Gilman will: "To Christina McIntire, who for several years has lived with my family (if she continues to live with us until my death), $1,000.00."[6] An extraordinary sum at the time.

Christina was surely Eleanor. Why the name Christina McIntire? Was Albert keeping his daughter a secret, not wanting to expose his having had a daughter out of wedlock? Perhaps he was afraid of again raising the spectacle of shame his family had been subjected to back in Ohio.

There is no record of a Christina McIntire's having lived in Portland before Albert's marriage to Ida in 1882; neither did she appear in any directory after Captain Gilman's death in 1891. Eleanor, it appears, left Portland at the age of seventeen, left Portland with a thousand-dollar inheritance and didn't look back.

She had witnessed the deaths of the elders, Laura and Captain Gilman, but her departure from Portland would have left her unaware of other family tragedies yet to come.

Chapter 2:

Gilman

On July 13, 1891, the *Oregonian* announced that Captain James Madison Gilman, at the age of sixty-five, had died of heart failure.

DEATH OF CAPTAIN GILMAN
Known Pioneer Passes Away After a Long Illness
Captain J. M. Gilman, a well-known pioneer resident of this city, who had been in poor health for some time, died of heart failure at 11:45 yesterday forenoon, aged 65 years. Captain Gilman was a native of New Hampshire and came to San Francisco in 1849 on a ship which brought out the machinery for the first steamboat which ran on the Sacramento River. He put the steamboat on the river and acted as the engineer for some time. He came to Portland in 1852, and since that time resided here continuously. He was an engineer on river steamers here in the early days, and was associated with Messrs. Ainsworth, Reed, and Thompson in organizing the Oregon Steam Navigation Company. He accumulated considerable property, among which is the hotel on First Street which bears his name. The Gilman house values to about $250,000. His wife died within the past year, and he leaves an only daughter, the wife of Mr. A. McKinnie. The funeral will take place tomorrow, at an hour and place to be named hereafter.[1]

The financial panic of 1890 was well under way when the captain died, and the Gilman family fortune was faltering. Albert, in the meantime, had taken charge of the family fortune and properties.

At the time of the captain's death, his extensive holdings were highly leveraged. His will indicated a meager $742 remaining in cash. From her father's will, Ida was to retain a monthly trust of $400, to be paid out of the estate. There appears to have been a sizable income stream available from various real estate assets, including rental income from the famous Gilman House. However, numerous creditors and lien holders initiated claims against the proceeds. These and other mounting failures pointed to Albert's deleterious management of the family assets. In the 1890 census, Albert was listed as a "speculator."

There is enough narration in the captain's will to indicate that Albert McKinnie did indeed speculate recklessly with Captain Gilman's money. For example, he mortgaged seven thousand deeded acres of valuable virgin timber located in Chehalis County, Washington. The will stated, "A. McKinnie hadn't enuf money to redeem the land and it went to the insurance company." The insurance company was the same Pacific Mutual Life Insurance Co. of which Albert McKinnie was an agent. One might well guess that this company was a conduit for laundering Captain Gilman's fortune into high-risk speculation. In those days, there was plenty of freewheeling going on throughout the country.[2]

Probate tied up the court for more than three years. Then, in the midst of all this, just twenty-eight months after her father's death, Ida succumbed on December 2, 1893, days after the birth of an infant son who died in childbirth. The *Oregonian* reported, "Mrs. A. McKinnie, the last of the Gilman family, died at her residence on Alder Avenue yesterday afternoon. She had been ill with heart disease for nearly a month. Her death was sudden and unexpected."[3]

Ida was thirty-four when she died. She and Albert had been married for just eleven years. Her passing left Albert with two children: Gilman, ten, and Laura, three. The Gilman deaths had come in too rapid a sequence: Mrs. Gilman's in 1890, the captain's in 1891, and Ida's and her infant's in 1893.

By the winter of 1893–94, Albert McKinnie had lost his Gilman family and had squandered the family fortune. He faced a mountain of debt and the care of two small children. He fled Portland for Wyoming. But before he departed, he placed his little girl, Laura, only five, at Saint Mary's boarding school.

Sadly, Laura did not live long. After only a year in the orphanage, she died of a heart aneurism—or, perhaps more descriptively, a broken heart—on November 11, 1896. It is not known whether Albert was notified or if any attempt was made to reach him. The internment permit was signed, "Cleveland Rockwell, Guardian." Cleveland Rockwell was apparently the family lawyer, as his name appears several times in the Gilman will.

A scathing article in a San Francisco newspaper reported the death of Laura, "a motherless little girl," laying blame on Albert's conduct as a father. The article stated that after Laura was placed in the orphanage, "Mr. McKinnie promised to pay for her tuition, but the sisters never heard from him again."[4]

Young Gilman, at the time of his sister's death, was thirteen. His father had already left Portland for Wyoming. His grandparents and his mother had died. And his older half sister, Eleanor, had forsaken the family and departed from Portland with a purse full of money. All of the illness around him, the deaths, and his father's absence had occurred within the space of six years. These were the dark shadows of Portland that stalked Gilman's early life.

Gilman had been left in the hands of an older couple, William and Heppi Spaulding, who were close friends of the Gilman family. William Spaulding and James Gilman were charter members and longtime trustees of the First Unitarian Church and active in local charities. Laura McKinnie's funeral was held in the Spaulding home.[5]

Albert's story, his intentions, his recklessness, and his apparent lack of parental character comprise a dark well of suspicion. He withdrew from a family in Ohio, expediently charmed and married the daughter of a wealthy Portland family, acted as an opportunistic agent for an insurance company in control of the family assets, co-opted his father-in-law into speculative land deals, mounted a hasty departure from Portland, leaving behind numerous creditors, and buried the three members of the prominent Gilman family who had embraced him. Finally, Albert McKinnie took liberty of his Portland children, as he had earlier taken liberty of Eleanor and Genevieve Hastings in Ohio.

One may observe that if the Gilman family of Portland had not welcomed Albert McKinnie to their home in 1882, its members might surely have enjoyed longer, more secure and more productive lives. However, these were the times when the vast country was opening up and on the move, and when family histories were being made and remade by chance meetings and auspicious arrivals. In this regard, the history of the Gilman-McKinnie family seemed particularly destined.

In his favor, after gravitating to the mining fields of southern Wyoming, Albert did not forget his son, nor did he forget Eleanor. Although no letters of Albert's were ever found, other letters, written later by Gilman and Eleanor, help surmise that Albert corresponded with Eleanor and arranged to have Gilman reside with her and her new husband, William Toomey, in St. Paul, Minnesota.

At the age of sixteen, Gilman said goodbye to the Spaulding family in Portland and boarded the *Eastbound Flyer*, arriving at St. Paul in the summer of 1900, where he was greeted by his half sister, Eleanor, and her new husband, William Toomey. Gilman remained with Eleanor and William for a year, during which time he attended St. Paul Central High School. Then, in early June 1901, at just seventeen, he boarded the westbound *Great Northern Flyer* heading for Chinook, Montana, a small town located in far North-Central Montana on the path of the Great Northern Railroad. Except for the regular passing of trains pulling passengers and freight across the endless Great Plains from St. Paul to Seattle, Chinook was isolated by the vast emptiness of Canada to the north and by the ancient, volcanic Bear's Paw Mountains to the south.

On the morning of his arrival, Gilman McKinnie was the lone passenger to disembark in Chinook. After two nights on the train, he eagerly anticipated a new adventure. Very likely, spring rains had left Chinook's main street in mud, and Gilman, wearing new boots, would have made his way gingerly up the hill from the depot. Lining the main street were several buildings—two hotels, a livery, a couple of saloons, a drugstore, a clothing store, and three general stores—and visible farther down was a Catholic church. A few horses and wagons idled along the route.

Main Street, Chinook, Montana, circa 1890

O'Hanlon Store, circa 1890

Gilman McKinnie, 1904

Florence McKinnie, 1904

Gilman looked for the Thomas O'Hanlon general store. He didn't know a soul in town, but in his pocket was a letter of introduction from Eleanor's husband, William Toomey, private secretary to James J. Hill, the builder and owner of the Great Northern Railroad. The letter was addressed to Henry O'Hanlon, who had recently taken over the store upon the death of his brother, Thomas. Thomas O'Hanlon had been a well-known pioneer in that part of Montana, and a close friend of James J. Hill. The letter was to assure Gilman a job in the thriving O'Hanlon business, which it did.

Gilman would flourish in Chinook. He had a companionable personality and ambition that won him many friends and set in motion a vibrant business. Like his father, he sought opportunity and enjoyed rapid success. Three years after he arrived, he fell in love with Florence Hankey, one of the sought-after girls in Chinook. They married on August 15, 1904, in a double ceremony with Florence's sister, Ethel, and Gilman's friend Earl Richards. Over the next seven years, four McKinnie children were born: Kenneth, Evelyn, Laura, and Ben.

Eleanor never forgot her half brother, Gilman, and seems to have corresponded from time to time with his wife, Florence. We shall learn later that Eleanor even made a surprise visit to Chinook in the fall of 1916.

Chapter 3:

William

Eleanor arrived in Portland, Oregon, at the age of about seven in 1882, and left at about the age of seventeen in 1891. Portland was where she spent her teenage years, and Portland shaped her future. It was a city founded by the likes of Captain James Madison Gilman, one of the many New England Yankees who arrived after the folks from the Midwest had traveled the famed Oregon Trail in search of rich farmland. The New England investors, recognizing Portland's importance as an inland port surrounded by a mother lode of natural resources, arrived with clutches of money, piety, thrift, discipline, and ambition. They built the churches, and the industries of trade, banking, and transportation, and Portland developed into a booming city.

Amid the growth of worldwide shipping, Portland's population tripled and tripled again. Included among its residents was a hard class of roustabouts, prospectors, lumberjacks, Chinese laborers, and seamen. Following close behind came saloon-keepers, gambling sharks, red-light madams, prodigal sons, and all manner of con artists and fleecers. These last gathered in Portland's haven of disrepute known as the North End, where small fortunes came and went. The neighborhood's most notorious business was that of the Shanghai, which operated with impunity for nearly fifty years. Unwary young arrivals, stupefied by laced booze, would awake onboard one of the merchant sailing vessels to a life of grueling seamanship while the Shanghai agent collected a hefty fee. Anyone venturing into the North End for excitement, adventure, and debauchery where drunkenness and ribaldry were the rule, might well have risked life and limb.

Eleanor, as Christina McIntyre, following her arrival in 1882, is documented as having lived with her father and his spouse, Ida, at two different residences, probably rentals. Then, after Mrs. Gilman's death on August 20, 1890, the McKinnie family moved in with Captain Gilman at 273 Alder Street. The *Oregonian* reported that Captain Gilman, who died only months later, on July 12, 1891, had been in poor health.

Although Eleanor's adolescent years were connected to the Gilman household and the sickness and deaths that occurred there, she would have also enjoyed her independence, enough to explore the frolicking environs of her wide-open, rambunctious city. Her curiosity might have beckoned her to skirt around Chinatown's nameless, spider-webbed alleys and venture into Portland's wicked North End. More likely, though, she would have been captured by Portland's numerous theaters. Portland had its own Broadway, along which bustled the Pantages Family Theatre, Cordray's Opera House, the New Market Theater, and a number of bawdy variety stages, such as the one in the capacious Erickson Saloon.

It was in one of those theaters that Eleanor, for the first time, encountered the young, vivacious actor Ben Teal, who was making his way through the West Coast theater venues of San Francisco and of Portland and Eugene, Oregon. Ben Teal, older than Eleanor by about seventeen years, was on his way to becoming one of the most successful early Broadway theater directors in New York City. Eleanor was not shy. Indeed, she would have made herself known. Her acquaintance with Ben Teal would not end in Portland.

Eleanor left Portland around 1891, in likely pursuit of a life in theater. There was a long stretch before her name appeared again. Somewhere along the way, she met her first husband, William Toomey. Most likely, it was in New York, where she seems to have started her career as a show-girl. There is no notice of her having success as an actress. A pulp fiction writer, in 1941, reviewed Eleanor's life in an article entitled, "The Jade of Diamonds." He wrote that "any burlesque director would have welcomed her curves in his stable. To top this off, she had a personality which marked her as an individual who expected a far better part than dancing in a chorus."[1]

In 1899, Eleanor chose a different role, as that of wife to a handsome, promising business executive from St. Paul, Minnesota. William Toomey was employed as the private secretary to James J. Hill, who founded and owned the Great Northern Railroad. As such, William was a well-paid rising star in one of the nation's premier industries.

Eleanor and William were married on April 19, 1899, at St. Mary's Church in St. Paul, Minnesota. She was twenty-four, William twenty-nine. The young couple could not have had a brighter or more secure future. The wedding ceremony was performed at seven o'clock in the morning, followed by a breakfast reception at the home of the groom's younger brother, John Toomey. Many prominent guests attended, and the *St. Paul Globe* glowingly described William as well-known and exceedingly popular young man," and Eleanor as "most becomingly gowned in her going-away dress of a dark-brown broadcloth. She wore a picture hat of white satin, covered with fancy braid and trimmed with turquoise blue velvet and pink carnations. She carried a white velvet prayer book."[2]

The marriage also marked Eleanor's first appearance in a public record since she had left Portland, and some very odd and curious details came to light. Her name was given as Eleanor McKinnie Forester Gilman. Where had the name Forester come from? As for her last name, she claimed title to the Gilman family history. She also took on her father's spelling: McKinnie. The *Globe* referred to her as the daughter of James Gilman, a prominent citizen of Honolulu, and one of the original Forty-Niners of the California gold rush. This was partly true. James Gilman was, indeed, a prominent citizen and a Forty-Niner, but not of Honolulu. Neither was he Eleanor's father. He was Albert McKinnie's father-in-law. Eleanor chose to dress the facts to suit her new persona.

The extraordinary early-morning wedding was to accommodate a quick honeymoon getaway by rail to tour the cities of Seattle, Portland, and San Francisco. The paper said that the couple left by private Pullman on that day, and that they would meet her "father," Mr. Gilman, in San Francisco. William was in for some surprises, not the least of which was that his beautiful and charming bride was a compulsive liar.

When honeymooners William and Eleanor returned to St. Paul from their three-week tour of the Northwest, they moved into a large, gracious Victorian house at 642 Lincoln Avenue. They also returned to a city reveling in the wonder of its own "gilded age."

James Hill had moved his large family into the famous Hill mansion known as the Summit, a magnificent red sandstone Romanesque home that dominated other fashionable hilltop structures overlooking the city. St. Paul and Minneapolis were the booming twin cities from which James J. Hill launched, by way of the Great Northern Railroad, an expansive agricultural and mining empire that crossed five country-size states all the way to Puget Sound. Jim Hill was the genius builder and singular driving force that moved millions of immigrants into that grand place. He became known as the Empire Builder, and multitudes would share in the accumulation of his vast wealth and heady endeavors.

Eleanor would have seen herself as born for the gilded age and as a princess of the empire. As such, she could not settle for the life of a Victorian housewife. Indeed, a St. Paul directory placed William and Eleanor in six different residences, all within five years. Eleanor's favorite abode appears to have been the fancy Aberdeen Hotel. Not long after her arrival, she would have observed with envy the Hill family living in luxury on the bluff overlooking St. Paul. It has been written about James Hill that, while conducting his business expenses in a somewhat spartan manner, he spared no expense in offering his family a lavish lifestyle. The Hill family, which included eight children, was an ever-present commodity for the society pages of the local press. Certainly, Eleanor would have devised a role for herself in that world.

Her new husband was in the right position, but William, though paid a generous salary, had not been born into any great wealth. He was a quiet, serious man who had launched himself into a promising career. One of the Great Northern ledgers of 1899 shows his monthly salary as $250, which by any standard of the time would have been substantial.[3] Eleanor, however, having acquired no fiscal discipline, and harboring an insatiable appetite for hotel living, ran recklessly through his paycheck without a glance toward the future.

William and Eleanor's marriage also spawned a twist of irony. The bride was given away by William's brother, John. Like William, John worked for Mr. Hill as a confidant and moneyman, but in a lesser capacity. The Toomeys of St. Paul were well known as a strong Roman Catholic family from Montreal, Canada. John was an honorary life member of the Knights of Columbus, and one of his sisters, Joan, was a nun. Eleanor soon found that she did not fit in well with the Toomeys. Her dissatisfaction brought stress and disruption into the household and caused her and William's estrangement from the Toomey family. As a consequence, William's career faltered. Within four years, John Toomey replaced William as Mr. Hill's private secretary and became the principal advisor to the James Hill family. When he died in 1942, his accomplishments and upstanding character received prominent attention in the local obituary notices.[4]

William's chance at a prominent place in the company had become tarnished. In the course of his emerging career as an executive of the Great Northern, he had encountered the ravishing, enchanting, and all-too-willful Margaret Busby—the stage name for Eleanor McKinney.

The royal battle of the Toomeys began only two years into their marriage. William and Eleanor no doubt began fighting behind closed doors soon after they moved into their first residence, as a consequence of William's attempt at braking Eleanor's rabid spending habit. When the conflict spilled into public venues, William suffered deep mortification. The final injury to this young Catholic gentleman, who had enjoyed considerable respect within the community, was to submit to the humiliation of a divorce, when divorce carried the stigma of public scorn.

The divorce decree was issued in the spring of 1904 and was rich in narrative. William claimed that, beginning early in 1901, Eleanor inflicted cruel and inhuman torment upon him. Her language was "habitually harsh, insulting, unkind, and threatening." She spared no reluctance in offering her abuse publically, often threatening to strike him, and nearly as often succeeding in the attempt.

Dinner party incidents at the Aberdeen Hotel were described in lurid detail. Eleanor must have loved to entertain guests, but, while doing so, she detested the presence of her husband. On one occasion, she heaped "violent, threatening, abusive, and otherwise improper language upon

[him] while dinner was in progress," and was so enraged that she threw and smashed a china cup.

Then, on Thanksgiving Day 1903, another party was held at the Aberdeen. Eleanor again "without provocation became violently enraged against William, addressing him with abusive and threatening language." She grew so unruly that, despite her husband's protests, she walked out on her guests and "left the said apartment for the purpose of taking dinner with a male acquaintance." On a third occasion, in the presence of a visiting friend, Eleanor addressed William with "contemptuous and profane epithets when he refused to promise the serving of liquor at the dinner party about to be held in the apartment that evening."

William went on to complain of numerous incidents of violence at home. Almost daily, Eleanor rushed at him with the intention of scratching, striking, and otherwise doing him bodily harm. Indecent and profane language always accompanied her assaults. Obviously, Eleanor was already well acquainted with the street.

The clinching argument for the divorce, of course, was her dalliance with adultery. While constantly making false charges of adultery in public against William, she, on the other hand, "frequently and without the permission or consent of her husband left the house on long visits to Chicago, New York, and other distant cities, and at one time went off to New York and remained there for five weeks." William went on to complain that Eleanor conducted "clandestine acquaintanceships and correspondence with men unknown to [him], and even received from them large sums of money."

The complaint closed with a chronicling of Eleanor's abuse of credit. She had accumulated "unnecessary articles of jewelry, clothing, and other commodities in thousands of dollars for which William had been compelled to pay . . . this to his humiliation and financial damage." William insisted that he made abundant provision for his wife's proper support, needs, and comfort, but said that, in the end, he had become "permanently and severely injured in health, depressed in spirits, and seriously troubled in mind and body, and that by reason of the conduct of the defendant, as above stated, the affections of the parties heretofore have become alienated, their happiness destroyed, and the legitimate ends of matrimony have not been and cannot be reached or realized." William concluded by stating that he had "always conducted [him]self toward the defendant as a kind, faithful, and affectionate husband."

The divorce was granted on October 14, 1904. Eleanor McKinnie Toomey was "barred forever from all right, title, or interest in all property of whatsoever kind belonging to the plaintiff William Charles Toomey now or hereafter."[5]

Eleanor and William had been living apart for six months prior to the divorce, William having resided at the Ryan Hotel, and Eleanor at the more upscale Aberdeen. Both would leave St. Paul, and make their way separately to New York City. But Eleanor, just before leaving St. Paul, took a parting shot. A prominent St. Paul physician, Dr. J. S. Bettingen, had, at some point in time, fallen under Eleanor's spell. He'd stumbled into an affair with her, and likely, in the intimacy of the moment, offered her marital encouragement. She hired a lawyer and filed a $25,000 breach-of-promise suit against the good doctor in the Ramsey County courthouse.

The Bettingen case opened on June 22, 1905, eight months after Eleanor's divorce from Toomey. Local papers ginned up the trial as a sensation. After all, Mrs. Toomey, the wife of a Great Northern Railroad executive, was a well-known social gadfly around Minneapolis and St. Paul, and her scandalous divorce from Toomey was still fresh in the eyes of the public. The courtroom was packed with local newsmen. Eleanor had brought the case to court and would display her talents. She would have her "stage."

Dr. Bettingen's lawyer, E. L. Durment, came prepared. He effectively skewered her character and her plot to humiliate the doctor. He first called two "hack drovers," who testified that on separate occasions each had taken Mrs. Toomey to a location in town referred to as "a resort on South Washington Street," emphasizing that once a gentleman companion had been with her. This, and other references to her nightlife, suggested that she was, indeed, well acquainted with the more opprobrious parts of town. When asked where she had been living since her divorce, she denied having residence anywhere near that locale but the inference had been made.

The defense also challenged various representations she made before the court.

Suspect, for example, were her real maiden name, her age, her origin, and the spurious accusations of infidelity that she placed on Mr. Toomey. She did, however, confirm her acquaintance with the Gilman family in Portland. She testified that her father had lived in Portland for twenty years, and that she had "lived with him until [she] left school."

"You lived at home?" Mr. Durment asked.

"Yes, with my father, my grandfather, my grandmother, and my brother and sister," she answered promptly.

When Eleanor testified in her redirect, she did, indeed, parade her talents. With a laced kerchief in one hand and a bottle of smelling salts in the other, she sobbed copious tears, weeping that she had been mischaracterized. She was the innocent divorcee who had accepted the promises of Dr. Bettingen, whom she had known for four years. They had become lovers. He had often spent the night with her at the Aberdeen Hotel. He had given her a necklace, et cetera. But the jurors didn't buy her performance. The verdict arrived on the evening of the seventh day, in favor of Dr. Bettingen. A morning headline on page 4 of the *Minneapolis Journal* announced:

MRS. TOOMEY LOSES

No money for Mrs. Eleanor M. Toomey's wounded heart. The jury in the scandalous St. Paul breach of promise case returned in verdict last evening in favor of the defendant, Dr. Joseph W. Bettingen. When the jury reported, Mrs. Toomey was in her room at the Merchants hotel. She heard the newsboys shouting, "Extra, all about the Toomey verdict!" She dispatched a Jap bellboy after a paper. Standing in the hall, breathless with excitement, she grabbed the paper from the boy's hand and read, "Mrs. Toomey Loses Suit." Then she nearly fainted.

"I am not shedding any tears over the verdict," she said last evening. "I bow to the decision of the jury, but I feel that I have been outraged by the statements made against my character. Within a few days I will go to Minnetonka to visit friends and rest up. The trial has been a terrible strain on my

nerves and tired me out. Next fall I shall be in court again and will then sue Dr. Bettingen for slander."[6]

The Bettingen scheme was the beginning of a chain of serial lawyer-client entanglements that would mark Eleanor's long career as a world-renowned mistress of the con. Soon after the trial, she caught a train for New York City. A reporter overheard her say, "St. Paul is nothing but a hick town, anyway."[7]

The scandal of William's divorce placed him in an unbearable position with the Hill family. Even so, he valiantly stayed on in a vain effort to rescue his torn reputation and restore some sense of balance and sanity. He kindled a friendship with someone he'd long admired, Gertrude Sans-Souci, highly regarded as a music professor and an organist at both the Cathedral of St. Paul and Saint Luke's Catholic Church. She also wrote popular songs, "most famously, 'When Song Is Sweet,' a little masterpiece of three pages, a truly folk-like art song in which the flow of melody, the climaxes, the harmony, all act in concert."[8]

William and Gertrude married on August 7, 1907. They moved to New York, where she set up a publishing enterprise for marketing her compositions. She sold one hundred thousand copies of her songs within a decade. William, after several starts, landed a position as an executive at a small film-producing company. A daughter, Ruth, was born in 1910. Then, tragically, on January 19, 1913, Gertrude fell ill with ptomaine poisoning and died. A memorial concert was performed in St. Paul the following year.[9]

On January 17, 1915, William Toomey, now age forty-seven, married once more. She was Jane Elizabeth O'Hara; age twenty-four, from a well-known Brooklyn family prominent in the construction business. They had a son, William C. Toomey, Jr. Then Ruth, William's daughter, for whom the Sans-Souci family had cared, joined the Toomey family.

William seems to have moved from one position of employment to another. He was an officer of the National Surety Company, vice president and general manager of the Mirror Film Company, and vice president and general manager of the Mutual Film Corporation. Then, in 1931, he took a position as an officer of the George Henriques Company, a securities investment firm.

Bad news came in April 1933, when the *New York Times* broke a story on a major stock and mail-fraud case. The New York State attorney general had placed an injunction on the George Henriques Company for making false representations concerning the stocks the company had been selling. William was arrested, along with two other company officers and several salesmen employed by the company. They had been involved in a boiler-room stock sales operation that preyed mostly on women. The public was reported to have purchased as much as $4,500,000 worth of inflated stock.

William and twelve others were found guilty on forty-three counts of mail fraud and conspiracy. William C. Toomey received a sentence of fifteen months in prison. Others received terms from one to three and a half years.[10]

Nothing more was heard from William until the announcement of his death on January 20, 1942. William died in Kings County Hospital in Brooklyn, New York, three weeks before the death of his older brother, John, in St. Paul, at age seventy-two. There was no published obituary for William.

Unlike William, Eleanor McKinney made a quick and extraordinary adjustment to New York City. Less than two years after her arrival in New York, in 1904, she married Broadway's theater director extraordinaire, Mr. Ben Teal.

Chapter 4:

Ben, New York, 1906

In 1905, New York City was approaching the apex of its thunderous population explosion. Almost overnight, the greatest immigrant movement in history would make the metropolis the population center of America. Out of these masses were wrung the many wonderful theatrical, musical, and storytelling talents that enshrined the city as the cultural landmark of the nation. Thousands of people moved onto the island of Manhattan every day. Eleanor McKinney Toomey, divorced, age twenty-nine, was one of them.

The vibrant center of theater and nightlife around the turn of the century was known as the Rialto, stretching along Broadway from Fourteenth to Forty-First Street, then, in short order, extending uptown from Forty-Second to Forty-Seventh Street, taking on the famous sobriquet the Great White Way. It was a mile-long entertainment mecca lit by arc lamps and climaxing around the voluminous gaudy lights of Times Square.

The New York history writer Anthony Bianco, in *Ghosts of 42nd Street*, recounts America's most famous street as having been lined with posh hotels, upscale and low-scale brothels, vaudeville houses, splendorous restaurants known as lobster palaces, and grandiose theater palaces—for example, the Olympia, "which consisted of three opulent auditoriums under a single roof—a huge 2,800 person music hall, and a smaller play house and concert hall—as well as a glass-enclosed roof garden theater up top."[1] Broadway became a river of all sorts of performers who jockeyed for position and dreamed of celebrity, many of whom were showgirls holding out for a chance to trap a rich husband. Among the thousands, Eleanor McKinney Toomey arrived with a consummate familiarity to the Broadway scene.

In St. Paul, at the Bettingen breach-of-promise trial, Eleanor testified that she had performed as a showgirl on the Rialto in the 1890s, before she had married William Toomey. Indeed, it may have been where they had first met. At any rate, having left St. Paul behind, Eleanor resumed her Broadway stage career, at the same time she positioned herself for another grasp at marital good fortune. She was no longer Eleanor; she resumed her stage name, Margaret Busby. To her theater pals, she was just Maggie.

What must it have been like to arrive in Manhattan and walk the Great White Way in the early 1900s? In *Ghosts of 42nd Street*, writer Bianco notes Charlie Chaplin's description of a disappointing daylight landing in New York City:

> *It was somewhat of a letdown. Newspapers were blowing about the road and pavement, and Broadway looked seedy, like a slovenly woman just out of bed. On almost every street corner there were elevated chairs with shoe lasts sticking up and people sitting comfortably in shirt sleeves getting their shoes shined. They gave one the impression of finishing their toilet on the street. Many looked like strangers, standing aimlessly about the sidewalk as if they had just left the railroad station and were filling in time between trains.[2]*

At night, however, Broadway awakened with blazing intermittent flashes of marquee theater lights and the brightly lit facades of the lobster palaces. Bianco recounts a 1911 Broadway travelogue:

> *To the turn-of-the-century New Yorker, 42nd Street was not a mere theater row but center stage of an after-dark pleasure zone nonpareil. "Broadway from 34th Street to 47th Street has been for the last few years the locality where the gay life of*

the metropolis has been most readily seen," Stephen Jenkins observed in his 1911 Broadway travelogue, The Greatest Street in the World. "Here are congregated great hotels, famous restaurants, and theaters. And the brilliant illumination by the countless electric lights has caused this section of the avenue to be called 'the Great White Way'. No stranger has seen New York who has not traversed it."[3]

This was the era of the opulent wealth of the Goulds, the Astors, and the Vanderbilts. It was the era of the Waldorf Astoria; the *New York Times*; the new Times Square; the Ziegfeld Follies; and the famous after-hours haunts of Rector's, Delmonico's, and the Knickerbocker Hotel. It was the era of the first Oscar Hammerstein, the grandfather-pioneer impresario and genius behind the dynamic growth of the New York theater industry, which gave birth to the Syndicate, a monopoly of theater owners who booked hundreds of road shows throughout the country and Europe. In its effect, if not in its wealth, the Syndicate rivaled the great "robber barons" and empire builders of the late nineteenth and early twentieth centuries.

As the theater world thrived, the turn of the century saw the rise of such personalities and greats as Diamond Jim Brady, Will Rogers, Charlie Chaplin, Harry Houdini, W. C. Fields, Buster Keaton, Al Jolson, Lillian Russell, Lillie Langtry, Sarah Bernhardt, Sanford White, and Evelyn Nesbit. Among them was a notable talent and ever-present personality whose fame glowed brightly for several years but then faded into obscurity. His name was Ben Teal.

One can only conjecture where Eleanor, now Margaret, first met Ben. As mentioned, they may have known each other as far back as when Ben performed in Portland, Oregon. When Margaret stepped onto Forty-Second Street in 1905, she already knew her way around and promptly joined a road show that took her to London, whereupon she jumped to another show that was under production by Erlanger and Klaw, the well-known operators of the Syndicate, which was the principal employer of none other than theater manager and director Mr. Ben Teal! Margaret's intentions toward him were swift and certain.

Under Teal's direction, the road show *The Rich Mr. Hoggenheimer* had just completed its tour in London and moved to Boston. While performing in Boston, Ben asked Margaret to marry him. This was only eighteen months after Eleanor's departure from St. Paul. Already she had wrapped herself in marital security for the second time. For Ben, it was his third walk up the aisle. A New York gossip columnist reported:

> *"Oh, sorrow and double gloom! Ben Teal, the man who promised himself to remain single after his second unsuccessful matrimonial venture, is reported to be married again.*
>
> *The word comes from Boston, where Teal is hard at work engaged in preparing 'The Rich Mr. Hoggenheimer' for a season on Broadway. Private telegrams from members of the company state that the ceremony was performed Monday, and that the blushing bride is one of the prettiest members of 'Mr. Hoggenheimer's' chorus."*[4]

Two weeks later, another columnist reported on their arrival in New York:

> *The Ben Teals are back in New York after a rather disjointed honeymoon and are ensconced very charmingly in Central Park South. The happy pair has shown a lot of courage in their choice of home, for they have set up lares and penates in Norma Munro's flat.*
>
> *Everybody is congratulating Mr. Teal on having won a charming wife, and the admiration all the girls feel for Margaret Busby in having landed the coy and experienced Ben Teal amounts to awe and reverence!*[5]

Although Margaret had put the twin cities of St. Paul and Minneapolis behind her, the newspaper boys there continued to follow the adventures of their very own scandalous darling. The *Minneapolis Tribune* reported the following on January 3, 1907:

MRS. BEN TEAL IS GRACIOUS HOSTESS
Woman Who Was Formerly Mrs. Chas. Toomey
Endears Herself High Up in Theatrical Profession.
Gossip from Gotham:

New York, Jan. 3. *A certain luxurious apartment in exclusive Fifty-Ninth Street West is often the scene of many brilliant "functions and socials." These affairs are not only notable because of the many scintillating gems that are displayed but also because the people who assist at them are extremely clever.*

And yet even these two requisites of smart society are of less immediate interest to the readers of these communications than the fact that the hostess at these gatherings is very well known in both Minneapolis and St. Paul. In fact, she was a resident of the latter city for six years, and as the wife of William Charles Toomey, formerly financial man of James J. Hill, was quite the social furor.

She is Mrs. Ben Teal now. Ben Teal, as all who are conversant with things theatrical must know, is the active manager of all the Charles Frohman productions. Mr. Teal married the former wife of Mr. Toomey about three weeks ago in Boston where he was at the time engaged in rehearsing "The Rich Mr. Hoggenheimer" company preparatory to its advent to Broadway, New York.

Mr. Teal must be a man of wonderful resources and power, busy rehearsing the latest Frohman success in Boston town, directing a score of other theatrical ventures here in this country and in London, Mr. Teal yet had time to woo the lady of his choice.

The wedding came as a surprise both to the friends of Mr. Teal and to the friends of Mrs. Toomey, who was known here as Margaret Busby. The former had become inured to the fact that "Ben" was to remain single for the rest of his life, and the latter had become used to speculating as to who was to be the next to succumb to the charms of their clever friend. But they never suspected it would be Ben Teal.

Mrs. Teal is a gracious hostess and has immeasurably endeared herself to those high up in the theatrical profession. On Sunday evenings her home is practically thrown open to the galaxy of theatrical stars shining on Broadway. Last Saturday afternoon Mrs. Teal gave an exquisite tea to a select number from The Rich Mr. Hoggenheimer Company.

The new Mrs. Teal is considered one of the best gowned women in New York, both in theatrical circles and out. She is frequently seen at dinners at Delmonico's and Sherry's and her costumes are always the objects of admiration.

Mrs. Teal will return to the stage next season—not because she has to but from choice—and it is rumored that she will be seen with Dave Warfield as leading lady in a new play.[6]

Ben and Margaret were married in October 1906. Ben was at the height of his career. He was forty-four, she thirty-one. Mr. Ben Teal had just staged his sixty-eighth play. In all, before his death in 1917, he staged eighty-three productions. Because Teal introduced numerous new special effects, lighting techniques, action sequences, and grand costumed spectacles, he became regarded as "the representative general stage director of this country."[7]

Until the advent of Ben Teal and his better-known contemporary David Belasco, staging plays had not been a well-recognized profession. Those who did it were called stage managers. Ben Teal raised the job to a new level and was recognized as the first Broadway theater director.

In a documentary of the theater, *Theater in America*, by Mary Henderson, she wrote that Teal "was without peer in his ability to move large numbers of extras around the stage."[8]

His more highly acclaimed big theater plays included *Hamlet* at the Metropolitan Opera House, *Sleeping Beauty and the Beast*, a highly successful musical, and the production for which he is best remembered, *Ben Hur*.

Ben Hur was performed before 194 New York audiences. One review claimed that "it was the most stupendous stage production in America." The show contained fourteen scenes in six acts. Teal commanded more than three hundred performers, some of them children, and numerous

Ben Teal, circa 1891

Ben Teal, Stage Manager.

Ben Teal, circa 1900

animals, including four teams of horse-drawn chariots that raced on an ingeniously designed treadmill against a moving panorama. The chariot scene was probably the most-talked-about event on Broadway at the time. The *New York Herald* review from November 5, 1899, was ecstatic:

> *The chariot race was more than realistic. It was real! The spectators were seemingly a part of the throng which sat in the great amphitheater at Antioch. The high-spirited horses raced as truly as did ever horses in the dust of the hippodrome. The straining necks, the swiftly moving legs, the foam-flecked breasts were no illusions of the senses. The rocking chariots, the wind-blown garments of the charioteers, the rumbling of the wheels, the clouds of dust, caused those who witnessed that race to lean forward and almost cry out with the multitude. The breaking of an axle, the loss of a wheel, the fall and ruin of Messala, amazed and enthralled. Then when Ben Hur, driver, had won, and the populace lifted up a tumultuous cry, those who were in the theatre joined in the cheers.*[9]

When the company of Klaw and Erlanger brought *Ben Hur* to London, it was, according to Teal, the first time a king of England had sat in the pit of a theater to witness a performance. In the *Sunday Telegraph*, New York, November 1, 1903, Mr. Teal described the performance:

> *I have rarely, if ever, seen an audience so moved from literally the beginning of the play until the final fall of the curtain. As the lights went out and that big theater with its vast auditorium became darkened and the first few notes of the invisible chorus were heard singing of the birth of the Nazarene, a hush fell over the audience, and from that time on until the end of the piece when not silenced and moved by what might be called the religious and majestic side of the drama, the story of which was being most beautifully told and unfolded, cheers and the most vehement applause rewarded the management and the player alike.*

> *At the end of the chariot race, which, by the way, we ran with sixteen horses instead of eight, as here, it seemed to me that pandemonium had broken loose.*
>
> *When the curtain finally fell on the series of tableaux which we present on the Mount of Olivet, for a few seconds there was a hush, then that big, splendid audience broke into cheers which lasted for several minutes.*[10]

Ben Teal remained a titan on Broadway, at least for a time. He was a prodigious, creative genius and a man accustomed to the sustained cheers of the audience. He had secured for himself a successful style of directing that was commanding and disciplined. His reputation was that of a martinet able to manage an army of stagehands and lines of chorus girls. The quality of his work was in demand. In one interview, Ben describes his work with the chorus girl:

> *The chorus girl in a big production has an immense amount of work to do, not the least of which is the necessity, where competition sets a killing pace, to keep herself in the best possible condition. Nothing else will be accepted. She cannot come to rehearsal with heavy eyes and lagging step. She must not stay away. She has simply got to be alert, clear-eyed, quick to apprehend every instruction. The chorus girl is no longer a place where a girl standing and looking pretty has achieved the purpose of her being. A great part of the new chorus girl work, which I must say without egotism was invented by me, requires tremendous assets of endurance and intelligence.*[11]

Ben Teal was a very busy and very affluent celebrity when he and his new bride moved into the expensive Norma Munro flat on Central Park South. Then, just a few months later, they gave it up and moved to even more comfortable digs at the Ansonia. The Teals also acquired, probably by lease, a home in Mamaroneck on the Hudson, and a "cottage" among the ocean mansions in Long Branch, New Jersey.

Margaret Busby, as the new wife of a distinguished man of the New York theater, stepped off the stage as a common chorus girl and assumed recognition as an influential matron of Broadway. She was, for a time, the go-to-girl for those ingénues who pined for the city lights. Certainly, this newfound status and celebrity along the Great White Way would seem enough to have satisfied her ego, as well as her appetite for a life of luxury. Sadly, it was not.

Chapter 5:

Frank

In the spring of 1907, the New York headlines flashed news of the Frank and Helen Gould divorce. The Gould family, starting with the family's patriarch, Jay Gould, represented the elite of New York's high society. Margaret Teal was drawn to the Gould divorce headlines. Intrigue, scandal, and gossip were the nutrients for her ruminations. A foolish and desperate scheme started to brew in her supple mind. It had always been her nature to store away nuggets of unseemly information, and by chance she had something on Frank Gould that could be woven into the Gould case and, if she played her cards right, might ingratiate her to Helen, as well as fill her pockets with some needed cash. The scheme was to frame Frank Gould with infidelity.

Frank Gould was the youngest of six children of Jay Gould, who had risen from a humble farm boy to become one of the robber barons of the late 1800s. He never quite attained the stature of J. P. Morgan, Andrew Carnegie, or J. D. Rockefeller, but, at his death, he had acquired profitable and influential connections with many of the largest railway operations in the country. He left a fortune to his large family, in addition to a spectacular estate, known as the Lyndhurst Castle, on the Hudson River.

Along with a very hefty portion of the vast Gould wealth, Frank inherited his father's cunning and self-centered ambition. He was an avid Francophile and proprietor of numerous French properties and businesses, most of which were casinos and hotels on the French Riviera. He became one of the original intercontinental playboys. When not in Paris

Lyndhurst Mansion, Gould Residence, Tarrytown, NY, circa 1880.

or somewhere on the French Riviera, he was often at the yacht club on Long Island Sound or on his yacht, *Helenita*.

Frank Gould and Helen Kelly met at the Jersey Shore in 1901, had a love-at-first-sight summer romance, and were married in December at the home of Helen's mother in New York City. Frank was twenty-three and Helen just eighteen. Two children followed in quick succession.

Frank and Helen came from different and strongly held religious backgrounds. The Goulds were Presbyterian. The Kellys were Roman Catholic. Helen's mother began to interfere with the children's religious training, insisting on a Catholic upbringing. The mother-in-law situation and Frank's intense jealousy over the homage men paid to Helen's youthful beauty fueled family dissent, and Helen became suspicious of Frank's free movements about the city.

When Frank and his pals took a yachting trip to Nova Scotia, Helen hired a private detective agency to keep an eye on him. The society rumor mill kept Frank in the public eye. There were rumors that he had been keeping questionable company with the up-and-coming Broadway song-and-dance bombshell Bessie DeVoe. The Gould troubles began to break in the *New York Times* in early May 1907.

Margaret Teal had risen as far as any showgirl could expect in the theater world of New York City in 1907 and 1908. But for her, having a place at the apex of Broadway's theater scene was not enough. There was a wide social boundary, a chasm, between the theater world and the world of the really well-to-do, and Margaret was envious. She had also allowed herself to get into desperate financial straits. The wonderful things that money could buy—her jewels, clothes, and furs—gave her life meaning. By July 1908, she was in debt by more than $4,000 (equivalent to $120,000 in today's money). Her creditors were on her tail, and she had already initiated a voluntary petition of bankruptcy. It was revealed in bankruptcy court that twenty-one creditors wanted relief from her spending voracity. Margaret was in debt to the Mrs. Osborn Co. for $1,100 worth of gowns. Apparently, none of this was known to Ben. Some of her creditors knew her only by her old stage name, Margaret Busby.

No other city in the world exhibited a more striking divide between the ends of the economic and cultural spectrum than did the city of New York on Manhattan Island at the turn of the twentieth century. The rich couldn't have been richer, more brash, more powerful, more opulent, and the poor more wretched, filthy, diseased, or crime ridden. The uptown silk-stocking district was far removed from the squalor of the riverfront hovels. The top-tier elites were the Livingstons, Mellons, Roosevelts, Astors, Vanderbilts, Rockefellers, Harrimans, J. P. Morgans, and Goulds. They lived in gracious and spacious luxury mansions. The poor amassed in overcrowded, disease-

Lower East Side, New York, circa 1900

and fire-plagued tenements on the infamous and dangerous Lower East Side. In the middle were the blue-collar and servant classes.

The Teals were of the bohemian class, for which eligibility into high society would have been taboo. Margaret was well fixed in that class, and if only she had been even marginally frugal and responsible, she could have enjoyed an enviable life of her own making. But her insatiable social ambitions got the better of her. She never saw herself as quite good enough.

She took a long look at the fanciful and wonderful world of the rich, and a horrified glance at New York's bleak and bedraggled, and decided that before it was too late she would have to take a long-shot gamble at financial recovery by playing to her advantage Frank and Helen Gould's marital troubles.

New York had become the upper-class-marriage capital of the country. As marriages among these families escalated, new bonds of social acceptance were established and moneyed connections strengthened. But if marriage was the high and proper vehicle for social success, divorce—something scorned and socially detrimental—was the very opposite. Divorce in New York, at the time, could be obtained only on proof of adultery. A divorce trial would be seen as a public disgrace and would seriously dismantle bloodlines and encumber the very important inheritance of money. A clergyman's highest charge was to keep the wayward within marital bonds. But, as these were people who were subject to the discipline of fidelity, they also lived gloriously and lavishly in one another's company and were easy targets for the pleasures of the flesh so readily available in the city. Indeed, the rigors of marital discipline tended to invite the practice of philandering. A mistress would necessarily be kept discreetly behind doors, and, as such, the knowledge of someone's paramour could be contained within a certain amount of social indifference.

Sometimes, though, marital problems became emotionally intolerable and the eruptions boiled over into the public arena. The divorce court offered the needed accommodation. "Marriage at all costs" began to suffer erosion. The thunder of marital discord rumbled under the surface of the inscrutable. The descendants of the Roosevelts, Vanderbilts, Whitneys, Mellons, and others began to suffer matrimonial dissonance that paved the way to the divorce courts.

Margaret Teal kept a curious eye on all of these comings and goings. When the *New York Times* broke the first story about the Goulds' domestic problems in early May 1907, Margaret was four months pregnant. She devoured the early reports with keen interest. Rumors of the young couple's quarrels persisted throughout the year. Then, on April 18, 1908, Frank moved out of the Gould mansion on Fifth Avenue and took up residence in the Plaza Hotel. By this time, Margaret was caring for six-month-old Ben Teal Jr., but she was undeterred. Motherhood would not interfere with her scheming!

Margaret felt certain that she possessed unique leverage in the Gould divorce. In her mind, she was holding an ace in the hole. What she believed and thought she could prove, was that Frank Gould and actress Bessie Devoe, the new star on Broadway, were not only acquainted but embroiled in an illicit affair. Months earlier, Margaret had subleased her apartment at the Glenmore to Miss Devoe! She was certain the apartment was the hotbed of Frank and Bessie's romance. She would find a way to convince Helen Gould that Frank was Bessie's frequent visitor.

Margaret may very well have had the goods, but providing convincing proof would be tricky. She would have to bring others into her confidence. Her first compatriot was Harry Mousley, a private detective and acquaintance. Next was her oldest and closest friend, Julia Fleming, whom she had known from her earlier days in St. Paul. The conspiracy began to take shape. Mousley would contact Helen Gould's lawyers after they had set their trap.

Margaret brought Harry Mousley to her suite at the Wyoming on July 13, 1908. On the same day, Julia Fleming (according to her own later confession) "just happened to come calling," only to find Margaret and Harry Mousley deep in conversation regarding Frank Gould's divorce situation, and his reputation as a rich playboy. It was at that point that Fleming was "innocently" brought into the plan. Fleming advised her coconspirators that she had known Frank Gould on a "hello, how are you" basis a year earlier, when she had run a ticket-and-newspaper stand at the Waldorf, where Frank had lived at the time. This was good news for the conspirators, as Julia could then provide an accurate description of Gould and his mannerisms, and Fleming signed on for the plot.

The next step was to bring in an outside accomplice, someone with an honest and faultless background who needed money, would perform in court, and would keep her mouth shut. Almost by happenstance, they recruited their foil. She was Miss Mabel MacCausland, an aspiring show-girl and casual acquaintance.

Mabel had for some time been working as a milliner's apprentice and had frequently delivered alterations to Mrs. Teal at the Wyoming. The milliner had allowed Mrs. Teal liberal credit for his services. But Margaret, of course, was long on promise and short on pay. She had gone into arrears by $150, and Mabel was directed to collect the debt. She visited the Wyoming several times, but Margaret's relentless charm and assuring promises always put off the diligent Miss MacCausland.

Three days after the conspirators began stoking their plot, Mabel called on Mrs. Teal again, this time to tell her that she had lost her position with the milliner, and to ask if Mrs. Teal would mind approaching Mr. Teal about getting her a job as a showgirl. It was an unexpected opening, and Margaret seized the moment.

"Mabel, you have come to see me at just the right time. I know how we can both earn ourselves some fast money."

"And how is that?"

"Well, you know how we have often chatted about the newsy Frank and Helen Gould divorce case, and how I figure he'd been seeing Bessie Devoe. Wouldn't Helen Gould like to know about that! She'd pay handsomely for that information."

"I suppose so."

"Well, Mabel, since Miss Devoe subletted my old apartment in the Glenmore, I know for a fact that Frank Gould comes and goes. What we need is an affidavit of proof. After that, we need to get it into the hands of Helen's lawyers. All you have to do is just swear in an affidavit that you have delivered services to Miss Devoe, that you have seen Mr. Frank Gould in Bessie DeVoe's apartment, and that you even once saw him come out of her bedroom! I could put $600 to $1,000 in your hands right away, and there would also be a nice monthly allowance, and a nice place for you in the country. Can you come by tomorrow? I can have everything ready."

"But I couldn't and wouldn't do such a thing. It's a lie. I don't know Frank Gould. I never saw him."

"Mabel, don't you need the money?"

"I came looking for a stage job. I won't be bribed. I have no reason to hurt Mr. Gould. I won't do it."

"Then, for heaven's sake, keep out of it entirely and don't say anything, or we will all be in jail. And don't for the world let Mr. Teal know."[1]

From here on, the story follows Mabel's courtroom testimony. She did not conspire in Margaret's skullduggery but rather appears to have been coaxed into a setup against her. Mabel revealed that when she left Mrs. Teal and went back to her own apartment, at 302 West Twenty-Seventh Street, she found her roommate, Ethel Conklin, with a Mr. Benjamin Katz, who had "just come to call." Benjamin was an aspiring young lawyer—the same lawyer, it turns out, who had coincidentally represented Miss Devoe in the subletting of her flat from Mrs. Teal.

Ignoring Margaret's demand to keep quiet, Mabel filled in Benjamin Katz about the content of her afternoon conversation. Katz then advised taking the story to Frank Gould's lawyers. But first, Mabel would have to revisit Mrs. Teal to confirm the fraud. This convenient meeting between Katz and Mabel seemed all too curious. Had Katz been working with Frank Gould and Bessie to derail Margaret's plot all along? Surely Margaret underestimated the cool Mabel MacCausland and the resources available to Mr. Frank Gould!

Mabel went back to Margaret's apartment the next day. She found Margaret with Julia Fleming and said, "Mrs. Teal, I have changed my mind. I will do it."[2]

Margaret and Julia were ebullient. They had, the previous evening, taken a cab downtown to meet and tempt two other stage girls with the same proposition. To their acute disappointment, they had been turned down flat. This, now, was a promising turnaround.

"Mabel, come back later, and we will go over the details with Helen Gould's private detective."

Mabel agreed and returned to the Wyoming that afternoon. Margaret introduced her to Harry Mousley. He was introduced as Mr. Stanley, who presented a detailed description of Frank Gould and instructed Mabel in her testimony. Mabel was to affirm that in March 1908 she had visited Miss Devoe in connection with her millinery-service, and that while sitting in Miss Devoe's apartment she had heard voices coming from the bedroom and had seen Frank Gould exit the bedroom and leave the apartment. Her testimony was also that she had seen Mr. Gould at the Glenmore on several different occasions. Mabel agreed that she would sign a statement to that effect. Mr. Stanley assured her that her affidavit would be approved by Mrs. Helen Gould's lawyers and that upon signing it she would receive her compensation. This would include $600 in up-front cash, a monthly allowance of $25, and an apartment in the country. Mabel agreed. Mr. Stanley would prepare the affidavit. Mabel promised to return the next day. She would sign and expect her reward.

Mabel did not return directly to the Wyoming apartment the next day; instead, she and her new friend Mr. Benjamin Katz made an appointment to meet the attorneys for Frank Gould.

Upon hearing Miss MacCausland's story, one of Mr. Gould's lawyers, Mr. Sullivan, accompanied Mabel and Katz to the office of Assistant District Attorney Smyth, where a full statement was made regarding Mabel's meeting with Eleanor's band of conspirators. Assistant D. A. Smyth assigned Detective Rayens to take Mabel back to the Wyoming. Upon arriving there, Detective Rayens positioned himself outside the apartment as Mabel entered.

Margaret greeted Mabel. "Please sit down; we've been waiting for you. Mr. Stanley will be here soon to take care of things."

Mousley arrived shortly. They discussed instructions about Mabel's testimony. Mousley had a photograph of Frank Gould. He then asked Mabel to sign a prepared statement of her testimony. She did so. At about that time, Detective Rayens rushed into the apartment.

"My name is Detective Rayens, of the New York Police Department. You are all under arrest and will be detained for further questioning regarding this transaction with Miss MacCausland. You will accompany me downtown to police headquarters."

Margaret Teal, Julia Fleming, and Private Detective Mousley were arrested on the early evening of Monday, July 20, 1908. Julia and Harry went willingly, but Margaret threw a violent fit of hysteria.

"I'm a new mother. I have an infant. I'm just regaining my strength. I can't leave. I'm innocent. I've been taken in by a ruse. My husband is Ben Teal, the Broadway manager. He will take care of this."

Detective Rayens decided not to take her in. Instead, Detective Lieutenant Beery was to stand guard at the Wyoming until morning. When Ben Teal arrived home late that Monday evening, he found a policeman outside his door, and Margaret inside, waiting anxiously. He listened to Margaret's version of what happened.

"Don't worry, my darling—I'll take care of it. My lawyers will represent you. You'll be back home before noon. Certainly, this is all a misunderstanding."

Early, the next morning, Margaret and her maid were taken by taxi to Assistant District Attorney Hart's office. Ben's lawyers were there for her. Julia had spent the night in the Mercer Street police station, and Harry at police headquarters. They all appeared together and were questioned for several hours, then taken to police court. After they had waited for an hour outside the courtroom, their case was called. Mabel MacCausland was on hand as well. The *Times* reported that "the MacCausland girl was dressed in a light flannel suit and a large straw hat. She appeared perfectly at ease, despite the fact that the two women prisoners glowered at her at frequent intervals."[3]

The courtroom was sweltering. Margaret was distraught and weak. When the defendants were finally called, she had to be helped to a chair. Magistrate Corrigan heard the case and held all three on a preliminary charge of subornation of perjury. Bail was set at $5,000. He announced that the maximum sentence for the charge could be up to five years in prison.

Harry would have to face the full charge because he was found with the false affidavit and a photograph of Frank Gould in his pocket. Harry had a lawyer, an ex–assistant district attorney, who was able to get him released on a bond.

The two women were held. Margaret's lawyers could not immediately come up with enough bond money to get them released, so Margaret and Julia sat in the courtroom hour after hour, watching a line of offenders of all classes pass before them. Ben Teal's secretary finally appeared, but not Ben. By four thirty, Ben still had not arrived. Margaret was on the verge of collapse. The police docket closed for the day. The magistrate prepared the bail bond so that the women could be released during the night if enough bond security could be obtained. They were taken to the city prison infamously known as the Tombs.

Margaret, anticipating a night spent in prison, had by this time completely broken down, crying bitterly into the shoulder of her maid, "Where oh where is Ben?"

Ben arrived after dark, having been detained by a rehearsal of the principals in his new play, *Fluffy Ruffles*, at the Criterion Theater, and found Margaret and Julia being held in the reception room at the Tombs. He rushed to comfort Margaret, then hastened to find a bail bondsman. Ben returned hours later and, along with a party of a dozen friends, escorted her home. But there was no bond for Julia. She was left cooling her heels. That was a big mistake.

Who was Julia Fleming? The *Times* described her as unattractive: "Mrs. Fleming wore a plain gown of light material and a large black hat. She is a large, dark woman, about thirty-three years old, with a ruddy complexion. She would not be called handsome."[4]

Julia had been a traveling companion and friend since Margaret's (Eleanor's) days as the young wife of William Toomey. She very likely accompanied Margaret when Margaret bolted from St. Paul on frequent escapades to New York. The *Times* noted that Julia indeed came from St. Paul. Julia testified that she had known Mrs. Teal for many years, and that she had been with her all through the time of her divorce action against William Toomey and the breach action that she had brought against Dr. Bettingen, the prominent St. Paul physician. She also stated that she had accompanied Margaret on four trips abroad. Surely Julia and Margaret, two birds of a feather, had enjoyed a history of furtive activities and adventures of questionable propriety.

Julia had already spent one night in the Tombs following her arrest on Monday. After three more nights as a prisoner, with no bail bondsman in sight, she had enough and decided to turn state's evidence. On Friday morning, Julia Fleming met with District Attorney Hart and spilled the beans. Yes, she had conspired with Margaret against Frank Gould. Her testimony aligned with Mabel's. It was Margaret Teal who had instigated and planned the whole thing.

The *Times* described Julia's resentful disposition:

> *Mrs. Fleming was angered at the failure of Mousley and*
> *Mrs. Teal to see that bail was obtained for her. Mousley was*
> *released on security procured by his counsel on the afternoon*
> *of the original arraignment of the three prisoners. Mrs. Teal*
> *was sent to the Tombs in default of bail with Mrs. Fleming,*
> *but her husband procured a bondsman for her after she had*
> *been locked up only a few hours. Mrs. Fleming, however, was*
> *allowed to remain in the city prison, where she still is, and this*
> *desertion so affected her that she announced to her counsel*
> *that she would tell everything that had happened.*[5]

Julia was released on reduced bail several days later. Mousley also turned state's evidence. Both would later testify against Mrs. Teal. The trial was scheduled for the following February.

Chapter 6:

The Gould Trial

Margaret Teal entered the Court of General Sessions on Tuesday, February 23, 1909, before Judge Foster. She was flanked by her lawyers, Robert J. Haire and Daniel O'Reilly. Ben was by her side throughout the four days of the trial.

The jury of twelve was seated after the noon recess. Mabel MacCausland was the first witness. Steady and composed, Mabel described Margaret's caper without missing a beat. In a clear, confident voice, she told how she had been coached and bribed to perjure herself in court, and how she had then forthrightly brought the unseemly matter to the authorities.

The next day, Julia Fleming turned state's evidence against Eleanor, confirming Mabel's account word for word. Harry Mousley did the same, adding that all along he had believed Margaret to be acting in good faith, with reliable evidence.

The prosecution discovered two other witnesses, previously undisclosed, who were called by the state: Blanche Hale, a hairdresser at the Lincoln Hotel who knew Julia Fleming, and Margaret Falk, a "colored" woman who was a dressmaker known to Mrs. Teal. Blanche Hale said that Julia had brought her to Mrs. Teal and had offered a bribe to sign a false affidavit against Frank Gould. Mrs. Hale told the jury that she needed money to visit and care for her ailing mother in Nova Scotia, and that Mrs. Teal's offer was very tempting. Blanche said that she was later visited by

Mr. Mousley and another man, both claiming to be lawyers for Mrs. Helen Gould, who needed to "test her ability as a witness." Margaret Falk testified that while calling on Mrs. Teal for a dress fitting, she had been offered a similar bribe not once, but twice, and both times had refused.

Just before the end of the day's proceedings, Judge Foster, at the urging of the assistant district attorney, ordered Margaret locked up for the night in the Tombs and withdrew her $5,000 bail.

On the third day, Mousley was recalled to the stand by the defense. Mousley added a couple of interesting unsolicited remarks:

"I was told by Mrs. Teal that she had sublet her apartment in the Glenmore to Bessie DeVoe, an actress, for $250 a month. I told her that $250 was an awful price, and Mrs. Teal said, 'That's what I told Bessie, but she laughed and said, "Frank Gould is paying for it; he can afford it."'

"Mrs. Teal also told me that at this time Bessie DeVoe exhibited a diamond-studded purse, saying that Frank Gould had given it to her."[1]

Margaret's lawyer Robert Haire, upon hearing Mousley's remarks, asked that the indictments be dismissed. This was denied, the remarks stricken as not pertinent. Haire then recalled Mabel MacCausland. She admitted that she had become friendly with Mrs. Teal over several months in order to get onto the stage, and that Mrs. Teal had gone out of her way to introduce her to several stage managers. She testified that, although she considered Mrs. Teal a friend, when the Gould plot was broached, she had to expose it through "a sense of duty." Then, curiously, Haire announced that the defense would rest without calling any further witnesses.

The assistant district attorney in his summary was sharp and caustic: "This woman is a vampire. She has designed the ruin of others. What mercy does she deserve?"[2]

The defense, in summary, characterized Maggie Teal as a good and much-wronged woman, against whom perjured witnesses had testified. Margaret, touched by her lawyer's summary, wept throughout.

The jury was given the case at 3:35 p.m., and deliberations went on into the night. At one point, the jury asked for a partial reading of the testimony. As the testimony was being read, Margaret pitched forward in her seat and nearly fainted. At 10:55, the foreman declared the jury deadlocked. The judge ordered the jury to reach a verdict. After another twenty minutes, the judge, hearing nothing, sequestered the jury for the night. Margaret retired to the Tombs.

Day four—the jury finally entered the courtroom with a verdict at 12:10 on Friday afternoon. Ben was at Margaret's side. She appeared to have given up hope. By unanimous decision, she was declared guilty. It was later learned that during the night the jury had been deadlocked at ten to two. One juryman wept for Margaret as the verdict was read.

Judge Foster said in his commendation, "Margaret Teal, you have had a fair trial, and the recommendation of the jury that you be shown clemency shall receive due heed from me. I will not add to your suffering by referring to your past record with which the district attorney has acquainted me. I have been very much impressed by the bearing of your husband during the trial and realize fully the appeal to the sympathies in the circumstances of your conviction. You deserve punishment, however, and the sentence of the court is that you undergo an imprisonment of one year in the penitentiary."[3]

Margaret swayed and nearly collapsed, sinking to her knees as attendants rushed to support her with a chair. Robert Haire asked for a stay of execution of the sentence until Tuesday next. Haire declared that he would appeal the case. The stay was granted. Twelve days later, failing an appeal, Margaret was sentenced on March 10, 1909, and confined to one year in the penitentiary on Blackwell's Island. She entered the penitentiary two days later.

Margaret was out of her league in taking on Frank Gould. Frank's detectives and lawyers appear to have been ten steps ahead of her. Margaret's shady overture to Mabel had backfired.

How convenient it was that Miss Bessie Devoe's attorney, Benjamin Katz, had appeared at Mabel MacCausland's apartment following Mabel's second cryptic meeting with Margaret. Mabel, seemingly in good conscience, having refused Margaret initially, at some point, went to Bessie, and Bessie went to Frank. When Mabel found Katz in her apartment with her roommate, she was only too ready to spill her story. Mr. Katz, with Frank Gould's men in the background, then set up the sting that brought down Margaret and her gang. In the end, Katz and Mabel were likely paid off and sent on their way, and Harry and Julia, likewise, were never heard from again.

Miss Bessie Devoe, Frank's suspected girlfriend and a darling of Broadway, who once played to everyone's favor in *A Chorus Girl* and *The Dairymaids*, also disappeared from the scene for a time. Bessie Devoe's amorous involvement with Frank Gould was never in doubt. Margaret knew what was going on, but her surreptitious contacts with Helen Gould's minions were left wanting. Despite all of Margaret's charms and devious maneuvers, she was unable to turn the gears in Helen's favor, or her own. Margaret Teal was duly convicted, and Frank Gould effectively screened out his own adulterous liability.

Not surprisingly, only months after the trial, Bessie DeVoe and Frank Gould again turned up in the *New York Times*. This time, it was Bessie's turn to go after Frank. The *Times* reported that Bessie would "publish sensational letters that Frank had written to her," letters that would sustain a breach-of-promise suit against Frank. Bessie's suit never again turned up in the news, and no New York theater credits were ever again bestowed to her beyond the last performance of *The Dairymaids*. It had been during her run of that show that she had rented that infamous Glenmore apartment from Eleanor Teal. She lived in the Glenmore until the end of the trial, a period of about fifteen months. Then Frank sent Bessie packing, and sailed off to France, where he purchased a luxury country home and a stud-racing-horse farm in Chantilly. His army of sentries had done their work.

Frank and Helen Gould were divorced on May 20, 1909, three months after the Eleanor Teal trial. Helen was granted sole custody of the two children, and Frank was given very detailed visitation privileges, down to the month, day, holiday, and specific hour. It was reported that this divorce decree was one of the lengthiest and wordiest ever handed down, because of its intricately negotiated custody provisions. It was a painfully enduring entanglement played out in public view for more than two years, made even more dramatic by the infused perjury trial of Mrs. Ben Teal.

A year after his divorce from Helen, Frank remarried. Again, his adulterous and abusive tendencies caused that relationship's demise. He married a third time, and this time it stuck. He remained faithful to his third wife, Florence LaCase, for thirty-three years; they were separated only by his death, on April 1, 1956. He died at age seventy-eight in the

French Riviera resort town of Juan-les-Pins, a seaside community he had built up to become the premier socialite watering hole of the Mediterranean. He owned villas, hotels, and gambling casinos, and was well known as a horse-show operator, a social bon vivant, a philanthropist, and a Knight of the Legion of Honor.

Frank Gould was born into wealth and prominence. Margaret Teal was born into insecurity and abandonment. And while Frank, as the scion of Jay Gould, rose above his miscreant state with the benefit of wealth and influence, Margaret had to compete with her wits and demons in a man's world.

When Margaret Teal entered Blackwell's Island Penitentiary on March 12, 1909, conditions were desperately decrepit, as were those of most New York City prisons, which, prior to reforms made in 1914, were publicly condemned as "little more than mediaeval."

Partly because of its nefarious name, the Tombs was the most notorious and dreaded prison in the city system. The ancient, gloomy structure with a "repellant Egyptian facade" was built upon the site of a pond that, having never been sufficiently drained, leached constant dampness. The fifty women's cells were smaller and darker than the men's and because of lack of drainage could not be cleaned properly. No decent bathing facilities were provided. Flimsy shower curtains offered only the pretense of any privacy. The hospital situation was such that not even the warden would enter, for fear of contamination. No direct sunlight or outer air entered the prison walls. Because of the lack of ventilation, temperatures could not be regulated. In the winter, prison occupants melted or froze, depending on location, and the only food that could be served hot was soup.

The Tombs held, at any one time, about four hundred prisoners. As many as fifty thousand prisoners passed through annually. Persons accused of crimes were confined until trial. Once sentenced, prisoners were sent to other prisons, unless scheduled for execution. These were hanged.

Prison conditions on Blackwell's Island in those days were considered little better than those in the Tombs. The obsolete buildings, having been constructed in 1832, were not built for humanitarian confinement but rather as structures from which prisoners would be unable to escape. In 1914, a new reform commissioner, Dr. Katherine Davis, described the prison cells as "wet, slimy, dark, foul-smelling, and unfit for pigs to wallow in." She complained that Blackwell's, like the Tombs, offered no light and no air, remarking that "the sanitary housing of a cow requires at least four hundred square feet of space, but that there wasn't that much space offered in three prison cells combined."[4] Medical care was described as desperately inadequate. One physician was assigned to the entire male population, and one nurse for the female prisoners. The task of providing medical care to nearly a thousand inmates by so few was impossible.

Charges of corrupt management also plagued Blackwell's Prison. The warden had a habit of collecting fines from the prisoners and depositing them into his personal account. Account management for these fines, as well as for the accounting of supply invoices, was assigned to selected prisoners. When asked about this, Warden Hayes said that such had been his long-standing practice.

Margaret Teal spent ten and a half months in this wretched environment. Her cry for release was unrelenting. Finally, on November 23, 1909, the court of appeals in Albany reversed her conviction just short of her twelve-month sentence. The reversal had been hard won by the dogged determination, dedication, and depleted fortune of her faithful and loving husband.

Chapter 7:

The Teals, New York, 1908–15

The heavy iron gates at Blackwell's prison slammed behind Margaret Teal just as Ben brought to a close two successful Broadway productions: *Fluffy Ruffles*, with 24 performances, and *The Queen of the Moulin Rouge*, with 160 performances. Margaret Teal's sorry public caper and imprisonment drew the curtain not only on her lavish and promising life but on Ben's illustrious career as well. He took leave of the New York stage entirely. It was a sacrifice he could not well afford. He knew that the theater business would wait for no one, and that new shows and faces would quickly eclipse the accolades of his accomplishments. Nevertheless, Ben accepted his fate and devoted every waking hour and all of his available assets to lobbying on Margaret's behalf.

As Margaret left for Blackwell's Island, dressed in silks and furs, Ben swore, "I'll get you out of that vile place if I have to give up all my other affairs to devote my time to the job." To the attendant reporters, he declared incredulously, "I'll clear my beloved wife's name if it takes my last dollar. I know how sweet and wholesome Mrs. Teal's character is. She's as innocent as a newborn babe, utterly incapable of such a crime."[1]

Weeks turned into months. Nothing good happened. Already in April, just weeks into Margaret's internment, Ben was forced into bankruptcy. He had paid out enormous sums in legal fees and had settled an avalanche of debt from Margaret's appetite for clothes and jewelry. At the same time, he had to pay for around-the-clock care of his infant son. Ben

had made countless visits to Blackwell's Island for Margaret's encouragement, and he journeyed often to Albany to curry favor for her release.

A man like Ben Teal would have had assets, but his wife's indulgences
had left him on a shoestring. He moved out of his expensive apartment
at the Wyoming into a modest house in the village of Mount Vernon, an
hour north of New York, on the Harlem line. Mount Vernon was founded
by John Stevens, a visionary community developer who built the village
in the mid–nineteenth century as a cooperative settlement for New Yorkers wishing to live away from the congestion, expense, and squalor of the
city. No doubt Ben saw Mount Vernon as a manageable refuge for himself
and his infant son, and as a retreat from his creditors as well.

Then, on November 23, 1909, two months short of Margaret's one-
year sentence, Ben's lobbying paid off. The court of appeals in Albany
ordered a new trial, which, due to a lack of credible witnesses, allowed her
conviction to be overturned. With this good fortune, the Teals believed,
they could once again hold themselves up to their admiring public. Margaret could once again parade into Delmonico's and the Sherry-Nether-
land in resplendent finery, turning the heads of familiar patrons. With
luck and hard work, Ben could resume his implacable presence on Broadway. But time would tell.

The new year began with uncertainty. Margaret's release from prison
restored the family unit, but Ben's reinstatement as one of New York's
preeminent stage managers was in doubt. Over the previous twenty-
seven years, he had enjoyed a remarkable theatrical career with seventy-
one very successful productions credited to his name. His reputation
had been widely acclaimed. He was truly, at one time, the busiest man
on Broadway, managing three and four productions at a time. Now, at
age fifty-five, he would attempt to reemerge as the titan who had perhaps
been forgotten.

Ben had been known as Mr. Teal, a man of boundless energy, discipline, integrity, and singular determination. It was said of his integrity
and character that he regarded good manners and propriety as the domi-
nant principles of the stage, and that sensuality should be diminished. His
motto was, "sanity, character, good taste—that is the trinity of musical
comedy."[2] And he alone among Broadway's managers and producers had

recognized and stood up for some of the basic needs of the players. He was, for example, the first manager to place the purchase of stage apparel in the hands of the producers. No longer did his subjects have to provide their own stockings, wigs, tights, and related necessities. But he could not escape his reputation as a martinet. His stage management was rigid, demanding, and on many occasions harsh and demeaning. Perhaps his abusive manner as an overbearing general had caught up with him. He had enjoyed respect and admiration among his peers, but because of his caustic discipline there were many among the actors who regarded him with derision. In 1910, it seemed, there might no longer be a place for him in this business.

The prison ordeal had all been an overwhelming burden of time and money. Ben needed work. Financial collapse knocked stubbornly at his door. Would he be able to count on Margaret? Could she resume her role as a mother? Had her confidence been shaken? Would she have enough patience? Had she learned a lesson or had she become hardened and embittered? All of these questions were on Ben's mind. He had friends, contacts, and a reputation for turning a profit. But would they all hold?

As it turned out, Ben had not been forgotten. Work was available, and things began to perk up. In April 1910, he directed *A Skylark* at the New York Theater. It lasted for twenty-four performances and secured him a leg up financially. But assignments were uneven, and big theater jobs were slow in coming. He was not noted for another major production until March 1912, when he staged *The Man from Cooks*, with thirty-two performances. There were other minor stage jobs and collaborations in and out of New York during this time. For a brief period, he acquired work in Cincinnati. Then he got a big break in August 1913, when he directed *Adele* at Teller's Broadway Theater, with 196 performances. He remained busy through 1915, with five more productions. Most notable, in addition to *Adele*, was *The Girl Who Smiles*, at the Lyric, with 104 performances.

Mr. Teal's return to the theater world was not as "the representative general of the Broadway stage." That singular status had slipped away. Nevertheless, he had achieved the comeback goals of financial recovery and name recognition. The eclipse of Ben's lofty position and status by the notable successes of other men, however, was a matter not lost on Margaret. For her, status mattered. Ben's devotion to her and his dedication to family life was not good enough. She was becoming restless.

Contentment and domestication had never been aspirations at all compatible with Margaret's restless disposition. Back in St. Paul, as the wife of William Toomey, she and Toomey had occupied seven different residences in the course of their five-year marriage, four residences having been hotel suites. In New York, in 1907, Eleanor and Ben's first domicile was the luxurious Central Park South Norma Munro flat, which came to be known as a consequence of a widely publicized breakup between the wealthy socialite Norma Munro and the popular Broadway actress Leslie Carter. The two had been close friends and had shared the fine apartment, owned by the Munro estate. Miss Munro's eastern end of the apartment opened to Miss Carter's western side—that is, until Miss Carter decided to marry Mr. Dudley Payne. Such a turn of affairs did not sit well with Norma. She had the doors that separated the two nailed shut from her side. She then proceeded to force eviction and sued her friend for back rent and utility costs. The coolness that arose between these friends became spicy fodder for Broadway gossip. The Teals, who had an inside track on theater gossip, benefited from the breakup. They moved quickly to acquire occupancy when Mrs. Carter-Payne moved out in October 1906.

It was at the Norma Munro flat where the *Minneapolis Tribune* found newlywed Margaret Teal entertaining the "galaxy of theatrical stars shining on Broadway."[3] Over the years, the *Tribune* boys in Minneapolis/St. Paul held a fascination for the former Mrs. Toomey, and kept tabs on her infamous career. Not surprisingly, the Teal domicile at Central Park West was short lived. Perhaps harmony with Miss Munro was impossible for the Teals as well—within three months, they moved to the Ansonia on the corner of Broadway and Amsterdam.

The Ansonia was the largest residential hotel of its day. Construction began in 1887 and was completed in 1904. It had 400 residential suites and 1,218 rooms. The Teals moved into a suite in January 1907. They would have enjoyed luxuries unheard of anywhere else. These included a pneumatic tube system that allowed tenants to exchange

The Ansonia, New York, 1905

news and gossip, Turkish baths, six passenger elevators, dumbwaiters that provided delivery to apartment kitchens, several restaurants decorated in the style of Louis XIV, two swimming pools, including the world's largest indoor pool, basement shops for upscale shopping, and a rooftop chicken farm that provided fresh eggs to the residents. There were even seals that frolicked in the lobby fountain.

A list of past residents and guests of the Ansonia "reads like a "who's who" of the art and entertainment world. Some of its most famous musical notables have included Enrico Caruso, Sergei Rachmaninoff, Igor Stravinsky, Arturo Toscanini, Gustav Mahler, Yehudi Menuhin, Lily Pons, and Ezio Pinza. Theatrical notables included Sol Hurok, Florenz Ziegfeld, Sarah Bernhardt, and Billie Burke. Sports-world legends Babe Ruth and Jack Dempsey lived there. Writers Elmer Rice, W. L. Stodard, and Theodore Dreiser were also residents."[4]

The Ben Teals lived no more than a year and a half at the Ansonia. The *New York Times* reported that "the couple moved rapidly from one apartment to another, and, in an effort to collect a bill against Mrs. Teal, the proprietor of the Ansonia is said to have had her followed by detectives."[5]

In 1908, they had settled in at the Wyoming, at Fifty-Fifth Street and Seventh Avenue. Debts were piling up, and creditors came knocking. It was at the Wyoming that Margaret initiated the unfortunate imbroglio that placed her in Blackwell's Prison for ten months. Indeed, throughout her life, a residence of about ten months seemed the norm for any one place, whether in a prison, a mansion, or a hotel suite.

The homecoming from Blackwell's Island in the winter of 1910 was not quite the return Margaret had in mind. Ben knew that the house in Mount Vernon, where he had been able to provide good and reasonable care for himself and little Ben, would not suit her. The remote village life was far removed from the posh existence she had enjoyed as a resident of the Ansonia and the Wyoming. They stayed in Mount Vernon for only part of the year and then moved into a Manhattan apartment owned by the same landlord. That, too, was unacceptable. A gossip columnist later in the same year noted that the Teals had launched "a lawsuit against Louise Livingston of Mount Vernon in the amount of $5,000, claiming that the apartment on Broadway and 109th Street was untenable by the presence of rats."[6]

Margaret's need for a fashionable lifestyle in the city begged Ben's attention. At first, Ben's halting financial resurgence was, for Margaret, agonizingly slow, but as job offers came in, Ben was able to ensconce Margaret in more and more upscale quarters. A social column in the *New York Star* reported on February 10, 1915, "Although we frequently see Mr. and Mrs. Teal on the Street of Streets, and they are often to be found at a Broadway hotel, their real living, Mr. Teal says, is done at their country home, Wayside Cottage on Griffen Avenue in Mamaroneck."[7]

Margaret faced the tedious role of responsible wife and mother. Her predisposition to the glamorous world of uptown Broadway grated against her domestic duty. The year that followed was a struggle for patience. Her mood lifted when, in 1912, they moved into the Ritz-Carlton Hotel, but her restless demons were not so easily assuaged. She awakened each morning glistening with new whims and ambitions. Ben, who was known as always being in strict control of the stage, came too easily under Margaret's persuasion. In 1912, she dogged Ben with a new, high-minded idea: they would adopt an older child, a sister for little Ben! Ben listened and obliged.

Late in 1912, Margaret, Ben, and Ben Jr., now five years old, entered the austere reception parlor of Saint Ann's Foundling Home on East Broadway. A little girl, Agnes Fitzgerald, age nine, was herded into the room, along with a dozen other foundlings, all "painfully scrubbed and clad in their stiffly starched best."[8] Little Agnes had been through this drill before, perhaps dozens of times, when someone wanted to adopt a child. Now, her eyes were immediately drawn to this gorgeously gowned lady, whose fingers were laden with diamonds and emeralds, whose neck was encircled by a string of beautiful pearls, and whose little boy was dressed in a velvet suit.

"I want this one!" cried little Ben. "I like her funny teeth."[9]

That was enough for Margaret. Early in 1913, Agnes joined the Teal family as Cynthia Marie Teal. Published news photos of Cynthia in her later teens show her as a very attractive girl. She did, indeed, have slightly protruding teeth, a feature more charming than distracting.

Suddenly and miraculously, Agnes became Cynthia Teal, a new girl lifted into a new world—for Agnes, a world of fantasy.

The Teals had, by this time, moved into a larger suite at the Ritz-Carlton. Margaret was happy and Ben foresaw happy days ahead. Cynthia became an amiable caretaker and playmate to Ben Jr. And with the backing of a new hit show, *The Wanderer*, Ben and Margaret would resume their appearances on *The Rialto*, receiving the well wishes of their friends at restaurants and chic cabarets. Ben's sacrifice had paid off. If any man had earned happiness, it was he. He could throw himself back into the profession he knew and loved. Perhaps, or so Ben hoped, Margaret could resume her role as a matron of Broadway.

In 1916, the Teals were not only "back in town" but sported ocean residences in fashionable West End, New Jersey, and on Long Island in Mamaroneck, New York. At both places they entertained hosts of friends, and Ben was known as a generous patron for those who came to him for help. He also formed a new theater company, the Times Producing Corporation: "Ben Teal, one of Broadway's most skillful stage directors of musical comedy, furnished the idea and the enthusiasm for the new organization, and associated with him are a number of men who believe there is a public for just such entertainments. Among these backers are the Pincus brothers, who control the Longacre Theatre, and the stock company hopes to install itself in this playhouse in September."[10]

The money and good times were finally rolling again. *The Wanderer*, directed by Ben Teal, had become a Broadway hit, with 108 performances, and Margaret was often seen at her favorite restaurants with friends. Most notable was her presence at the Waldorf, where the maître d' greeted her with noted cordiality.

Chapter 8:

A Funeral, 1917

Sustaining the good life increasingly challenged Ben's productivity, and Margaret met with disdain any bridling of her spending. As fast as Ben could earn it, Margaret spent it. This, of course, was nothing new. Since her arrival as his new bride in New York City in 1907, Ben had reluctantly abided her extravagance. Within a year of their marriage, Margaret, on her own, filed a voluntary petition of bankruptcy in the US District Court, in which she put her liabilities at $4,379 and her assets as nothing. This occurred in March 1908, without Ben's knowledge. Twenty-one creditors were mentioned, among them jewelers, a candle company, a silver company, a cab-and-stable company, and numerous shop owners. Then, in July of the same year, just as Margaret was being investigated in the Gould divorce case, Ben was sued by a fashionable dressmaking establishment for unpaid purchases of gowns, wraps, a coat, and a laced bodice, in the amount of $1,040. In 1908, these were serious transgressions. On the heels of these legal pressures, Ben faced, in 1909, legal forays surrounding the Gould trial and Margaret's impending stay in Blackwell's Prison. While Margaret languished in prison, Ben was left with no choice but to petition the court for bankruptcy, this time in his own name with liabilities of $12,069, and again no assets. He also humbled himself to lean on his friends. For example, the *New York Sun* reported that he owed the famous songwriter Jerome Kern $200.[1]

Upon Margaret's release from prison, she resumed piling on debt. By the time 1913 rolled around, she again applied for a bill of bankruptcy—once again without Ben's knowledge. Margaret had become well accustomed to the bankruptcy drill and other means for covering her debts. A human-interest piece published years later in the *Chicago Herald Examiner*, recollecting the notorious life of Margaret Eleanor Teal, noted that at one point during this period of her life, "an insurance company showed ungallant curiosity over the destruction by fire of Mrs. Teal's heavily insured automobile."[2]

As Ben's stature and fortune returned and the Teals' glamorous life in New York City seemed more assured, domestic tranquility in the Teal home withered. Margaret's restless forays and restless avarices were not to be sacrificed for the mundane life of a mother and homemaker.

Although Ben struggled to marshal both his marriage and his career, Margaret continued to slip away from him. At the age of sixty-one, Ben was more energetic than most men, but the late-night theater hours and his young wife's social and material addictions sapped his vigor and strained his health. More often than not, Margaret was escorted home during the wee hours without him.

In October 1916, Margaret left New York for a long train ride to the West. Things were getting too hot with her New York creditors, and she needed to escape the pinch. She was accompanied by six-year-old Ben Jr. and a female friend. They got off at Chinook, Montana, and paid a surprise visit to her half brother, Gilman McKinnie, and family.

Perhaps she included Chinook on her travel itinerary in hopes that a visit would elicit favorable attention from Gilman. Gilman, though, had little to share at that time. Stepping off the train station platform, she would have encountered living conditions somewhat wanting. Even though Chinook was a booming little agricultural community with three hotels, a couple of restaurants, three churches, and a newspaper, Eleanor, as she was known to the family, could not have been very much impressed. And, though warmly greeted by Gilman's wife, Florence, and their four children, she would have been discouraged by their small ranch house outside of town.

She may have stayed a night or two, or until the next train stopped. Gilman would later write in a letter to his father, Albert, that she claimed to be on her way to Portland. She had to get to Portland, she said, because Albert was dying. Later events indicate that there may have been some truth to Eleanor's story. However, confirmation of the true impetus behind her trip came in a letter to Gilman two months after her visit.

George A. Hoffman
Counselor at Law
135 Broadway Corner Cedar Street
NY, NY

G. McKinnie, Esq.
Chinook, Montana
11 December 1916

My dear sir:

For at least two years I have known Mrs. Eleanor M. Teal and off and on have rendered service to her. During the past two months, I have done many things for Mrs. Teal, to protect her and her interests. As you must know, she has been short of funds and all along has told me that her father, Mr. A. McKinnie, would assist her financially. I have been told by Mrs. Teal that her father lived at Butte (Montana) part of the time and Honolulu the rest of the time, but I have been unable to obtain from her his complete address. As there are numerous matters in my charge for Mrs. Teal and some of which require prompt attention, I certainly would appreciate it very much indeed if, upon the receipt of this letter, you would telegraph me at my expense, and furnish me with the full name and address of Mrs. Teal's father so that I can communicate with him by letter, telephone or telegraph. Of course, this letter is written to you in confidence and I am going to ask you to treat it in the same way.

Yours very truly,
George A. Hoffman

Gilman may have replied to Mr. Hoffman. If so, it was probably with-out the requested information. Then, days after receiving the Hoffman letter, Gilman received another surprise. It was a letter from Albert, the father he hadn't heard from in more than fifteen years. Albert's letter is lost, but Gilman's carbon copy in response was not. Gilman complained about Eleanor's October visit and how he had been fleeced in the amount of "several hundred dollars." He also advised his father that, despite his long, anguishing absence, he was forgiven, that he must come home to know his grandchildren and live out his remaining years, and that there was plenty of room in their newly built house. A year later, Albert took up the invitation. He arrived at Christmas 1917. Within three months, he died of stomach cancer and was buried in Chinook. He left behind only a stack of defunct mining certificates. There is no indication that Eleanor had been advised of his death.

As indicated by the date on the Hoffman letter, December 11, 1916, Eleanor, again Margaret, had returned to New York. It seems unlikely that she would have gone all the way to Portland. If she had, she would not have found her father there. The letter that Gilman had received from Albert came from New Mexico.

Upon arriving home in New York from her trip west, Margaret Teal would have faced a very unhappy husband. Ben Teal had learned of an ongoing affair Margaret had been conducting with the maître d'hôtel at the Hotel Astoria. The affair had been cooking for most of a year. The heat of that affair was probably another reason for Margaret's scramble out of New York. The man's name was August Schneider. In March 1917, Ben filed a $50,000 alienation-of-affection suit against Schneider. For Ben, the last straw was when he learned that Margaret had instructed their daughter, Cynthia, to call Schneider Father. Ben was also desperately short on cash. Along with the suit against Schneider, he filed a schedule of bankruptcy, showing liabilities of $16,245 and assets of $1,500. The $50,000 suit against Schneider was important to his solvency, as well as to his pride.

"It isn't true!" Margaret pleaded, when Ben confronted her about Schneider. Whether it was true or not, it brought about the final breakup. Ben filed for divorce. Then, within weeks, before neither the suit against

Schneider nor the divorce could come before the court, Ben suffered a severe attack of gallstones. An operation was performed. Three weeks later, Ben died while in recovery at Stern Sanitarium. His friends said it was really a broken heart that killed him.

Ben Teal never completely recovered the stature he enjoyed prior to Eleanor's imprisonment as the renowned stage director of *Ben Hur*. Others had come along to master the craft. Well-known names were Hugh Ford, Herbert Gresham, and Julian Mitchell. The most famous was David Belasco, whose reputation eclipsed all others. Ben, while still hanging on, had lost too much ground. Thus, when notice of his death was published in the *New York Times* on April 24, 1917, it was printed as a subtext to a more flattering obituary, that of popular comedian David Montgomery, of whom it was said:

> *Not since the funeral of Charles Frohman have so many men and women of the theater gathered to honor the memory of one of their number as assembled yesterday afternoon for the funeral services of David Montgomery. The chapel of Frank S. Campbell at Broadway and Sixty-Seventh Street was filled with actors and actresses and men and women representative of every branch of the theater, while many who could not find room within stood outside.*

Added to the bottom was a short paragraph about Ben Teal's death:

> *The funeral of Ben Teal, the stage director, was held yesterday at 10:30 o'clock at the Church of the Blessed Sacrament, Broadway and Seventy-First Street. The services were largely attended by theatrical folk.*[3]

Those "theatrical folk" would have been moneymen—owners, producers, and investors. The actors and actresses whom Ben had hired and fired at will, and had moved around a stage like chess pieces, attended the other funeral.

Despite Ben Teal's reputation among actors as an abusive and abrasive

Ben Teal, 1917

stage director, he was the best thing that had ever happened to Margaret. He was mature, practical, aspiring, successful, disciplined and devoted. And, for Margaret, Ben's investment in the glamour and nightlife of the new century was everything she needed to assuage her capricious aspirations.

His loyalty to her and his discipline had held their demanding marriage and roller coaster lives together for eleven years. His untimely death was, in a sense, his final act of sacrifice, for Margaret was spared the anguish of a gossipy and chafing public divorce. Did Margaret grieve that Ben had died more of a broken heart and a collapsed career than of an attack of gallstones? To Margaret's credit, she spared no expense in arranging a worthy send-off for a once-renowned personality of the theater.

The funeral service was conducted at the Chapel of Carleton Winter-Bottom, at 111 West Twenty-Fourth Street; from there, guests proceeded to the Church of the Blessed Sacrament, on Broadway, for the offering of a solemn requiem Mass. Ben's body, as reported in the *New York Times*, was to be placed in the receiving vault at Woodlawn Cemetery in the Bronx, and then later removed to Portland, Oregon.

Again, the recurring connection to Portland is a poignant reminder of a family sentiment that must have been imprinted on Margaret's early life. She seems to have had in her mind, at least in passing, the intention of interring Ben in the cemetery plot occupied by the late Gilman family of Portland. But Ben's remains were never sent. He was buried in the Honeysuckle section of Woodlawn Cemetery. His burial at Woodlawn would have been appropriate, as Woodlawn is famous as a final resting place for many prominent figures in the history of New York. Very likely the internment was not Margaret's decision, but one that had been left to the patrons of the cemetery when further directions from Margaret were not forthcoming.

Ben's funeral cost the extravagant sum of $8,000. It was an expense that Margaret could not and would not meet. She was strapped even for enough cash to shelter herself and her two children. Ben had just gone into bankruptcy. There was nothing left for his funeral or for his family's survival. He died penniless. She would have to devise a plan for escaping the debt, and for escaping town.

Margaret, Cynthia, and little Ben returned to the Ritz-Carlton, where, Margaret knew, she was on a short leash. In the weeks following the funeral, she set about Fifth Avenue to dazzle shop owners into crediting her with thousands of dollars' worth of gowns, furs, and jewels, and then pawned enough to buy train tickets to Galveston, Texas.

Chapter 9:

Galveston, 1917

Margaret Teal, widow of Ben Teal, the first full-time Broadway the-ater director, was about to skip town. "Pack up," she announced to Cynthia and Ben Jr. "We're going where money grows on bushes."[1]

As an avid reader of the New York newspapers, Margaret kept a keen eye on the prosperity of the nation. She would have known that the great Texas oil boom got its start on January 10, 1901, outside Beaumont, Texas, when the largest gusher in North America burst forth on a little hill famously known as Spindle Top:

> *All of a sudden, a noise like a cannon shot came from the hole, and mud came shooting out of the ground like a rocket. Within a few seconds, natural gas, then oil, followed. The oil gusher, greenish-black in color, doubled the size of the drilling derrick, rising to a height of more than 150 feet (about 50 meters). This was more oil than had ever been seen anywhere in the entire world. Captain Lucas had been hopeful that this well might produce five barrels per day. In fact, this well, "Lucas 1," flowed at an initial rate of nearly 100,000 barrels per day, more than all of the other producing wells in the United States COMBINED!*[2]

By 1903, more than four hundred wells had been drilled side by side on the dome of the great Spindle Top gusher. Big oil, independents and "wildcatters" rushed to Texas. Within a few years, the large oil companies became the familiar giants of Texaco, Gulf, Amoco, and Humble. Southeastern Texas was awash in oilmen and roustabouts who followed the action from field to field. Dusty Texas towns turned into small cities accented with scores of newly erected Victorian hotels. The headlines across the country, almost daily, reported the progress of "black gold."

After devouring the headlines, Margaret Teal, scenting the oilmen's money, boldly packed up her little family and set out for Texas. She knew trains. She had been the wife of a railroad executive and had traveled the country from one end to the other, often in private coaches. She would have bought first-class fares at Penn Station for herself and her two children in tow. Ben Jr. was now nine, and Cynthia was thirteen. Margaret's gamble would have required that they travel in style. She and her little troupe walked out of the Ritz-Carlton unnoticed with a trunk full of Fifth Avenue's finest "borrowed" clothing, which she'd kept in reserve from the New York pawnbrokers. She might have purchased fares on the famous *Broadway Limited* to Chicago, or she might have taken a more direct route to St. Louis on the *St. Louisan*. Either way, once in St. Louis, they would have transferred to the Missouri Pacific's *Sunshine Special*, which took the Teal family into the Texas oil cities of Dallas, Fort Worth, and Houston. It was a train that became famous in the lore of railroading.

> *See that engine rollin'*
> *She's ballin' in the jack,*
> *Her wheels hummin' Dixie*
> *And her headlight on the track.*
> *Watch that engine swayin'*
> *While she's comin' down the line,*
> Sunshine Special, *she's right on time.*[3]

Train travel between 1912 and 1938 was known as the "heavyweight era," the era of the big steam engines. The better passenger trains were equipped with six to eight "through" cars, including an observation

Sunshine Special

Pullman, a compartment Pullman, two all-drawing-room Pullmans, and an elegant Harvey dining car. Formal dress in the dining room was expected, if not required. Eleanor would have been used to this kind of fare and would have worked it to her advantage.

The entire trip from New York to Galveston would have taken about seventy-two hours. The Teals, though, made stopovers along the way as their train crossed into Oklahoma and into the oil territories. While the oilmen prospected in the oil fields, Maggie Teal prospected for an oilman. The new hotels were the fields of her endeavor. As she paraded in her finest regalia in the various hotel lobbies, the children were kept locked in their rooms. The reward of an appealing prospect of some permanence, however, was kept wanting. Oilmen were a transient lot.

Margaret did not meet her man until she got to Galveston, an island city that, seventeen years earlier, on the morning of September 8, 1900, had been struck by the deadliest hurricane in history. A tidal surge of fifteen to twenty feet washed over the entire city, swallowing 3,600 homes and killing six to eight thousand people.

The brave, visionary survivors decided to rebuild. A permanent concrete wall was built along a large portion of the beachfront, and millions of yards of sand were dredged from the ship channel to raise the entire city and its remaining structures an amazing seventeen feet. The new Galveston became one of America's foremost engineering marvels.

In 1911, area businessmen raised enough money to build the Hotel Galvez, which became a symbol of prosperity that restored the city to its former glory. It was at this hotel, in late summer 1917, that Eleanor, who was at the end of her rope, finally hit pay dirt.

Chapter 10:

Hotel Galvez, 1917

A year after its construction, the Hotel Galvez had already become known as the Queen of the Gulf. An elegant, circular garden drive approached the grand entrance, facing the Gulf of Mexico. A long veranda overlooked the plush grounds. A mahogany-beamed ceiling accented the spacious main lobby. Richly upholstered furniture in shades of cranberry and green surrounded an antique mahogany guest bar nearby. Walking gingerly across the polished granite floor, three new hotel guests—an attractive woman and two well-groomed but hungry children—approached the front desk.

As she had done already at previous hotels along the way, Mrs. Teal checked in herself and her children under aliases, this time as Genevieve Thompson, the widow of the popular Broadway author and composer Jack Thompson of New York, and her children, Jack and Marie Thompson. The only Jack Thompson known to New Yorkers at that time would have been a fledgling boxer who had made a couple of headlines on the sports pages. Maggie had a knack for inventing aliases, a habit she would increasingly employ throughout her life.

She kept a close grip on the children. She might have left them in New York, perhaps with a friend. Supporting their needs and paying their way was a burden that would seem to have made her peculiar quest that much more difficult, but they were her burdens; she owned them—and there was no other family available.

It is comforting to believe that Margaret, upon the death of her husband Ben, had become anchored to her role as a mother, that she loved her children, and that she alone must provide for their welfare. And surely a recollection of her own childhood should have influenced her against revisiting the same curse upon her offspring. In a letter that she would later write to her half brother in Montana, she expressed resentment toward the father who had abandoned her: "I owe all my unhappiness to our father. . . . No father could treat his own children as he did and get away with it."

But whatever redeeming emotional attachment she may have felt, Margaret also used Cynthia and Ben Jr. as innocent pawns in her unremitting mission to land a rich husband. She would arrive, in Galveston, as the beautiful, forlorn widow who had been left to care for two fatherless children.

Alone in their room, Margaret sternly cautioned the children. For the time being, they would stay put. She reminded them that she was Genevieve Thompson, that they were to use their new names, Jack Thompson and Marie Thompson, and that they were not to talk about their trip to Galveston, or about their real life in New York. But this no longer sat well with Ben Jr. He was exhausted from this long ordeal and just wanted to be himself.

"I don't want to play this game, Mama. My name is Ben Teal, and I'm keeping it!"

Margaret flew into a rage and beat him, saying, "You're a brat, and you'll do as I tell you!"

An angry outburst was always the wedge of choice when her children or anyone else stood in her way. The children submitted, and Margaret Teal prepared herself for Galveston society as Genevieve Thompson.

She cut a svelte figure in her tropical dress and brimmed sun hat as she entered the main-floor loggia. She was used to turning heads and had cultivated a walk that spoke of elegance and sophistication. At the age of forty-two, she could still present a portrait of innocence and beauty.

The hot summer season at the Hotel Galvez was quiet. The larger crowds of wealthy visitors to the therapeutic waters arrived mostly during the winter months. But throughout the year, the hotel offered oil-industry

Hotel Galvez, 1911

executives and those of associated businesses a frequent second home. Galveston's deep-water channel made it the most important seaport city in Texas and a hub of American business. More than one thousand ships called on the port annually. Cotton, wheat, and oil moved into and out of Galveston. Most notably, it was the hub for steamboat tanker transportation coming from Mexico's booming Gulf Coast oil fields.

An attractive, beautifully dressed woman strolling alone through the rich halls of the Hotel Galvez would have caused a murmur among the male guests. Genevieve Thompson took a seat in the elegant lobby restaurant, which provided an expansive view of the beach and the ocean horizon. She was not alone. Others were cooling themselves under the great fans as well. She walked to the veranda. She paused to take in the views, knowing that a handsome, well-dressed gentleman, sitting alone in the restaurant, had taken notice. She waited.

The encounter seemed natural enough. He introduced himself as Dr. George Paddleford. He was tanned, wore spectacles, and spoke confidently, with a quiet Western accent. They sat, and he ordered glasses of wine. She learned that he, like she, had lost a spouse, and that he had the care of an only son, who was the same age as Ben Jr. More important, Dr. Paddleford held the position of general superintendent of a large Mexican oil company in Veracruz, Mexico. His employer was Edward L. Doheny, the well-known California oil magnate, who almost single-handedly had discovered and developed the vast oil riches of the Mexican Huasteca rainforest along the Gulf of Mexico. What could be more perfect?

When Genevieve Thompson returned to Cynthia and Ben Jr., she was beaming, "I have just met a rich man, and I'm going to land him!"

Two wide-eyed children stared back in a kind of suspended disbelief.

As for Dr. Paddleford, he couldn't believe his good fortune. He had just met an attractive, charming, sophisticated widow from New York City who seemed to like him. For the first time in a long time, his heart jumped, and he felt fully pleased with himself.

Chapter 11:

Cynthia

Cynthia and Ben Jr. stayed in the hotel room alone, as directed. It had been a long, hot, hungry, tedious afternoon and evening. After their days and nights on the rails and their stays in various hotels, Cynthia had all but exhausted hope. Her mother's resources were near depletion. With a burden of worry, she hoped fervently that this beautiful Galveston hotel would not fail them. Margaret, though, was excited and heartened. She knew in her heart that she had reached her vein of gold!

Ben Jr. awoke from a restless sleep when his mother finally returned. She was flush with excitement and certainty about landing a rich man. Her triumphant entrance brought relief and a cautious thrill of anticipation. They would meet Dr. George Paddleford in the hotel dining room for breakfast the next morning.

Then Margaret laid out instructions. They were to keep to the story. There would be no mention of their past and no mention of Ben Teal. Just keep quiet and be gracious. And their names from now on would be Genevieve, Marie, and Jack.

Cynthia submitted to her mother's direction. It was a lesson that had been well forged with threats and beatings over the past four years. But beneath her submissive veneer, she kept a storehouse of self-determination and self-preservation. Now thirteen, she had not entered the Teal family without a well-developed character. The Sisters of Charity who had raised her from birth as Agnes Fitzgerald had instilled in her discipline and a sense of right and wrong. Little Agnes, as she was known to the nuns, was intelligent. She had learned to read and already possessed a talent for writing. She also loved to sing. The sisters were well known for the singing they brought to the foundling home. The songs that Agnes had learned were to become Cynthia's treasures. And she had been taught deportment, the art of bowing politely, and walking correctly—all of which served her well now, as she learned her place as Eleanor's obedient daughter.

The New York Foundling Home had been for little Agnes a secure and loving place, as it was for the thousands of abandoned and dispossessed children of New York whom the sisters saved, including iron-basket babies and those brought in from any number of service agencies and locations throughout the city. As they arrived, the sisters and workers recorded assigned names.

Cynthia was not an "iron basket baby." Her mother had reportedly given birth at the maternity hospital of the foundling home. She would have been one of the thousands of unwed mothers who had found birthing refuge and care, and may have been one of the hundreds of mothers who remained in support of their child for a short time before submitting the child to the orphanage.

Cynthia remained Agnes Fitzgerald, an orphan, until the age of nine. Then, as has been said, she stood in a reception line with other older children and, to her wonderment and surprise, was wanted by an elegant family who, on the prescribed and anticipated day, ushered Cynthia Teal, newly adopted and bundled in a new velvet coat and cap, and a new pair of shoes, into a waiting carriage that took her into a world of lights, restaurants, theater, and the bustling energy of New York City.

It was not the city she knew, but the city as it was known to Ben and Margaret Teal and their son, Ben Jr., the eager little boy who had voiced his animation when he'd said, "Mommy, I want that one!"

At first, relieved from the regimentation of the Foundling Home, and for a while thereafter, Cynthia must have felt an amazing new sense of freedom and luxury. She certainly would have been awed and captivated by the excitement of all the venues and surroundings that had always been so close, yet now were so new to her. Broadway, with all of its sounds, sights, colors, and frenetic energy, had suddenly replaced a very

drab world. It wouldn't be long, though, until the exhilarating thrill of release would rust over through long periods of confinement and boredom in the Teals' uptown apartment.

Margaret Teal's design for the adoption of an older child was much more oblique than altruistic. She really wanted someone to amuse, care for, and attend to little Ben. Cynthia, five years older than Ben Jr., provided a solution, and it was a gamble that worked. Cynthia was responsible and understood her place. And her new mother's confidence in this arrangement was only augmented by her domineering control.

As it turned out, for a time, the arrangement was fortuitous. Cynthia developed a kinship with and affection toward Ben Jr. and learned the manners and sophistication of the city. And Maggie Teal, fairly relieved of responsibility, could rise at midday to pamper herself in preparation for another night on the town.

Mr. Ben Teal, in all of this, had been upright and responsible. Although a very busy man, he had taken care of the family. There was a maid for

Margaret and a tutor for the children, who became accustomed to city life and to carefree summer weeks in luxury homes rented at Mamaroneck on the Long Island Sound, and at West End on the Jersey Shore. For a time, it had been a whirlwind world of theater, restaurants, and new friends. Now, four years after her adoption, Cynthia's New York life was dramatically interrupted and her name in Galveston had suddenly changed to Marie.

As Cynthia, now Marie, entered the formal Hotel Galvez dining room, along with her mother, Genevieve, and her stepbrother, Jack, to have breakfast with a new acquaintance by the name of Dr. George Paddleford, he rose to greet them. The children, of course, had been well instructed in fine dining, thanks to Ben Teal. Their manners were impeccable. Surely the doctor would have been impressed. Likewise, the children were drawn to this handsome, charming man who had the commanding confidence of a successful businessman, and the comforting presence of a doctor.

After breakfast, Marie walked out of the Hotel Galvez into a bright, sunny Galveston morning, well fed and delighted at the prospect of an afternoon with Dr. Paddleford on a yacht named *Casiana*.

Chapter 12:

George

George Edgar Paddleford was born on October 19, 1874, the youngest of four children, in Mendocino, California, a logging settlement perched on a bucolic headland rising over the Pacific coast two hundred miles north of San Francisco. His father, Benjamin, had migrated from New Hampshire to the northern coast of California in the 1850s, along with many other New Englanders who engaged in the lucrative northern California lumber industry.

Benjamin became the superintendent of a sawmill in Big River, the town's name before it became Mendocino. He married Mary Jane Walsh, ten years younger, who came from the small town of St. Catherine in Canada. They lived most of their lives in Big River, retiring to San Francisco in their later years. Mary Jane died on September 3, 1917.[1] The timing of her death nearly coincided with George's chance acquaintance with the attractive New York widow who introduced herself as Genevieve Thompson. Indeed, George may even have been in transit from his mother's funeral at the time.

As a young man, George followed the ambitious nature of his father. His inclination, however, was not toward the hard, manual business of lumbering but rather toward an academic life. His parents and teachers recognized his ambitions in this realm and encouraged him to enter the University of Southern California. In June 1904, at the age of thirty, George graduated with distinction from the College of Medicine. An

Dr. George Paddleford, 1904

honorary banquet was held for the twenty-four members of his graduating class at the Hotel Angelus. The toasts and addresses to the class were effusive. It was noted that the College of Medicine at USC was the only college on the Pacific Coast whose graduates had all passed the state examination.[2]

As a disciplined New Englander, George would have taken to heart his responsibilities as a new physician and would have channeled a life of decency and discipline. However, he was not one to miss a good time, and, meanwhile, he had fallen in love with a girl named Edna Stetson, the daughter of Albert L. Stetson, a widower and prominent citizen of Los Angeles. They were married on August 2, 1904, shortly after George's graduation from the University of Southern California, in the Stetson home. In September, after a two-week honeymoon in San Francisco, the young couple moved into a temporary Los Angeles apartment on South Grand Avenue. George was quickly hired by California's entrepreneurial oil tycoon Edward L. Doheny as a field surgeon for the Mexican Petroleum Company, more than two thousand miles away on the Gulf of Mexico. Edna, they decided, would stay in Los Angeles until George could find a suitable residence near the Tampico oil fields.[3]

In 1905, months later, the young couple traveled by train to the beautiful basin city of San Luis Potosi, centered in the high central plateau, rimmed by the distant Sierra Madre mountains, and blessed with a comfortable, semiarid climate. It was an ideal location for George and Edna's first Mexican residence. Cathedrals, shrines, temples, lavish colonial villas, and government buildings steeped in Spanish heritage displayed the monumental wealth that had been derived from the historic mining of silver and gold in the district. And, like all Americans and other foreigners engaged in the capitalization of Mexico at this time, the Paddlefords were welcomed as privileged guests. George Paddleford could not have provided Edna with a more secure and beautiful haven for the first year of their marriage.[4]

Dr. Paddleford's assignment as a physician to the workers in Doheny's oil fields required train travel from San Luis Potosi to the port of Tampico, two hundred miles eastward on the Gulf Coast. Although the trip to Tampico was slow and torturous, the magnificent scenery of the valleys, mountains, and deep gorges of the eastern Sierra Madres made up for it. The most treacherous leg was the eighteen-mile pass through Tamasapo Canyon, a construction masterpiece that forced the train up steep grades and around hairpin rim turns against vertical cliffs hundreds of feet high. The eight-to-ten-hour trip to sea level was a drop of more than six thousand feet. Approaching from the distance, George would have found the verdant Huasteca rain forest a beautiful and welcome sight.

However, upon arriving at the Cerro de la Pez (Hill of Tar) oil fields, thirty-five miles outside of Tampico, the doctor would have faced a hot, sticky jungle punctuated with incessant mosquitoes, where he would have to live for long stretches without his bride in San Luis Potosi.

Despite these challenges, as weeks passed into months, Dr. Paddleford quickly established himself as a respected, exemplary leader and an indispensable addition to the disease-infested, injury-afflicted environment of the Mexican Petroleum Company community known as Camp Ebano. As one of the surgeons, he was instrumental in the organization of hospital, medical care, and sanitation systems servicing more than

three thousand unskilled Mexican workers, hundreds of skilled techni-
cians, managers brought from California, and all of the workers' families
as well. No expense was spared in providing for the health and domestic
welfare of the camp. The Mexican Petroleum Company gave George Paddleford high marks in its annual report of 1916:

> Dr. George Paddleford entered the service of the company a
> dozen years ago as a surgeon, and was located at Ebano. He
> soon developed a rare ability in business details and the han-
> dling of men. When the general manager looked for a gen-
> eral superintendent, Paddleford was the logical man. He has
> made good at every point, and now is to have a steamship
> named for him, which may carry his name to every port of
> industry in the world.[5]

It was nearly a year before Edna Paddleford arrived at Ebano from
San Luis Potosi. Anticipating the chafing petulance of the Huasteca
rainforest, she was pleasantly surprised by the housing and comforts
provided at the camp. A description of Camp Ebano was written in a
book authorized by the Mexican Petroleum Company:

> In February 1901, a railroad spur was built to facilitate the
> delivery of material to the places selected for drilling and
> building a camp. The site chosen is strikingly picturesque;
> the buildings cover the summit and flanks of a cone-shaped
> hill known as Cerro la Dieha, and there is probably no better
> equipped camp today in Mexico. There was installed imme-
> diately an ice and cold storage plant to provide pure water
> and proper refrigeration for meats; in a short time there was
> built, in addition to the necessary offices, a boiler and black-
> smith's shop, and a large supply warehouse. Good houses were
> constructed of brick or wood for all employees, and a large
> recreation room, which is without any rival in the Republic of
> Mexico. Water was brought through a six-inch line from the
> Tamesi River, which is about fifteen kilometers from the camp

*at Ebano. Under the direction of a medical doctor appointed
by the Company, a hospital was built and equipped.*[6]

Edna made the best of Camp Ebano. There were other wives with
whom she could share the adventures of living in a beautiful rain forest,
with its paradise of exotic plants and birds, and conversely with whom
she would also bear its discomforting heat, torrential downpours, pes-
tilent insects, and poisonous snakes. Their social life was accompanied
by plenty of good food and drink, although Doheny, as a general rule,
forbade alcohol. There were bridge games, table tennis, and other rec-
reational activities. The town of Tampico provided shopping, festivals,
churches, and a library.

George and Edna took a break from the jungle just a few months
after they had settled into their domicile at Ebano. Edna's sister, Florence,
was to be married to Mr. George Hazard in Los Angeles on August 7, and
Edna insisted that they attend. They arrived in mid-July 1906 to enjoy a
month of vacationing and visiting before returning to Mexico. They also
purchased a large house, located at 539 South Western Avenue.

A little over a year later, in November 1907, Edna told George that
she was pregnant and that she would return to Los Angeles to have her
baby. She delivered a son, George Stetson Paddleford, on August 7, 1908.
George and Edna returned to Mexico with their new baby, and enjoyed
family life and the safety of Camp Ebano for five more years. However, by
1914, the Mexican Revolution was in full swing.

The foreign-owned oil companies along the Gulf of Mexico operated
outside the revolutionary central corridors of Mexico. Geographically,
the Golden Lane was walled by the Sierra Madre Oriental Mountains and
the forested terrain of the Huasteca. As a result, the gulf oil enterprise
never suffered an attack of wholesale destruction. The revolution brought
fame and glory to Mexico's antiheroes—Pancho Villa, Emiliano Zapata,
First Chief Venustiano Carranza—and others who rode in roughneck
revenge against the Federalist government, crying out, "*Viva la Revolu-
cion*"—even though the Revolution, "from 1910 to 1920, killed one million out of fifteen million Mexicans."[7]

Although the coastal oil fields were skirted by the onslaught of the

Mexican Revolution, constant vigilance was required. The pumping stations, derricks, tracks, storage, and miles of pipeline were not entirely left untouched by raids, banditry, and sabotage. Hundreds of thousands of dollars had to be paid out for protection. By this time, the Golden Lane included oil companies other than Doheny's Mexican Petroleum Company—principally, the British company, Eagle Oil, owned by Sir Weetman Pearson, who would become well known and admired for his work in Mexico as Lord Cowdray. Protection required cooperation among all the operators along the gulf.

In 1914, the oil fields narrowly escaped calamity when a large contingency of First Chief Carranza's Constitutionalist forces managed to congregate outside Tampico and line up against the Mexican Federalists garrisoned along the Panuco River. Americans and other foreigners, numbering nearly two thousand, were caught in the middle, plagued by fear of a devastating crossfire and an unleashing of oil that could spread a firestorm throughout the forest.

The US Navy was summoned to the shores of the gulf. Refugees poured into the harbor, filling available American, British, and German vessels. The oil company managers, holding out hope, felt that as long as the American fleet sat offshore, neither Carranza's nor Huerta's army would initiate an all-out-destructive battle. Then, on April 21, 1914, to the shock of the remaining American residents, the American Fleet pulled out of Tampico. Orders were confirmed that American Admiral Mayo was to leave Tampico and embargo a German arms shipment entering the port at Veracruz. Tampico citizens, two hundred miles to the north of Veracruz, received news that 126 of their fellow countrymen had been killed. The mood in Tampico turned ugly. Americans left to carry on without military protection and who were spread throughout the oil fields had to be evacuated. As general superintendent of operations for the Mexican Petroleum Company, George Paddleford played a key role in dealing with the Tampico incident.

The evacuation of Tampico required quick, decisive leadership. George Paddleford, who had been watching the tempest develop for some months, shepherded his wife and young son aboard the SS *Edward Doheny*, in mid-March, bound for Galveston. From there, Edna and young George returned permanently to their home in Los Angeles. With his family safely out of the country, George returned to help oversee events as they might develop in Tampico. When he saw that he was left to manage an evacuation of hundreds of his employees from the oil district without the benefit of a robust American military, he rose to the occasion. His leadership role was gratefully witnessed by a company employee, C. H. Melton, in the *Los Angeles Evening News*:

> *I believe we were the last of the Americans to leave the city under the protection of the Stars and Stripes, for on Tuesday, 31 women and 99 men, employees of the company and their families, were loaded into the American yacht Wakiva, ready to be carried out to the United States battleships. Then they were given orders by the commanding officer of the Mexican battleship Bravo that if the Wakiva lifted anchor they would turn their guns on them.*
>
> *George E. Paddleford, general superintendent of the company, then made arrangements with the German and English gunboats anchored in the river to come to their rescue, which they quickly consented to do. The employees of the yacht consented to the American flag being taken down, and the German and English flags raised. As soon as the flags were hoisted on the staff that previously held the Stars and Stripes, the boat pulled anchor and glided out of the river to the waiting refugee boats stationed several miles out at sea.*
>
> *You people up in this country cannot realize the humiliation the Americans felt in having to be protected by another flag. Too much cannot be said in praise of Mr. Paddleford, our general superintendent. He saw that every employee of the company was safely taken from the city and he was among the last to leave Tampico. Throughout the entire day, with the assistance of the two yachts Wakiva and Wild Duck, he collected members of the company in a radius of a number of miles around the city and by Wednesday noon had them safely onboard the American boats.[8]*

The Tampico and Veracruz incidents in the spring of 1914 were indeed almost incidental footnotes to the great ten-year Mexican Revolution, except, of course, to President Wilson's administration and to the Americans who lived and worked in the oil fields along the Gulf Coast. General Superintendent Paddleford and his workers and comanagers who had been evacuated would have to wait through a cooling-off period until such time as they would be permitted to return.

Paddleford had his hands full. The Tampico incident was more than an international incident; it was an ongoing business and human turning point that he would have to manage. The disruptions that followed the Tampico and Veracruz incidents seriously challenged the managers of the oil fields from one end of the Golden Lane to the other. Reports of banditry, intimidation, and threats by insurgent rebels signaled a rolling crisis. One returning witness, Mr. A. Speliney, owner of a small oil company, wrote about the troubles: "Property is taken from Americans by the warring factions. Free license, I granted, to rob Americans of money, provisions and crops, horses and cattle. This is often done at the point of a gun, and intimidation is practiced generally."[9]

In the midst of the chaos in Tampico, Edna wrote in February 1915 to say that she was again pregnant, but George and other executives were already back in Mexico, as it was imperative that superintendents and managers maintain their managerial positions over the oil fields. In October, George received an urgent message to return home. Edna was seriously ill. He returned in haste. Days after his arrival, on October 26, 1915, both Edna and her baby girl died in childbirth.[10]

George laid to rest his beloved wife and daughter at San Gabriel Cemetery in Los Angeles, left seven-year-old George S. Paddleford in Los Angeles, under the care of his aunt Florence, Edna's sister, and returned to the Tampico oil fields, where the Golden Lane continued operations at a time when Mexico's central corridor became more immersed in war and political turmoil than ever.

Chapter 13:

A Gusher

Events were happening quickly in Mexico. At the end of 1915, two weeks after George buried his wife and daughter, Pancho Villa's Division of the North fell to First Chief Carranza's Constitutionalists. Villa fled to the hills with a handful of fellow bandits, fuming with revenge.

George Paddleford was summoned back to Tampico. Something new and extraordinary was brewing in the oil fields. Under way was a drilling operation that, if successful, might surpass the production of all other wells combined.

One of Doheny's early Mexican acquisitions was a ten-thousand-acre tract of rolling hills pockmarked with hundreds of asphalt seepages. It was thirty miles into the jungle. High hopes were placed on a site named Cerro Azul No. 4. Holding tanks and pipelines had been built in preparation. On a stormy night in February 1916, cold rains slashed at the derrick's rigging. As evening fell, a low, unfamiliar rumble from deep inside the earth superseded the hammering of wind and rain. The men ran for their lives. In minutes, an explosion of gas blew the derrick and drilling tools into the night sky. Flying steel mixed with the rain. As dawn broke, a fountain of oil creased the sky and the landscape was drenched in ebony for miles around. It took ten days to cap the flow. The black lakes surrounding the tower surrendered half a million barrels of reclaimed oil, and the hydrant yielded more than two hundred thousand barrels per day. Production from Cerro Azul No. 4 continued for fourteen years.[1]

The gusher challenged Doheny's men. Transporting, holding, refining, and exporting became an extraordinary undertaking. A million dollars per week in profits flooded into Doheny's corporations. Oil transport depots needed to be constructed on both sides of the Atlantic. The gusher made George Paddleford and the other executives wealthy men, and Doheny one of the richest men in the world.

The Golden Lane required more protection. Doheny's Mexican Petroleum Company, Lord Cowdray's Eagle Oil Transport Company, and other newly formed companies scrambled to garrison this part of Mexico. Under General Manuel Peláez, Doheny's hired gun, the company's security forces swelled to an army of six thousand. Manuel Peláez and his prominent family, of Spanish heritage, were long-established hacienda owners in the Huasteca region. The family benefited from leasing large tracts of land to the oil companies. George Paddleford acted as a liaison to General Peláez in order to keep his loyalty. At the same time, it was necessary to placate the interests of Carranza's government. Dealing with these factions, along with labor strikes and persistent vandalizing, was an ongoing bedevilment to all oil company managers. Over time, while engaging in his management capacities, Paddleford struck up a personal friendship with General Peláez—one with lasting consequences.

Meanwhile, Pancho Villa, who had been seething in the hills of Chihuahua, learned that Mexico's new oil gusher would enrich American pockets. He went on a fuming rampage, recruiting followers and robbing the countryside. One of his bandit patrols, on January 17, 1916, stopped a train and in cold blood murdered sixteen American miners. This was followed by a raid on a hacienda owned by William Randolph Hearst. Seemingly out of control, Villa then crossed the border with a band of Villistas and, on March 9, shot up the town of Columbus, New Mexico. It was a firefight that killed seventeen US citizens. Villa's apparent mad intent was to unleash a war with the United States and rekindle his role as Mexico's heroic defender. The bait was taken, and on March 15, 1916, the US Army, under General "Black Jack" Pershing, with "4,800 men, 192 officers, and 4,175 pack mules and horses, crossed the border to capture or kill Pancho Villa."[2]

General Pershing thrust deep into Mexico, thinning out supply lines over hundreds of miles. His soldiers suffered cold, heat, thirst, and hunger.

Mostly, they endured intimidating frustration for their efforts. The Mexican peasants were not about to give up their hero. Villa seemed to be a ghost. After eleven months and three hundred miles of punishing marches into the cold winter mountains of northern Mexico, Pershing was ordered to stand down. Pancho Villa remained Mexico's populist hero at large. In February 1917, Pershing's army marched out of Mexico.

In many ways, 1917 was a pivotal year. First Chief Carranza, the white-bearded governor of the state of Coahuila, had taken control of a greater proportion of Mexico, and the United States recognized him as Mexico's de facto president. Carranza called for a national constitutional convention. The centerpiece of the 1917 Constitution was Article 27, which called for a return of all natural resources, including oil and minerals, to the nation. Years of legal battles followed. Finally, in 1938, Mexico nationalized the gulf oil fields, but by that time Doheny and company were gone.

General Pershing's troops, after seven months in suspended agitation and continual training at the Mexican border under Pershing and his second in command, Lieutenant George Patton, were ordered to embark on a greater mission. On April 6, 1917, the United States entered World War I.

The Cerro No. 4 oil well couldn't have come in at a more opportune time. "The demand for Doheny's oil products skyrocketed as the war continued. . . . During July 1917, his Huasteca Petroleum Company shipped 1,301,590 barrels of crude to buyers throughout the world. At this point, Doheny could move nearly 100,000 barrels a day to points across the globe via his fleet of thirty-one tankers."[3]

In that same year, Doheny's Pan American Petroleum and Transport Company launched six new tankers. One was the SS *George E. Paddleford*, launched at Wilmington, Delaware, on April 18. "It was the first of our new steamers to go into service, and our first American-built ship. She is to sail in June, with a cargo of 55,000 barrels."[4]

Edward Doheny was riding high on the profitable oil tankers laden low in the water. The Tampico oil fields hummed with expansion and production. "Tampico tugs, launches, and barges worked as they [had] never worked before. Everything that can carry freight or tow a barge is working almost day and night. The freight to the Panuco, Topila, and southern fields is increasing daily. Every vessel arriving from the States brings freight to the oil fields."[5]

These were very heady times for Doheny and his executives, many of whom, like George Paddleford, made their homes in Los Angeles. George Paddleford's returns to Los Angeles, since Edna's passing had been far less frequent. In Galveston, in the summer of 1917, at the Hotel Galvez, when he had never been busier in his career, George Paddleford, on his own, embraced a relationship with a young widow with two children from New York. She was beautiful, intelligent, flirtatious, and sophisticated. He felt young again. He'd enjoyed an unexpected and welcome respite from his duties. Meeting Genevieve was an awakening from a personal life that for too long had been swallowed up by work and numbing sorrow. He carried these thoughts on the day the Doheny yacht *Casiano* pulled out of the Galveston harbor heading back to Tampico.

He and Genevieve had talked of meeting again in New York, and she had promised to call him. Indeed, by 1917, the embers of their brief summer romance in Galveston still smoldered. Genevieve Thompson and her children had taken him in, and he felt certain that she was taken with him as well. He was flattered by her efforts at keeping in touch.

Their relationship was momentarily interrupted when, on October 30, a distressing event brought him up short. One of the company tankers ran aground off the coast of Tampico. It was the SS *George E. Paddleford*! But good luck prevailed. The entire crew was rescued in very dangerous turf, the great tanker was pulled out, and by December it was back in service. With this good fortune on his side and with a brief slackening of company duties, Dr. George E. Paddleford married Genevieve Thompson on December 18, 1917. The marriage was performed by a justice of the peace in Houston, Texas.

In later years, George might have looked back and thought the grounding of his namesake vessel an omen to heed. No such reckoning was given at the time. His ship had been righted. For the marriage, though, rocky shoals lay ahead.

Chapter 14:

Hollywood

A blue California sky greeted Dr. George Paddleford and his new family as they stepped out of the Santa Fe La Grande station into downtown Los Angeles. They breathed deeply the floral breeze that brushed across the lush Los Angeles landscape.

Less than a year had passed since Aunt Eleanor had scrambled out of New York City one late night onto a southbound train with her trunks, her two children, and an obdurate self-assurance that recovery was but a horizon away. She inhaled not only the California air but the success of

La Grande Santa Fe Station

having transported her family from one world to another. Dr. Paddleford, with pride and hope in his heart, felt blessed with his bright new family.

The driver motored easily down wide, tree-lined Sunset Boulevard to the corner of Sunset and Laurel. George escorted Genevieve, Marie, and Jack up the long walkway to their new home, a large California ranch with a deep-beamed front porch. They were met by George's sister-in-law, Florence Stetson Hazard, sister of George's first wife, Edna. Standing with Florence was George's son, George Jr., who rushed to his father. He was the same age as Jack.

Eleanor, now Genevieve, saw safety and security and already felt the familiar hint of adventure. She had gambled on safety and won. She was a winner. She had succeeded, she knew, on a foundation of lies, but she was good at that. Deception had always been a useful ally. Their arrival had been welcoming and the atmosphere inviting. This time, so far away from her past, she would make it all work.

George's housekeeper had obviously put extra effort into their homecoming. An enormous bouquet of flowers announced a large flowing dining and living room. There was champagne, a bowl of fruit, and a table setting for six. After George gave the grand tour, they sat down to a sumptuous lunch. The little group became acquainted. The boys made friends quickly and easily. Cynthia was excited. She had her own room. Genevieve soon turned the conversation to the location of nearby shops. Tomorrow they would need to go shopping.

Dr. Paddleford was generous. Overly so. He'd encouraged her to open accounts in the best stores. With Cynthia, now Marie, at her side, Genevieve set off early the next morning for a long day of shopping downtown on LA's Broadway. The driver would load the packages. She'd thought ahead. Soon she would announce her presence to Los Angeles society. The details of a grand reception began to form in her mind as she meted out her list for the day's spree.

Like a match to gasoline, Genevieve Paddleford burst onto Hollywood's swanky department stores and shops. By the end of her first week in Los Angeles, she had accumulated a new California wardrobe, not only for herself but for Cynthia and little Ben as well. She opened accounts at Hamburger and Sons, May Company, J. W. Robinson's, and Bullocks.

She strolled into the luxurious Alexandria Hotel, home of two of Hollywood's favorite jewelers, Harry Winston & Co. and the Laykin Diamond Company. She might have brushed by some very prominent Angelenos in the movie business. In particular, a familiar guest at the Alexandria was Charlie Chaplin. Other movie greats seen around town included Mary Pickford, Douglas Fairbanks, Marion Davies, Lillian Gish, Greta Garbo, John Gilbert, Al Jolson, Buster Keaton, Lionel Barrymore, Samuel Goldwyn, and Louis B. Mayer.

It was 1918, and the movie business was on the verge of overshadowing the California oil bonanza. The lust for oil that had erected hundreds of oil derricks across the LA landscape gave way to the creative voyeurism of the movie palaces. Brilliant production entrepreneurs who had come out of very modest backgrounds gambled on the magic of Thomas Edison's Kinetoscope. The new movie business burgeoning in those sunny hills would soon become known around the world as Hollywood. Feature-length movies had already captured hungry audiences. More than six hundred movies would be produced in 1919. The first movie stars were born, and great movie palaces had sprung up in Los Angeles and New York. Even fan magazines had hit the streets.[1]

Genevieve Paddleford found herself relishing the familiar world of entertainment. She would find a way to make herself known in Los Angeles. There was so much to do! She devoured the society pages and began to write two lists of names. One would come from the society pages of the *Los Angeles Times*, the *Los Angeles Evening Herald*, and the more gossipy *Los Angeles Examiner*, owned by William Randolph Hearst. That list would include those upper-class, established residents who had not yet embraced the movie crowd. They were the wives of bankers, publishers, orange growers, oilmen, builders, and so on. She would garner the other list of names by combing the new movie-fan magazines.

For Genevieve, names were currency. Names well dropped could establish credit, elevate status, and secure an invitation. She had used this currency in acquainting herself with George Paddleford. From the divorce case that would eventually follow, court documents revealed that when George met her "she told him she was the half sister of Mrs. Claus Spreckels, Mrs. Jacklyn, and Mrs. Moffat, all prominent in California social circles. She also represented that her father, R. A. H. McKinney, was a capitalist worth millions."[2]

Aunt Eleanor, the new Genevieve, had married well. She had accomplished more than her hopes. George Paddleford was a rich doctor, socially prominent, handsome, kind, and generous. He had been a lonely widower whose heartstrings were easily plucked. She had long learned to play a man's heart as a virtuoso. She could love this man, but how wonderfully convenient it was that he must spend weeks at a time away from home. And by capitalizing on pretty Cynthia's magical voice and charm, she would focus on entertaining. If there was one thing she knew how to do well, it was how to put on a show. Everything was falling into place as she set out to draw in the crust of Los Angeles's social elite. Yes, she could love a man, but to be the center of attention was her real delight.

Chapter 15:

The Paris of Mexico

Great new serpentine vessels stretched across the Atlantic horizon in the early 1920s, destined for world ports. Many of these were owned by the Pan American Oil and Transport Company and supervised by George Paddleford.

Oil had replaced coal as the fuel for general transportation worldwide. From 1919 onward, unprecedented investments were channeled into Gulf Coast terminals, pipelines, storage tanks, pumping stations, refineries, and ships. More than one hundred different companies were by then engaged in drilling and construction. Dr. George Paddleford was at the center of what was, at the time, one of the world's largest construction projects. The greatest project, the Panama Canal, had just been completed in 1914.

Tampico, twenty years before the oil boom, was a sleepy, removed, unremarkable old Mexican town. By 1920, its scattered population of 17,000 had increased to 135,000 city inhabitants. The arrival of the industrious foreigners—Americans, English, Germans, Canadians and Dutch—changed Tampico into a cosmopolitan city. New shops, stores, social clubs, and lodges, mostly American, as well as a variety of newspapers, allowed foreigners a familiarity of home. Foreign investments were made in schools, hospitals, and roads. Tampico had become the Paris of Mexico. Tampico's Spanish plazas and architecture, accentuated with cast-iron balconies, were reminiscent of New Orleans. The centerpiece

Tampico Cathedral

of Tampico, the stunning neoclassical Cathedral of Tampico, located in the Plaza de Armas, was built largely with funds provided by Edward Doheny, a devout Catholic.[1]

But Tampico, not unlike any boomtown, had its dark side. There was squalor. During the oil boom, thousands of migrants were crowded into slums, their shanty shelters built on stilts next to swamplands.

"The native itinerants suffered the most unhealthful conditions. In one rooming house, 57 people lived in sixteen rooms. In another, 2,100 people lived in thirty rooms. . . Migrants raised chickens in the city to supplement their diets. The mortality rate also rose with the population. In 1910, it was forty-one deaths per one thousand people; in 1917, it was sixty-six per one thousand. Little, except for the high wages and the expectation someday to move on, made up for the unhealthful conditions of living in Tampico's slums."[2]

Dr. George Paddleford's personal life came second to the oil action around Tampico. The boys, however, George Jr. and Ben Teal Jr. (Jack, as he was called then), in their teens, apparently visited the oil region often, while on breaks from school. George was close to these boys, and, for them, Tampico must have been an adventure. For a time in their lives, they were inseparable.

Genevieve also visited Tampico and stayed at Camp Ebano, sometime in 1919. However, it was a visit not without mischief. She certainly could not have been happy in the sultry, steamy oil environment of the camp. It was later revealed in Dr. Paddleford's divorce decree that her social meddling and milling while in Tampico almost cost him his job. In her state of discomfort and yearning for Los Angeles, she spread a malicious rumor that the general manager of the Mexican Petroleum Company, Mr. William Green, found Dr. Paddleford's services no longer satisfactory. This kind of meddling seems to have been an irresistible flaw in her character. She had treated William Toomey with similar maliciousness.

Hearing the rumor for himself, Dr. Paddleford offered his resignation. It was not until later that he learned the rumor had been Genevieve's invention, seemingly a connivance to get her and Dr. Paddleford out of Mexico. With tearful innocence, she gushed her sorrow. In the end, she got her way and left for Los Angeles alone to resume the favors of Dr. Paddleford's generosity and to carry on as one of one of LA's emerging socialites.

While Genevieve Paddleford and her daughter, Marie, were riding the social circuit and entertaining musical guests in the Paddleford home, a tragedy struck in Montana. Genevieve's half brother, Gilman McKinnie, at the height of his business career, along with a wool buyer from Boston, were both killed when their car left the road outside Chinook on June 26, 1920. They had just made a deal with a large sheep-ranching operation. Gilman's funeral was attended by folks from miles around the county. The family recollected a mile of cars struggling through a rainy day on the muddy road to the cemetery. Florence was inconsolable for months. The family, though, finally pulled together. Florence's children and later her grandchildren would always regard her as the strong matriarch of the McKinnie family. Eleanor, living in California as the wife of George Paddleford, was never notified. The name Genevieve Paddleford was unknown to Florence at the time.

Back in Tampico, Dr. George Paddleford became more deeply involved in negotiations with General Peláez, who wanted more for his services. Coveting his independence and defying Carranza's Constitutionalists, Peláez fought for regional autonomy with money he could extract from the oil companies. Doheny called it extortion, but Peláez commanded an efficient and reliable strike force that proved highly valuable against other rebel factions that would demand extortions of their own. Peláez demanded more and better weapons. But because of the US embargo, the oil companies could not ship arms directly. Instead, cash was filtered through the company to the general for purchasing smuggled weapons. Paddleford had to personally assure Peláez that while President Wilson willingly recognized the Carranza government, Carranza's army would not get new weapons, only ammunition replacements. Peláez's trust in Paddleford was critical to protecting the company oil fields. Paddleford was able to assuage his temperament.[3]

George Paddleford plied these turbulent waters. He was not the only senior decision maker on the ground. There were as many as thirty other senior managers and superintendents who were dedicated to the Mexican Petroleum Company and its subsidiaries. George Paddleford and William Green could, arguably, have been closest to the action around Tampico. Green was in charge of the terminal operations, and Paddleford ran the transportation systems all the way up the Atlantic seaboard from the Tampico fields to Portland, Maine, as well as to Europe and South America.

It is of little wonder that the busy superintendent had no time or inclination to check the background of the woman with whom he had fallen in love and married only months after their meeting. However, as the madness that stalked Mexico for so many years finally ground to an end and, one by one, its warrior luminaries were assassinated—Zapata in 1919,

Carranza in 1920, Pancho Villa in 1923, Alvaro Obregon in 1928—and the foreign-owned oil industry gradually began to shut down, Dr. George Paddleford, in 1921, returned to Los Angeles. Only then did he realize the crushing truth: Genevieve was not the person she claimed to be.

The revelation convulsed into a scandalous divorce suit that stretched across the LA newspapers for months, and for years to come, the divorce and the name Genevieve Paddleford would supply grist for newspapers across the country.

Chapter 16:

Leaving LA, 1921

The president of Mexico in 1938 was Lázaro Cárdenas. He bent to the demands of the labor unions and nationalized Mexico's petroleum industry. By then, gulf oil had already been in a serious state of decline for more than fifteen years. In 1923, oil prices and production fell precipitously, exhausted oil fields became subject to saltwater seepage, and thousands were left unemployed. What precipitated nationalization was the workers' alignment with the state. "More than anything, the demands of organized petroleum workers brought an end to the operations of the private foreign oil companies in Mexico. Days before President Cárdenas decreed the oil expropriation, the oil workers had begun to seize control of the oil installations. He had no choice but to expropriate. He did so during a dramatic nationwide broadcast on 18 March 1938, a date many Mexicans associate with the economic independence of Mexico. . . . The foreign oilmen were stunned."[1]

Edward Doheny had seen the future, and in 1925 he sold his Mexican oil interests to Standard Oil of Indiana. Meanwhile, Dr. Paddleford, having already returned to Los Angeles in 1921, found that the family he had nurtured from a distance failed to offer the homecoming he'd expected. Almost immediately, he encountered a dark truth that would unravel his life, a truth that would tarnish his standing in the community and consume his spirit. Dr. Paddleford had been duped.

Three years had passed since the day George had moved his new family into his Hollywood home. For three years, Genevieve Paddleford had engaged in Hollywood's fashionable lifestyle, easily employing her social talents well honed in New York as the former wife of Ben Teal. She also discovered that she could ride the coattails of Cynthia's vocal talents. Cynthia's blossoming popularity enabled the two of them to make the Paddleford name notable in society pages and gossip columns.[2]

George learned that the woman who so lavishly spent his money harbored a past that he could not abide. He found out that Genevieve Thompson was really the widow of Ben Teal and had been a convicted inmate at Blackwell's Island prison.

Although Genevieve had indeed made a name for herself over her three years of marriage to an executive who worked for Edward Doheny in the oil fields of Mexico, she did not quite seem the typical country-club wife of a notable executive. Where had she come from? Her pronouncements seemed exaggerated from the start. Certainly, people talked. Cynthia wrote in her memoir that a friend alerted George to his suspicions about Genevieve, and that prompted George to hire a detective agency.

For a while, he kept Genevieve's secrets to himself, but the truth was that George had been supporting a fraud. Not only was she an imposter, but she was an angry, bitter, and totally distrustful woman. If he could divorce her quietly, perhaps he could avoid the humiliation he might face from his colleagues and friends. When he finally confronted Genevieve, she went into a hysterical eruption.

For a brief period, the Paddlefords put up a front for the public, but both agreed that a separation was required. Genevieve decided that she would ensconce herself in New York City as the wife of a wealthy oil executive. She would arrive in style, and she would expect "suitable accommodations."

Cynthia notes that she and Genevieve traveled by train while Dr. Paddleford motored cross-country with the two boys and trunks of luggage. There were two cars. George drove one, and the other was driven by Genevieve's manservant, whom Cynthia referred to as Joe. Genevieve and Cynthia would have traveled in a first-class Pullman from LA to Chicago on the *Santa Fe California Limited*, then from Chicago to New York on the *Broadway Limited*. It was important to Genevieve, for appearances, that her husband arrive with two limousines bearing her trunks.

Genevieve and Cynthia Marie's train trip across the United States was long—at least three days—but it was far from uncomfortable. They would have enjoyed fine dining, maid service, scenic views from an observation car, and many opportunities to engage socially.

The motor trip would have been long and arduous, though for the Paddleford boys it was probably an adventure. There were scenic mountains, deserts, endless plains and fields, and countless towns along the way. The long journey connected a series of named and unnamed roads, mostly unimproved, that, taken altogether, became known as the Lincoln Highway.[3] George and his small company would have traveled only during daylight hours and would have carried food, water, and gasoline. Genevieve would have crammed in as much luggage as possible and would meet her caravan of trunks as it pulled up to New York's Plaza Hotel.

It had been five years since Genevieve, formerly known as Margaret "Maggie" Teal, had mysteriously disappeared from Broadway's social

Plaza Hotel, circa 1920

scene. The gossip circuit must have been electrified over her mysterious disappearance at the time, wondering, "Whatever became of Margaret Teal?" Little did her former friends and acquaintances know that Maggie Teal had long transposed herself into the wife of a wealthy Californian, and that she and her daughter, Cynthia, had recently moved into the Plaza Hotel with trunks liveried by the chauffeurs of two limousines. In time, as the notoriety of the Paddleford divorce coursed through the Los Angeles and New York newspapers, Maggie Teal's former New York friends would gasp at the revelation that Maggie Teal resided at the Plaza as the wealthy Genevieve Paddleford.

Dr. Paddleford, it seems, left the Mexican Petroleum Company either by resignation or by taking a very long leave of absence. Perhaps he'd been allowed a partial leave of his business duties. The Mexican oil bonanza had peaked in 1921. The Doheny operations could well have afforded Dr. Paddleford a sabbatical. There is an unfortunate shroud of mystery surrounding the affairs and movements of many executives who worked for Edward Doheny. Doheny's biographer Margaret Davis noted that Doheny's wife, Estelle, burned his personal papers on the evening of his funeral in September 1935, and that his descendants refused to be interviewed. She writes, "I was told that it would be next to impossible to unravel the historical details of Doheny's complex and contradictory life."[4]

Jonathon C. Brown, author of *Oil and Revolution in Mexico*, writes in a correspondence about Doheny, "I suspect that his business papers were also destroyed or simply thrown away when Pan American sold out to Standard of Indiana."[5]

Dr. Paddleford's domestic affairs, though, crop up again and again in the local press. Curious scandal seekers were drawn to reports of charges and countercharges in the Paddleford divorce. Even years after the divorce decree, issued on July 20, 1923, the Paddleford name appeared frequently in the newspapers across the country as a consequence of Genevieve's misadventures, much to the dismay of the Paddleford family.

Chapter 17:

An Unfortunate
Misunderstanding

The social and musical worlds of New York, Los Angeles, and London are reeling from the stagger of an astounding discovery—the rich and dignified dowager who had captured the most conservative sets in these respective cities by her display of wealth and her elegance stands revealed as a woman with a past out of a living melodrama of men, millions, divorces, and society.[1]
— Indianapolis Star, *March 12, 1922*

Genevieve settled into the Plaza Hotel during the first week of October 1921. The Plaza, unaware of the recent scandal surrounding the Paddlefords, recognized only Genevieve's reputed wealth and elegance and accepted her without question. She quickly got to work by making selective contacts in the musical world of Manhattan on behalf of Cynthia and quietly entertaining new guests in her fashionable hotel suite. Her goal was to build an operatic career for Cynthia and a life for herself among New York's intellectual elites. Notable among the musical contacts Genevieve lined up for Cynthia were Viennese prima donna Madame Maria Jeritza and American soprano Geraldine Farrar. Both expressed interest in promoting an operatic career for Cynthia. Genevieve looked forward to eventually lifting the eyebrows of the social elite who'd snubbed her as Broadway's Maggie Teal. At the same time, she would shield herself from old Broadway acquaintances. She gambled that none of her former associates along Broadway would suspect that the elegant Mrs. Genevieve Paddleford was the long-lost wife of the impresario Ben Teal.[2]

But that was not to happen. Genevieve got in the way of her own tenuous plans. She ensconced herself and her two children at the Plaza for three months, hoping to hold on to Dr. Paddleford's generosity. Predictably, things really started to unravel when Genevieve's manic attraction to New York's fabulous shops brought her the kind of attention she wished to avoid. But she couldn't stop spending. And bills, those fluffy promises that were so easily laid to one side, began to pile up. A newspaper story that circulated months later described what happened when one creditor decided that she'd had enough.

Wealthy persons, like everyday folk, are often slipshod about paying up their accounts, as any Fifth Avenue merchant will tell you. Mrs. Paddleford had shopped extensively. Among the places she patronized was the millinery establishment of Marie La Tour, on Fifty-Eighth Street. And according to Madame La Tour, she did not pay the bill. So Madame sent it to her lawyer, and he issued a summons.

"Say, do you know who this party is?" demanded the process server, an old-timer with a keen memory for faces, when he returned from the Plaza and a brief interview with a prettily miffed lady.

"Sure, said the attorney. "She's Mrs. Paddleford. Her husband made barrels of money in Mexican oil, and she's got enough to pay this bill a thousand times over and not miss it."

"Well, maybe she's Mrs. Paddleford now, but the last time I saw her, she was Mrs. Ben Teal, and had just finished a stretch on the Island" was the astonishing reply.

As the news of Mrs. Paddleford's identity began to leak out, here and there, in New York, none were more amazed than old friends who knew her when she was Mrs. Ben Teal. Even her own

lawyers and the lawyers of her husband had not suspected the
secret she had kept for five years and which, but for a little lax-
ness over a millinery bill, she might still have locked in her heart.[3]

As it turned out, the milliner's bill was substantial. Genevieve owed her
$1,645.51.[4] The news spread through the gossip grapevine. As Genevieve's
past was increasingly laid bare, Dr. Paddleford began meeting with his
divorce lawyers. As the crest of Genevieve's wave as the wife of a wealthy
Los Angeles oilman began to crash, her mind, never without a conniving
thought, had to consider alternatives. Quickly realizing a stand-by strategy,
she turned again to Cynthia, still Marie. She saw in front of her an opportunity to entrap a new husband, not for herself but for her daughter.

Genevieve had been parading herself and Marie around the elegant
Plaza Hotel and the finest neighboring restaurants and concert halls with
an eye toward introducing her as an up and coming concert artist. But
establishing recognition for Marie was taking time, whereas currying
favor with New York's apparent well-to-do was immediate. Genevieve's
talent in this regard was unmatched.

One of Genevieve's early encounters at the Plaza was with a young
man who presented himself as an Australian cattle king. His name was
Edward Jeffries Naughton. Genevieve and Marie met with him and his
friend Raymond Brownlow on several occasions. Genevieve was thoroughly impressed, but a hoax was being hatched. Cynthia, in her memoir,
recalled the agonizing months of November and December 1921 as laden
with deceit, desperation, and disgrace. She told how she was "kidnapped
and doped into matrimony." She told the story of her furtive marriage to
Edward Jeffries Naughton, which occurred in New York City on November 15, 1921. The following notice appeared in the *New York Times*:

Naughton—Paddleford
Miss Cynthia Marie Paddleford, a daughter of John Paddleford
of Los Angeles, Cal., and Edward Joseph Naughton, a cattle
man of Australia, were married yesterday at the Municipal
Building by Michael J. Cruise, City Clerk. The bride gave her
age as 19 and Mr. Naughton gave his as 33.[4]

Cynthia Marie's age is entered as nineteen. She was a seventeen-year-old minor. She was not the daughter of John Paddleford; she was the daughter of Ben Teal. The notice had all the markings of Genevieve's duplicity. However, this chicanery drawn up between her and her hackneyed friends in this sad marital scheme backfired. On the one hand, Genevieve Paddleford, returning to her name as Margaret, learned that her wealthy Australian cattle king was bogus. On the other hand, the bunco boys from England simultaneously found out they were being flimflammed by Mrs. Paddleford. It was a case of both sides being hustled into a bizarre dupery—a tragic-comedy. As for Marie, she returned to her mother's flat, ashamed, disgraced, and alone.

December brought even more consternation. Near the end of the month, it became urgent for Genevieve to return to Los Angeles. Somehow, she'd slipped up. She had signed over to Dr. Paddleford power of attorney, which had allowed him to put their Laurel Avenue house up for sale. When learning of a pending sale, she rushed back to Los Angeles to sue for her share. Upon arriving, she and Marie checked into the Ambassador Hotel. They would return to New York as soon as her lawyers set aside the sale. In order to make her case, Genevieve falsely claimed that she had not authorized the power of attorney.

When reporters caught up to her, she remarked, "The whole matter was an unfortunate misunderstanding. The power of attorney was requested by Dr. Paddleford to facilitate the rental of our Hollywood home. While I was out, Marie, my daughter, found the telegraphic order prepared by me, and sent it without my knowledge, after I had changed my mind. The suit was brought to correct the situation only. Dr. Paddleford and I are in touch with each other and in harmony. He is now in Bakersfield. There has been no domestic trouble between us."[5]

While in LA, she would also lay stake to any personal belongings left in the house. However, the stores that held her in debt got there first and placed guards around the house to restrain her from touching the property. More litigants got in line, and more guards were stationed. The *Los Angeles Times* reported that a large jewelry account, an account from a department store, and an account for expensive gowns were included in the group of litigants.

The house itself, according to the same report, was purchased by Dr. Paddleford's lawyers, who then arranged a transfer agreement of sale to General Manuel Peláez of Mexico. For a time, Genevieve's lawyer succeeded in tying up the property.[6]

Ben Teal Jr., or Jack Paddleford, as he preferred to be called, seems to have been lost in the shuffle over his mother and sister's three-month escapade in New York City. It appears that Jack had returned to Los Angeles with Dr. Paddleford and George Jr. There was no account of his having remained in New York during those last three, ominous months of 1921. But by mid-January, Jack was back in New York with Genevieve and Cynthia. He would again have to share with Cynthia more of their mother's misadventures. When the Plaza Hotel began pushing for settlement against their prolonged stay, Genevieve checked out, promising that her queen-size bill would be covered by Dr. Paddleford, and then checked the family into a brief stay at the Ritz-Carlton where she planned her next move. They would escape New York in the dark of night—reminiscent of the train journey commenced six years earlier from New York to Galveston. This time, they'd board a luxury liner for Europe.

Chapter 18:

Deposed in LA

Back in Los Angeles, the Paddleford vs. Paddleford divorce theatrics had begun to be played out in newspapers across the country. Charges and countercharges flew between the principals. Dr. Paddleford's docket of complaints revealed the causticity of his suit. A final judgment of divorce finally came in his favor on July 25, 1923.

The entire Paddleford divorce suit filled an astonishing 110 pages. His extensive complaints were filed, along with Genevieve's countercomplaints and denials. Her amended complaints were twice filed and twice denied. The depositions, along with Genevieve's pitiful rebuttals, read like a narrative in a dime-store novel.

The divorce suit stated that defendant Genevieve Paddleford:

> *since the date of said marriage, has treated plaintiff George Paddleford in an extremely cruel and inhuman manner:*
>
> *That on occasions too numerous to mention, said defendant stated and represented to plaintiff and to plaintiff's friends and acquaintances and to the public in general . . . statements that were false and known to be false and fraudulent and made for the purpose of inducing friends and acquaintances to believe that defendant was a reputable woman of good family, moving in good society and accus-*

tomed to the luxuries of life. That thereafter friends and acquaintances learned that each and every one of said statements and representations were false and fraudulent and that by reason thereof plaintiff suffered great mental pain and anguish and became physically ill.

That she represented to be the widow of Jack Thompson; that she had a daughter whose name was Marie Thompson and that she had a son whose name was Jack Thompson; that she was a half sister of Mrs. Claus Spreckles, Mrs. Jacklin, and Mrs. Moffatt, of San Francisco; that she was the daughter of R. A. H. McKinney and that said R. A. H. McKinney was worth fifty million dollars; that she was a sister of Price McKinney; that she was a sister of Nell Fonda and that Nell Fonda was at one time married to Harry Hammerstein, but was now the wife of a son of the founder of the Mallory Steamship Company; and that all her life she had unlimited money for herself and was accustomed only to the luxuries of life.

That after their marriage, said defendant asked for large sums of money aggregating $10,000; and represented that her said sister, Nell Mallory (formerly Nell Fonda), owed defendant the sum of $26,000 and exhibited an instrument purporting to be a promissory note of said Nell Mallory, signed with the name of Nell Fonda, and stated that if plaintiff paid sum of $10,000 to defendant's credit in her bank, she would repay said sum as soon as her sister paid said note; and that defendant showed plaintiff certain large apartment buildings in the city of New York representing that said buildings belonged to her sister, Nell Fonda Mallory.

That within one year after their marriage, defendant stated that her father owned certain valuable properties in the United States and that she herself owned large tracts of land in North Dakota and other portions of the United States, and that her son and daughter each owned valuable properties and had large sums of money; and that if plaintiff would advance sums of money for the education and support of her *children, said defendant's father would repay such sums so advanced. That defendant exhibited numerous letters purported to have been written by her alleged father, R. A. H. McKinney, in which the said R. A. H. McKinney stated that he would reimburse plaintiff for all moneys expended for the support and education of defendant's children. That he believed each and every of said statements and relying thereon paid out moneys beyond his means for the education and support of defendant's children. Each and every representation was false, and each and every of said letters was written by defendant and not by defendant's alleged father.[1]*

Then came Dr. Paddleford's most startling complaint: the egregious accusation made that he had once abused and molested Marie. In her memoir, Cynthia wrote that Genevieve, sulking and seething in their Plaza Hotel suite, came up with a scurrilous maneuver. She was forced to write a letter to Dr. Paddleford threatening to expose him of the crime. Her refusal to do so unleashed a thrashing with a mahogany lamp stand. The letter was written and signed. It became one of the depositions in the suit. It read in part, "My winning card is when I take the witness stand and tell the world of the evening you ruined me, during my mother's absence." Genevieve also later floated among Dr. Paddleford's friends her accusation that he had ruined her daughter and that he would spend time in the penitentiary for his act. It was such an outrageous accusation that Judge Charles Crail dismissed it without question. Crail, who would later decide the case, was sickened at the accusation and of the despair found therein.

The filed complaints against Genevieve continued:

That on occasions too numerous to mention, during the years 1920 and 1921, defendant called plaintiff a "son of a bitch," a "bastard," a "hound," and a "cur" and called plaintiff's relatives "bastards," "whores," and "whorehouse mistresses."

That in July 1919, at Long Beach Island, defendant told plaintiff that she had taken poison, and that again in the

summer of 1920, at Los Angeles, California, she said she had
taken dichloride of mercury tablets; that each of said state-
ments was false and was made by the defendant for the pur-
pose of harassing and frightening plaintiff.

That during the years 1918–1922, defendant, without
consent or knowledge of plaintiff, on occasions too numerous
to mention, stated and represented to tradespeople that she
was a person of great wealth and that plaintiff was a man
of great wealth and gave her large sums of money, and by
such statements induced tradespeople to charge quantities
of jewelry, wearing apparel, furniture, and other goods, and
that representations were made by defendant for the pur-
pose of obtaining goods, wares, and merchandise without the
intention or ability to pay for the same. That many of said
tradespeople sued plaintiff and caused him to be pursued and
hounded by process servers and bill collectors.

That during the month of December 1921, defendant
stated to her daughter and to other persons that she had spent
the night in a room in a hotel with a certain man other than
plaintiff and had received therefore the sum of $3,000.[2]

Eleanor Margaret Genevieve Toomey Teal Paddleford was certainly
an infidel and had numerous affairs and consorts throughout her years.
Only a few made the headlines: the prominent St. Paul doctor against
whom she filed a breach-of-promise suit (later dismissed) while married
to William Toomey in St. Paul, and, near the end of Ben Teal's life, the
headwaiter at the Hotel Astor, August Schneider. Throughout her life, she
was a magnet to men.

Again, Dr. Paddleford's complaints:

That in August 1922, defendant was arrested on the charge of
obtaining goods of value by fraudulent means by the police of
Vienna, Austria, and thereafter was extradited to Lucerne,
Switzerland. That defendant was imprisoned in Lucerne, Swit-
zerland, for some months. That the news of defendant's arrest

and imprisonment was published in many newspapers in Europe and America, and which arrest became known to plaintiff's friends and acquaintances, and that by reason of facts afore said plaintiff suffered great mental pain and anguish.[3]

Dr. Paddleford complained further that Genevieve's lies regarding her name and her failure to disclose past husbands caused him to lose friends and acquaintances—and jeopardized his employment. Genevieve had lived with him in Tampico in 1919, and, as noted, while there she had maliciously spread a rumor that the general manager of the Huasteca Petroleum Company, Mr. William Green, found Dr. Paddleford's services no longer satisfactory and that Paddleford was about to be removed. Paddleford surprisingly stated in his complaint deposition that he'd lost employment with the Doheny oil enterprises in Mexico, and that he had tried and failed to seek employment elsewhere. This, then, his final complaint:

That on occasions too numerous to mention, during the year 1922, plaintiff endeavored to secure employment in order to support himself, but that on each and every occasion he was informed by the person to whom he made application for such employment that such person could not consider his employment for the reason that defendant's actions and reputation as herein before alleged, had become so notorious that plaintiff's connection with any business enterprise would be injurious thereto, and that by reason of defendant's actions as hereinbefore alleged, plaintiff has suffered the loss of all his money and property and has been unable to earn money with which to support him and that he is now dependent upon his relatives and friends for such support.[4]

There is evidence that Dr. Paddleford returned to the oil fields following the divorce decree in 1923. Certainly, he resided in Los Angeles for many months of anguish until then. When the Mexican Petroleum Company was sold in 1925, it is unknown whether Dr. Paddleford returned as an employee of the new owner, Standard Oil of Indiana.

Finally, the concluding decree of divorce:

*That by each and every of the statements and acts of defen-
dant as hereinbefore alleged, plaintiff has suffered grievous
mental pain and anguish and his health has been greatly
impaired.*

*Wherefore, plaintiff prays that the bonds of matrimony
heretofore existing between plaintiff and defendant be dis-
solved and for such other and further relief as to the court
shall meet.*[5]

While the divorce complaint, signed by Dr. Paddleford's attorneys, Horace S. Wilson and George W. Stephenson, laid bare Dr. George E. Paddleford's humiliation, it bears repeating that twice before in her marital history, Genevieve had punished her husbands with the guile of a temptress. Both William Toomey and Ben Teal had suffered similar wreckage.

The final decree of divorce could not be issued without allowing Genevieve her chance to engage in a last stand against the decree. She returned from Europe on January 31, 1923, three weeks after her scheduled appearance. Her lawyer successfully pleaded that severe storms in the Atlantic had delayed her appearance and that she needed more time to prepare. When reporters caught up to her, she said she had a lot to say, in order "to get right with the public—and to be exonerated of the unjust charges that have been brought against me by Paddleford during my absence. And you might tell 'em that I've come back to fight to clear my name of these cruel things that have been said of me. I am going to fight this divorce to the limit. I'll play a Mrs. Stillman* on him and get a divorce myself after he has failed."[6]

Upon returning from her yearlong misfortunate lark in Europe, Genevieve had to wait six months in Los Angeles before learning her fate in the final decree of divorce. During that period, she not only had to fight the decree but also, more pitiably, had to support herself. That part of the story, and her son, Ben Jr.'s, dramatic testimony before the divorce court, is still to come, as is the story of Genevieve's misfortunes in Europe, where she attempted to reestablish herself and her resources during the preceding year of 1922.

*Mrs. Stillman: According to Wikipedia, in 1921, James A. Stillman filed for divorce, saying that his wife's youngest child was the daughter of a half-blood Indian guide from Quebec. His wife denied the charges and accused him of fathering two illegitimate children with chorus girl Florence H. Leeds. After five years, the court refused the divorce, saying that he had misbehaved. His wife then filed for divorce but withdrew the contest after receiving a $500,000 necklace. They sailed to Europe to receive counseling from Carl Jung. The court case cost him more than $1 million, but they ultimately remained married.

Chapter 19:

Arrested in LA, 1922

An itinerant New York family accompanied by a manservant boarded the SS *Paris* on April 26, 1922, for a six day transatlantic voyage to London and Le Havre, France.[1] The family was impeccably dressed; no one could possibly have suspected, based on their appearance, that they were not from New York's finest lineage. But they were really a homeless family boarding a luxury cruise ship on a veritable shoestring. Their ship, the *Paris*, was the largest of the French fleet and billed as the most modern and luxurious transatlantic steamship in the world. They came onboard at the last minute, following a week of harrowing whirlwind skirmishes, the suspense of which is detailed in Cynthia Teal's memoir.

SS Paris Leaving New York, circa 1921

A luxury cruise allows its passengers the suspension of worries and torments. That would have been particularly true on the *Paris*, where every need and desire was met with a flick of a wrist. "Dining on the *Paris* was excellent, her service superb, and the living spaces were divinely comfortable and luxurious. French Line ships had enormous appeal in the 1920s—'floating bits of France itself,' as one brochure aptly stated. Service and accommodations were fine, but the cuisine was its most outstanding feature; it is said that more seagulls followed the *Paris* than any other ship in hopes of grabbing scraps of haute cuisine that were dumped overboard."[2]

Genevieve Paddleford's passport identified her as Margaret McKenstreet. Cynthia and Ben Jr. were registered under the name McKinney. Their servant, once identified in a news clipping as Joseph DeNorie, was referred to frequently by Cynthia only as Joe. The boarding officer challenged the validity of the passports, but Genevieve's persuasiveness ruled the day. She really was Margaret McKinney, age forty-eight, and was by now well accustomed to the art of persuasion, which she would continue to use without reservation to secure any advantage.

Nearly halfway through their passage, Margaret paraded a story that her purse and all of her money had accidentally fallen overboard. The gypsy story spread like wildfire among the passengers, many of whom had fallen under her garrulous charm. Her fellow passengers rushed to her assistance. According to Cynthia, one French viscount was especially persuaded.

With several hundred dollars newly fleeced, the family had enough money upon arrival to check into the Hotel de Crillon, one of the most historic and exclusive hotels in Paris. However, only one night's advance payment meant that their stay at the Crillon would soon be in dispute unless Margaret could perform some new magic—which she did, but that, too, shall be left for Cynthia to unravel in her recounting.

Their stay in Paris was no more than a few days. Perhaps the jewelers and shopkeepers there were reluctant to advance credit on the merchandise Margaret wished to purchase. In any event, she and the children left Paris and made their way to London, where Margaret, as anticipated, found the shops more agreeable. Her shopping and pawning of expensive women's merchandise kept them there for nearly a month.

With several trunks full of purchased wares yet to be pawned, Margaret jostled her crew off to Brussels. Then, after a few days of shopping, they hit the road again, making stops at various towns and cities along the way, ending in Vienna. To keep ahead of investigators from Paris and London who were asking questions, Margaret changed names at every new hotel along the way.

It was in Vienna where things fell apart. At first, the attractive family was received with welcome accreditation. She was again Mrs. Genevieve Paddleford, the wife of a wealthy American oil baron. Thanks to a collection of reference letters that she had gathered carefully over the preceding months in New York, the family was graciously accommodated among Vienna's upper class. Of special note was one letter of introduction to the famous composer Franz Lehar, composer of "The Merry Widow" and idol of the City of Music. He escorted them to the opera and introduced Genevieve to Vienna's prominent citizens. While in Vienna, Genevieve, having acquired so much favor, made fast work of its finest shops. She bought thousands of dollars' worth of lace, furs, apparel, and jewels.

Cynthia was aghast. "Sooner or later, Mother, we'll be arrested; the police in all those countries must be looking for us now!"

"Nonsense, my child," laughed Mrs. Paddleford. "We'll leave for Canada. Once we're there, it will be a simple thing to smuggle our trunks across the border. I'll be able to sell this stuff for more in New York than the shops over here ask. We'll be rich, Cynthia—rich, I tell you. I'll have more than enough to fight Paddleford's divorce."[3]

On June 9, police from Paris, Lucerne, and Vienna raided their room at the Grand Hotel. Genevieve had waited too long. Her plan had collapsed. The arrest hit newspapers across the country from New York to Los Angeles. On June 11, 1922, the *San Francisco Chronicle* reported:

> *Genevieve Paddleford, who claims to be the wife of a wealthy California oil trader, is under arrest here in connection with a number of fraudulent operations in which businessmen of Lucerne, Paris, and Vienna were the victims. Eleven trunks containing costly furs and other goods alleged to have been*

obtained illegally were seized, as well as two silver mounted
vases bearing the mark of the Ritz-Carlton hotel, New York.[4]

Genevieve's month-long stretch in Vienna's prison brought her
low. In early July, she was taken to the prison hospital. Most likely, she
feigned illness to create sympathy. Around that time, the Swiss embassy
demanded that she be extradited. The Viennese officials were having
their fill of Mrs. Paddleford. She promised that a $15,000 check from
her husband was already in transit to cover her expenses. Herr Ungar,
the department-store owner who was holding bills for furs, lingerie, and
gowns, and who had taken the children under his wing, sent several cables
to Dr. Paddleford regarding the missing check. The *Los Angeles Times*
reported a reply sent to the prefect of police in Vienna: "Deny sending
Mrs. Paddleford any money and she knows it. I will not be responsible
for her debts."[5]

Questioned by the *Times* after he sent his cable to Vienna, Dr. Paddleford replied, "Mrs. Paddleford's troubles do not concern me. I've had
enough. If the Vienna police choose to keep her, I shall have no objec-
tions. My only concern is that none of those bills are sent to me. I want to
forget Mrs. Paddleford."[6]

A week later, the *Times* also reported that Dr. Paddleford "had made
a complete money settlement with her and will do nothing to aid her in
this recent predicament."[7]

Newspapers in Vienna at the time of Genevieve's arrest were making the plight of the stranded children a cause célèbre. According to the
Times, "numerous families, through sympathy for the youngsters, offered
to take them off the hands of the police."[8]

Cynthia, in her memoir, gives Franz Lehar credit for her passage
back to America; however, the *Los Angeles Times* reported that "there
arrived by post from Paris a cable from Dr. Paddleford announcing that
he was sending wire funds to cover the cost of the children's return to the
United States. The police have prepared passports, but Mrs. Paddleford's
extradition is demanded by Switzerland for process in Lucerne."[9]

Ben Teal Jr., now Jack Paddleford, was, by all indications, returned to
Los Angeles. He was fourteen years old. As for Cynthia, the *Los Angeles*

Times reported on September 27, 1922, that she was "now a resident of New York."[10]

The eleven trunks that the Viennese police confiscated were opened and inventoried. Through the efforts of a lawyer assigned to Mrs. Paddleford, the contents were returned to the defrauded merchants of Vienna. That was enough for the Viennese officials to dismiss her case and honor the extradition the Swiss embassy sought. The Swiss were not so eager to dismiss their case against Mrs. Paddleford. She spent five months incarcerated in Lucerne, awaiting trial before the Swiss criminal court.[11]

The Lucerne jail—a four-story, block-style building in the heart of the picturesque city—was built in 1862 as a humane answer to locking up criminals in various medieval towers. Prison conditions for Genevieve would not have been so markedly improved over those originally intended. She would have been held without daylight for twenty-two to twenty-three hours daily, her diet sparse, her shared cell tiny, her mattress hard and thin. Only her obstinate will would have stood her while waiting on the court.[12]

Her case was finally called in the first week of December. The merchants of Lucerne charged that Mrs. Paddleford had defrauded them out of expensive merchandise valued at 37,000 Swiss francs. Her lawyer again appealed to Dr. Paddleford, urging him to send money. The lawyer told reporters that $600 would square everything, but Dr. Paddleford "refused to give his wife a single cent." Her lawyer also reported that he was paying for his client's board in jail. The jewelry, he said, was returned, but the merchants refused to take back the lingerie, gowns, and wraps.

Remarkably, when the decision came down, the criminal court found there were no grounds for charging Mrs. Paddleford of a crime. As several newspapers reported, the angry merchants would have to follow up with a civil case. On December 12, 1922, Genevieve "walked calmly out of jail as the court convened."[13]

Chapter 20:

Back in LA, 1923

Aunt Eleanor was a wily, crooked woman with an engaging, though domineering, personality—the kind of woman who could take over a room. Like all seasoned crooks, she succeeded in her dupery and fraudulent ways most of the time. When caught and thrust through the front door of a prison, she had to pay the price, but with her theatrical skills she more often than not could locate a back door.

Theatrics had managed the Lucerne lockup. Upon her release, she had to find a way home. The American embassy in Zurich, based on her required appearance at the Superior Court of Los Angeles, fixed her papers and means for passage.

When accosted by LA reporters, she explained the "rumor" relative to an arrest while in Vienna, Austria:

> "I was not arrested for shoplifting or on any criminal complaint whatsoever," Mrs. Paddleford declared yesterday. "I was quizzed in Lucerne, Switzerland, relative to passing under two names. I had the name of Mrs. George E. Paddleford on my passport. At a hotel in Lucerne I signed my name as Mrs. Ben Teal, a name I have used professionally at times, as my daughter's name is Cynthia Marie Teal, receiving this name from my first husband."[1]

Her attorney backed her up by producing a statement he'd obtained from thecriminal court in Lucerne:

> We herewith give testimony to be delivered to Mrs. Gen-
> evieve M. Paddleford from Los Angeles, California, that the
> attorney general of the canton Lucerno has made neither an
> accusation nor a motion against Mrs. Paddleford on a charge
> of shoplifting. Sig. Kaufman, Chancery of Criminal Court,
> Lucerne, Dec. 11, 1922.[2]

Mr. Philip Cohen spoke about the cross-complaint that he would file on Mrs. Paddleford's behalf to answer the charges against her:

> In due time, after I have been able to delve more fully into
> these charges, my client will be acquitted in the public mind
> and before the court when the matter comes to trial of the
> ridiculous charges which have been brought against her.[3]

The Los Angeles Times published her denials of these "ridiculous" charges:

> That she was arrested in Vienna on a charge of shoplifting
> and served in a European prison. That she beat her adopted
> daughter, Cynthia Marie Teal, concert singer, into signing a
> statement that her foster father, George E. Paddleford, had
> attacked her. That there was ever such a statement meant to
> benefit her in the divorce. That she served ten months in the
> Tombs prison on Blackwell Island for perjury in connection
> with the famous Gould divorce case in 1907 and 1908, as she
> is accused. That she gave gifts to other men, as the divorce
> complaint declares."[4]

Mrs. Paddleford's cross-deposition would deny every complaint and assertion Dr. Paddleford made. The case stalled before the court by amended complaints and amended countercomplaints. As she waited through those six months for the final decision, troubles gathered. She had to find a way to support herself. So she resorted to her old ways and went shopping.

Two weeks after her arrival in LA, she moved into what was described as a sumptuous house at 6864 Bonita Terrace in Hollywood. The house seems to have been rented and occupied by a mystery "boyfriend." The owner, Mr. Raymond W. Smith, said that "Mrs. George McKinney" moved into the house without his knowledge by permission of the former tenant. He said that she had made a small down payment and had agreed to sign a two-year lease. Even before signing the lease, Mrs. George M. McKinney went on a shopping spree to furnish the house at 6864 Bonita Terrace. It wasn't but a month after she'd moved in that a sortie of disgruntled Hollywood and Pasadena merchants compared notes on Mrs. McKinney's real identity, means, and promises, and on March 10, a Friday evening, with a warrant in hand, the police and merchants launched a raid on the premises.

The raid lasted through the next day. At least seven merchants carted off merchandise, valued at more than $10,000, that they had sold to Mrs. McKinney. Moving vans, touring cars, and drays all lined up to convey the goods that had appointed the home in luxury. Warned that the merchants were to reclaim their merchandise or expect immediate payment, the *Times* noted that the unmasked Mrs. Paddleford "offered no objection to the removal." Nothing remained in the house late Saturday except a phonograph and a sewing machine. The blinds were drawn, and Mrs. Paddleford was nowhere in sight.[5]

On the night Eleanor—Mrs. McKinney or Mrs. Paddleford—was brought in for questioning, she named the famous ragtime bandleader Jelly Roll Morton as her boyfriend. Jelly Roll performed around town nightly between 1917 and 1922. He and his common-law wife, Anita Gonzales, ran a "hotel" called the Anita. Later in 1922, Jelly managed the Wayside, referred to as an "amusement park" and featuring Jelly Roll's six-piece band four nights per week.[6]

Jelly Roll Morton was a larger-than-life character, not unlike Genevieve Paddleford. They were both show folks, always dressing the part. Jelly even wore an embedded diamond in his front tooth. Both loved

Jelly Roll Morton

the stage. Both boasted and stretched the truth. It was said about Jelly Roll that his "cockiness" was ever present. Their commonality as harbingers of the night made it very likely that Aunt Eleanor knew, or perhaps even was a casual friend of, Jelly Roll. In an acclaimed collection of recorded interviews with musicologist Alan Lomax, one response from Jelly implied no romantic relationship between them: "The tracks were treating me very dirty these days and, somehow, my luck in California was running out. . . . Some woman in Pasadena was arrested for stealing her employer's furniture and, when the police asked her who was her boyfriend, she named me. Down at the jail, when I actually met the woman, she admitted she had never seen me."[7]

Another source referenced the same occurrence in a slightly different quote, not attributed to Jelly Roll: "A woman stole furniture in Pasadena, and JR was arrested in connection with the case. When asked who her boyfriend was, she said JR. But when confronted by JR in the jail, she corroborated JR's testimony that they were not acquainted."[8]

Shortly after the raid on Bonita Terrace, Jelly Roll Morton left Anita Gonzales in LA and moved to Chicago, where in 1923 he made a name for himself by composing and recording on the Victor label. His Red Hot Peppers band became a sensation.[9]

Although speculative, the idea that Jelly Roll Morton was the former tenant who permitted Mrs. McKinney access to the house at 6864 Bonita Terrace remains quite credible.

Chapter 21:

Hectic in LA, 1923

Los Angeles was closing down around Mrs. Paddleford. Was it a mad compulsion that led her to rent a house and deck it out with furniture, or was it a front, a strategy meant to elevate her standing in Dr. Paddleford's divorce case? Whatever it was, it was too little, too late. She moved into the house on February 12 and was thrown out on March 10. Four days later, the *Los Angeles Times* reported, "Philip Cohen, attorney for Mrs. Paddleford, filed notice of withdrawal from the case yesterday. Pressure from other business was given by the attorney as his reason for the withdrawal."[1]

Complaints lodged by the merchants led to Mrs. Paddleford's arrest on March 22. Her movements from Bonita Terrace to her arrest are unknown. She may have been with a friend. The *Los Angeles Times* reported that Mrs. Paddleford was picked up by the police at the corner of Fourth Street and Grand Avenue just as she was about to enter her car. Ben Teal Jr. was with her and later placed in the care of Major John E. Quinn, commandant of the Urban Military Academy. The arresting officer reported that Mrs. Paddleford verbally remonstrated against her arrest. Several merchants had sworn and signed the complaint. She was charged with grand larceny, and bail was set at $10,000. Unable to post a bond, she was locked up in LA city jail.[2]

New questions crop up. How did she get a car? How was it that Ben Jr. was in the car? Where had he been? Where was she going? How had she managed to dupe so many creditors? The police answered that last question. "Her method, according to Detective Lieutenant McMahon, was to call the manager of the store by telephone, give the name of a customer well known to the management, and ask that credit be given to a certain woman. In making her purchases, Mrs. Paddleford is asserted to have used many aliases, going at times, it was said, under the names of McKinney, Teal, McKenstreet, Erwin, Tall, Toomey, and Thompson."[3]

A preliminary hearing was held on March 29. Until then, Genevieve sat in jail. Five shopkeepers testified that Mrs. Paddleford had obtained goods by misrepresentation, stating that she would pay for the goods upon receipt of money that she expected from the East in a few weeks. A trial date was set for June 18. Mrs. Paddleford pleaded to be released on her own recognizance, promising to appear for trial. True to her prowess at bluffing, she convinced the district attorney to buy her promise and grant her release.

She immediately hired a new attorney, Mr. A. L. McDonald, to represent her in court, as well as to prepare a countersuit against Dr. Paddleford. Shortly thereafter, she left town, breaking her court promise. On May 18, a bench warrant was issued for her rearrest. "The district attorney's office declined to state the reason for the issuance by the superior court of the bench warrant, but declared it was desired to have her brought to court and placed under heavy bonds."[4]

Genevieve went missing. On June 18, the day scheduled for her trial on the charge of grand larceny, she did not appear. Proceedings began without her. The *Los Angeles Times* reported that "Mr. McDonald presented to the court a letter recently received from his client on stationery of the St. Regis Hotel, Mexico City. Mrs. Paddleford stated that she would kill herself before she would return to Los Angeles, as she believed that she had no chance of obtaining justice in the courts of this city."[5]

Genevieve, now a fugitive from justice, stated in her letter that she went to Mexico in search of her son, fifteen years of age, who had been kidnapped by her husband, Dr. George Paddleford.

In the meantime, Dr. Paddleford's lawyers had prepared their briefs for the divorce hearing, scheduled for July 20. His lawyers had for some months held in their possession a consequential signed affidavit received from Cynthia Teal, sent at the time of her return to New York City from

Switzerland. It stated that she had "abandoned and renounced [her] foster mother and was willing to bare [her] own tragic life to assist Dr. Paddleford in his divorce action."[6]

In an amendment bristling with a new complaint, Dr. Paddleford
charged Genevieve with having intimate relations with "a number of
men here and in other parts of the country and had mulched them out
of large sums of money, under threat of exposure. On one occasion, Dr.
Paddleford complains, she spent a night in a hotel with another man and
then forced her victim to turn over to her $3,000 under threat of expo-
sure. He also learned that she obtained a considerable sum from another
man in the same manner after assuredly telling her victim that she was
being followed by private detectives and that they both would be arrested
unless he gave her sufficient money to bribe the operatives."[7]

Genevieve, even as a fugitive from justice, fought back through her
new lawyer, Mr. McDonald. The *Los Angeles Times* reported on one of
her more bizarre attempts to trump Dr. Paddleford's charges. McDonald
brought a countercharge stating that when Genevieve was held in the
Los Angeles jail, she'd met another Genevieve, a Miss Genevieve Albitz, twenty-one, convicted of passing bad checks. He presented an affidavit signed by Miss Albitz stating that Dr. Paddleford had conducted
improper relations with her in January. It read:

> *Miss Albitz met Dr. Paddleford in a downtown hotel and
> started a flirtation with him. She declares he drove her home
> and on the same evening called her back and took her to a
> roadhouse, where much alcoholic liquor was imbibed. A few
> days later, at Dr. Paddleford's request, she called him by tele-
> phone at a downtown club and on that evening accompanied
> him to a Los Angeles hotel, and spent the night after they had
> registered as man and wife. A few days later he tried to per-
> suade the girl to go with him to Mexico, as his wife, promising
> her, she says, every luxury. Miss Albitz charged that Dr. Pad-
> dleford embarrassed her by openly making love to her while
> riding in a limousine and the driver overheard the doctor's
> remarks and can be obtained as a witness.*[8]

This, of course, was another one of Mrs. Paddleford's shams, which resulted in a charge of subornation of perjury, in addition to the charge of grand larceny. Subornation of perjury was a familiar charge for which, years past, in the Frank Gould case, she had spent ten months in the women's penitentiary on Blackwell's Island.

On June 20, the day Mrs. Paddleford was to appear in court to face charges of grand larceny by the Hollywood shopkeepers, the superior court of Los Angeles heard the divorce case of *Paddleford vs. Paddleford*. Witnesses were called. Genevieve was nowhere in sight, her whereabouts unknown.

The first witness to appear before Judge Crail was a sad and serious teenager, fifteen-year-old Benjamin Teal Paddleford. A *Los Angeles Times* reporter wrote, "He was cast up in Los Angeles last night, a helpless cork on a marital whirlpool. His unruly hair was combed back. His face and arms were tanned by work in the fields of a ranch where he had been 'hiding out,' he said, from Mrs. Paddleford. He also said, 'the greatest treasure a boy can have is the right kind of mother . . . there ought to be a court just for boys like me. If a boy's home is unhappy, and he sees his mother doing the things I saw my asserted mother doing, there ought to be some way for him to get out of it. I wish I had had a judge I could have gone to, and have him help me out of this mess.'"

The *Times* reported that Benjamin was old for his years. When asked what he was going to do, he confirmed that he liked Dr. Paddleford, "but she broke him. I wish I might have a guardian who would give me a happy home and educate me." In his heart, surely, Ben Jr. would have been grateful if he could have returned to the Paddleford home and family.

Benjamin went on to tell of flights from the police, of intrigues to capture wealthy men, of traveling all over Europe and the United States. He told of how he was forced to change his name to Jack Thompson before meeting Dr. Paddleford. "I was mad," he said, "and I wouldn't do it, so she called me a little brat and beat me. When in Europe, every time she went to a different city, she took a new name. It was in Paris that she got taken in good. She met a four-flusher who said he was a prince. He looked it. She thought he had money, and he thought she was rich. They both found out their mistake and separated in a hurry."[9]

Benjamin Teal Paddleford

Benjamin's tutor, Joseph "Joe" DeNorie, backed up his testimony. He added some other details. "Quite often she would not return home until five o'clock in the morning. Once, here in Los Angeles, I remember having seen her go in a bathroom with Keith McLeod with only a bath towel around her."[10]

Mrs. Paddleford's former housekeeper in New York, Mrs. Regina Mettler, declared that she had seen Mrs. Paddleford go into her room with men several times. "She often ordered cocktails from behind closed doors. What went on in the room, I don't know. She had many men friends and often entertained them in her room."[11]

Finally, Dr. Paddleford based his case on the affidavit signed by Cynthia Teal in which she declared that Mrs. Paddleford had "sworn that she was going to have Dr. Paddleford sent to the penitentiary for having had improper relations with [Miss Teal]."[12] Cynthia stated that she had always been under the domination of her foster mother and compelled to do her bidding, and that the note she wrote implicating Dr. Paddleford was written under compulsion after she had been beaten.

After two hours of hearing the affidavits and other papers introduced as testimony, and hearing the witnesses, Judge Crail granted the decree of divorce without hesitation.

Dr. George Paddleford had freed himself of the torment that wrecked his reputation. Cynthia was free of her foster mother, at least for the time being. And, it appeared that Benjamin, also free of his mother, might receive the friendship and guardianship from Dr. Paddleford that he longed for. As for Genevieve, she was a fugitive.

Chapter 22:

Europe, 1924–27

For a year, Mrs. Paddleford's trail ran cold. Then, on April 2, 1924, this headline appeared in the *Los Angeles Times*: "Divorcee Is in Trouble Once More." It turned out that Genevieve was wanted in Paris for bank fraud. The report cited a dispatch from the Paris police to the New York police seeking information on any outstanding warrants for her arrest. In turn, the local police in New York wired the Los Angeles police asking for information regarding any outstanding warrants for her arrest in LA. Yes, they were told, Genevieve Paddleford was wanted for jumping bail on a charge of grand larceny and subornation of perjury dating back to May 1923. The dispatch from Paris said that she was wanted for obtaining articles worth 60,000 lire. These had been acquired in Venice from pretended credit on a Paris bank. Her whereabouts, according to the Paris dispatch, were unknown, but she was thought to be in Vienna, Austria.

The same *Los Angeles Times* article reported that Genevieve had claimed a new husband. Such an occurrence, if true, could have been possible only between June 1923 and April 1924. It was a story she would tell often over her succeeding years. Newspapers were all too willing to recite the tale. His name, Eleanor said, was William. H. Howells, a millionaire railroad builder in Egypt. She claimed that while married to Mr. Howells she had lived in one of the largest villas in Cairo, had been served by a retinue of servants, and had worn jewels worth fortunes. Her husband, she said, had provided for her a prenuptial trust of $12,000,000. She had also commanded three palaces on the Nile and a townhouse in Alexandria.

When asked about Mr. Howells's whereabouts, she replied that he had met with an unfortunate accident: his Rolls-Royce had careened over a cliff near Alexandria. The $12,000,000, however, would be forthcoming.[1]

What was not a fantasy but startling in its truth was that on this second grand tour of Europe, she was accompanied again by her daughter, Cynthia Teal. How could Cynthia, who had been through so much, who had published her *Confessions,* and who'd once vowed safe any further contact with her foster mother, have been once again persuaded to rejoin Genevieve in a repeat tour of Europe? The sentiment and determination revealed in her *Confessions* had signaled such a notion as preposterous. Had Cynthia's life become humdrum? Genevieve was dangerous; however, she offered excitement and just maybe a path back to the theater. One wonders, how was Genevieve able to find her, and why?

The *Los Angeles Times* report from April 2 failed to mention that Genevieve traveled with a companion. But eight months later, on November 20, 1924, the *Times* reported that a mother along with her daughter were caught and arrested in Zurich and charged with swindling a hotel out of 150 francs ($30). They were later identified as "Mrs. Genevieve Paddleford and daughter, who have been involved in a number of police incidents in Vienna and Switzerland during the last two years. They registered in the hotel as Miss Healy of London and Miss Clay of California, but carried passports under the name of MacKenney, mother and daughter."[2]

The hotel clerk reported that Miss Healy and Miss Clay checked into the hotel with several trunks and that upon checking out, they needed to borrow 150 francs ($30). Miss Healy told the clerk that her money, in the form of a check, had not yet arrived from Geneva. With a small loan they would proceed to Geneva to obtain the money needed to settle her bill with the hotel. The clerk willingly vouchsafed the loan with a ring that Miss Healy removed from her finger. Becoming suspicious, he had the ring examined and found it bogus. The police caught and arrested the mother-daughter pair at the train station.[3]

The arrests in Zurich occurred nearly two years after Genevieve had bolted from Los Angeles to seek, she said, her young son, Ben, whom she believed to be in Mexico with his stepbrother, George Jr., and stepfather, George Paddleford. But her sojourn in Mexico was brief. She instead sought and found Cynthia. The likelihood of that contact could have come about only through her Los Angeles divorce attorney, who would have had access to Cynthia's address.

Once again, Genevieve and Cynthia bounded off on another unbridled tour of Europe. They reportedly "arrived in Switzerland after having toured the world by way of Vancouver, Shanghai, India, Egypt, Italy, and Munich, and she [Mrs. Paddleford] did not have a cent to her name"[4] when they were arrested in Zurich.

Oddly, of the several news reports announcing their arrest in Zurich, none identifies Genevieve's young "modest" traveling companion as Cynthia Teal. Cynthia had published her *Confessions*, which had been syndicated across the country. She had claimed her independence and renounced her adoptive mother. One wonders whether Genevieve had had access to Cynthia's *Confessions*, which was published in late 1922, while Genevieve, back in Europe at the time, was sitting it out in a Lucerne prison. Genevieve was not released from Lucerne and out of Europe until February 1923. Could she have missed the syndicated story? It seems possible. As soon as she arrived back in the United States, she engaged in the Paddleford divorce and bollixed herself up in the Bonita Terrace house caper. Very likely Genevieve had read it—in a state of fury—and had brought it, hand in hand, to Cynthia, wielding it as a cudgel of guilt.

A very curious article appeared in the *Washington Post* on April 6, 1924. It appeared just four days after the *Los Angeles Times* reported that the Paris police were seeking information on Genevieve Paddleford:

Long Missing Girl, Thought Found, Again Disappears
Adopted by Mrs. George Paddleford, Wife of Oil Magnate
Special to the Washington Post

> *Maspeth, L.I., April 5—There is a mystery in this town. "Who is Cynthia? What is she?" are questions the neighbors are asking one another. Handsome limousines with chauffeurs in livery and fashionably dressed women, all inquiring about Miss Teal or Miss Norton, puzzle them. Many have seen the strikingly pretty girl, but few know her and those who do refuse to talk of her.*

Miss Charlotte Norton, who is alleged to be Miss Cynthia Teal, the adopted daughter of the wife of Dr. George Paddleford, Los Angeles millionaire and partner of E. L. Doheny, has disappeared.

The story that Miss Teal left her foster mother's wealth and luxury to share the destiny of her own mother, Mrs. Schmayer, residing in Maspeth, and that she obtained a position as a telephone operator in the Murray Hill exchange in New York City, seems in some respects to be true.

A Miss Norton, a most beautiful girl, did work in the exchange and left abruptly, last Monday afternoon, saying that her brother was sick in Los Angeles. But there is no Mrs. Schmayer in Maspeth.

The candy store owner before whose place the automobiles are said to have stopped adds to the mystery. Questioned today, she said: "Of course, I know Miss Norton. But I won't tell you one word about the child. She is being hounded and is in hiding." And the lady refused to say anything further.

If Miss Norton is Miss Cynthia Teal, she was born in the charity ward of a New York hospital, reared in a home, and then adopted by the one-time famous theatrical producer, Ben Teal, whose wife has since become Mrs. George Paddleford. Tiring of life on the coast, Cynthia Teal deserted her foster parents and came east to support herself. In a romantic chapter of her life she discovered her real mother, whose name is supposed to be Mrs. Schmayer, of Maspeth, with whom the girl went to live.[5]

More questions. Why had the *Washington Post* become interested in Cynthia Teal at this time? Who was Mrs. Schmayer? Did Cynthia reside above the candy store? Was Mrs. Schmayer really her long-lost mother? What about the limousines? And how could Eleanor have still wielded such a commanding influence over Cynthia?

A ship's manifest from the SS *Caledonia* recorded her eventual return voyage from this second tour of Europe. It revealed that Cynthia Teal, born August 4, 1904, in New York City, sailed from Glasgow, Scotland, arriving at the Port of New York on December 19, 1926. Her address was listed as 3 Putnam Place, Nutley, New Jersey.[6] It was, indeed, Cynthia who entered into Europe as Genevieve's companion. Their first grand tour of Europe, in 1922, lasted only six months. This, their second, was a two-and-a-half-year European escapade, but with news reports few and far between. The report of the Zurich hotel arrest did not disclose the terms of their confinement. One might guess that Genevieve's usual bold assertions and regal poise as an American aristocrat had gotten them off easy.

After the arrest in Zurich, Genevieve and Cynthia were not heard from again for another year and a half. It was not until May 29, 1926, that they were picked up in the mountainous town of Innsbruck, Austria.[7] For months, they had successfully carried out scam operations across Europe without cost. The report of the Innsbruck arrest, however, referred to one previous arrest, without accompanying detail, in the western Polish city of Posen (Posnan) where they had been held for two months on a charge of embezzlement.[8]

The Innsbruck police now held the two women on a warrant issued by the police in Berlin. The *Los Angeles Times* reported:

> *With dignified gray strands of her bobbed hair and with her beautiful, modest-looking daughter at her side, Mrs. Paddleford descended on Berlin's most fashionable hotel, registering as Mrs. McCormick Howells of 340 Park Avenue, New York, and daughter. This name and the lady's volubility impressed Berlin's rue de la Paix [Kurfürstendamm, Berlin's famous avenue]. It [the Avenue] disgorged its beautiful gowns and hats. The asserted millionaires ordered an $8,000 trousseau for herself and daughter. When most of the goods were delivered, the ladies motored from the hotel and never returned.[9]*

The *New York Times* report added that photographs were taken of the arrested couple at Innsbruck and rushed to Berlin. The photographs showed them entering the jail in the clothes they had "bought." The report said that Genevieve and Cynthia dressed themselves with as much of their new trousseau as they thought would pass inspection. They were wearing about $2,000 worth of clothing. "When the guests left the hotel one morning, a detective was notified that both women seemed stouter than usual and immediately investigated their rooms, which he found bare, except for an old satin frock. . . . When they were arrested in Innsbruck, they were wearing the costumes acquired in Berlin."[10]

At the time of their arrest in Innsbruck, Mrs. Paddleford blurted out a strange tale about having met with an automobile accident on the Austrian border, where practically all their baggage had been destroyed. Perhaps the Berlin merchants were able to recover their losses and all parties, including the police, were willing to accept the stories of this volatile, weeping woman. Once more, it seems, mother and daughter were allowed their release.

Genevieve and Cynthia were constantly on the move, their travels touch-and-go. Cynthia, by this time, was no longer the reluctant tagalong teenager she had been four years earlier; she was an all-too-willing adult accomplice. Judging from the virtuous eloquence expressed in her written *Confessions*, she must have found herself cringing often at the life she was leading. At the same time, so it seems, she relished the occasional stolen luxuries to which she had become so accustomed and possibly addicted.

Genevieve had a hold on Cynthia. She could hold people, even powerful men. The martinet Ben Teal himself had been no match for her. Certainly, the innocent waif from the New York Foundling Home was easily brought under control once more. At the same time, a vulnerable, needy young woman remained conflicted by her moral judgment, and had become accustomed to her wants and desires.

Six weeks later, on July 17, 1926, the *London Times* reported that the pair was held and questioned by London police for false statements made to a Home Office customs officer while applying for emergency passports. Apparently, Genevieve had refined her credit scam by allowing creditors to hold their passports as collateral. Then they would rush off to secure new emergency passports, each time misreporting their personal information. The London office researched the issuances and found fraud. Their last passports, for example, had been issued in Spain bearing the names Margot McKinley Howells and Marie C. Howells, but in London she gave her name as Mary Allen McCormick and her daughter's as Marylon Dorothy McCormick. "Mrs. McCormick, in the witness box, said that her real name was Mary Allen McKinley, which was her maiden name, born in London, Ontario, Canada . . . and that her husband, Mr. McCormick, was known in the literary world as William Howells . . . and that she herself did literary work under the name of Margot Howells."[11]

The prosecutor pointed out other discrepancies and observed that no one could believe their stories. No subsequent reports were found in regard to any incarceration. The passport incident occurred in July. Cynthia boarded the SS *Caledonia* for New York in December. Between July and December, she was very likely incarcerated in London. No prison record emerged. Genevieve arrived three months later, on March 27, 1927, aboard the SS *Letitia*.[12] In London, they must have been handed separate sentences.

No record has been found to account for Cynthia Teal and Genevieve Paddleford's ever having met again.

For seven months after Mrs. Paddleford arrived in New York, nothing more was heard from her. Then, on October 28, 1927, the *Los Angeles Times* reported that Mrs. Paddleford had been held for six months in Salinas, California, on a charge of grand theft, under the alias of Mrs. Grace Potter. She had been accused of trading a fur coat to a shopkeeper in exchange for clothing. The merchant said that the articles taken on account far exceeded the value of the coat.

Genevieve was tried in Salinas on November 23 and found guilty of obtaining money under false pretenses by a jury of nine men and three women. "The woman who is said to have received a palace on the Nile in Egypt and a large estate in northern Africa from one of her former husband's heard the verdict calmly but went into hysterics later. She alternately babbled of her luxurious past life, shouted wildly, and wept. She was taken to a Monterey County hospital."[13]

After the SS *Caledonia*, which registered Cynthia Teal as a passenger, docked at the port of New York City, the name Cynthia Marie Teal never showed up in any newspaper or public record. Her fate remains unknown. The fate of Eleanor/Margaret/Genevieve McKinney/Toomey/Teal/Paddleford, however, would continue to unfold.

Chapter 23:

San Quentin, 1927

Cynthia Teal disappeared. She walked away from a New York pier into the great city on December 19, 1926, never to be heard from again. So it seems. Or, perhaps, she did not disembark from the SS *Caledonia* at the pier. Cynthia wrote in her *Confessions* of 1922, "One step and I could plunge out of my misery into dark forgetfulness! I rose from my chair, giddy with a great temptation."

Cynthia had talent and she had dreams, but fate had thrown her a curveball. After December 1926, her name could not be found in any census reports, published directories, or vital records. Her name no longer appeared in newspaper reports. Genevieve Paddleford never again mentioned her name in public. Cynthia had simply disappeared. She would have left the European continent again penniless, disillusioned, defeated, and haunted by doubt and fear.

A female passenger's name was entered on the SS *Caledonia* manifest next to Cynthia's. She was Mary Wilson; age forty-nine, from Newark, New Jersey. Perhaps, returning together, they had become friends. Cynthia had claimed to live in the town of Nutley, New Jersey, just a short bus ride from Newark. Was a connection made? The reader of Cynthia's *Confessions* might only hope.

When Genevieve Paddleford was arrested in Salinas, she gave her name as Grace Potter. She had been held in the Salinas jail for six months before admitting to be Genevieve Paddleford, the name that would tag her for most of her life. Her movements had been extraordinary. After departing at the pier in New York, she went on the lam for two months, swindling her way across the country to California. Several articles appeared in various newspapers covering her arrest in Salinas. She recited a favorite story over and over, that "she had been living in Oriental splendor in Cairo, Egypt, having married W. H. Howells, a wealthy ship owner, who had one of the largest establishments in the Egyptian city, a retinue of servants, and jewels worth fortunes, and that Mr. Howells had left her $12,000,000."[1]

After a jury of nine men and three women found Genevieve guilty and she was sent to Monterey County Hospital, a strange thing happened. It was revealed that Genevieve had not been alone in the courtroom. A male friend had sat in the gallery. "He had checked into a Salinas hotel under an alias, but was later identified as Walter J. Belding, age sixty-seven, wealthy Stockton man."[2] He had been in close consultation with Genevieve's attorney, Henry L. Corson. After the jury found Genevieve guilty, Mr. Belding returned to his hotel room, fell ill, and was rushed to the hospital, the same hospital where Genevieve was taken for her outbreak of hysteria. He died there the next day. It was reported that he owned a theater in San Francisco and was a boyhood chum of Ben Teal.

"Mr. Belding died yesterday of apoplexy brought on, physicians said, by excitement attendant on efforts to save from prison Mrs. Genevieve M. Paddleford."[3]

Genevieve lost an apparent benefactor. Nothing more was recorded about the mysterious Mr. Belding, other than that he was an heir to the Charles Belding estate, "which had large holdings in San Francisco and Stockton." Throughout her life, Eleanor called on friends to bail her out of tight jams. The enchantment her friends had for her was such that she could not be forgotten or ignored. Somehow, Walter Belding had found her and rushed to her defense as a last gasp of friendship.

Judge Treat handed Genevieve an indeterminate sentence of up to ten years in San Quentin prison. A *Washington Post* article reported that she was conveyed to prison in an ambulance. "Her physician, Dr. Henry Murphy, informed the court that his patient was suffering from serious rheumatic ailments."[4] A *Los Angeles Times* report said that because she

Genevieve Paddleford, 1927

complained of rheumatism in her legs, she had to be carried from the county jail on a stretcher. The San Quentin prison physician then, over the next two days, conducted mental and physical tests, without conclusion. Genevieve entered prison on November 29, 1927. As it turned out, she earned the questionable distinction of being the first female prisoner to enter the newly built women's ward at San Quentin.

"Mrs. Genevieve Paddleford traded her name today for the prison number 44428, as the first step she should take in readjusting herself to a sentence of from one to ten years for grand theft."[5]

San Quentin State Prison is California's first prison, and the only prison in the state that is used for executions. Prior to the construction of San Quentin, convicts were held in severe degradation on prison ships. The gold rush of 1849 ushered in the need for a land prison. Completed in 1854 by prison laborers, San Quentin resembled a medieval bastion of cruelty, its architecture a medieval fortress with Doric columns, arches, bell towers, minarets, heavy oak doors, and two-foot brick walls. Over the years, it has held, at any one time, close to six thousand prisoners, nearly doubling its intended capacity. In November 1927, ninety-seven women prisoners followed Genevieve into the new ward.

Surprisingly, Genevieve served only six months at San Quentin, her conviction reversed. Her lawyer had filed an appeal in the State District Court of Appeals and was able to claim before the court that the prosecutor had failed to show that Mrs. Paddleford was unable to pay for the material she was convicted of obtaining by fraud. Had Genevieve found yet *another* benefactor to foot her legal fees? Apparently so.

Two months into her incarceration at San Quentin, another man, claiming to be an old friend from her halcyon days as the wife of Dr. Paddleford, arrived as her knight in shining armor and announced to Warden Holohan his intentions to marry Genevieve, even while she remained a prisoner. He gave his name as Dr. F. L. R. Silvey. When interviewed outside the grim gray walls by a reporter from the *Oakland Tribune*, he blushed and said, "I proposed to her by telegram, and she accepted by mail. I'd marry her here if the law would allow. But in any case, I'll marry her as soon as she is free to marry. I'd wait forever."[6] Several news outlets carried the story. The headlines attracted attention: "Cupid Can't Even Get in San Quentin," "Fiancé Wants Convict Freed," "Locksmith Gets Laugh on Lovers."

Dr. Silvey approached the warden with his intentions in January 1928 and was summarily dismissed. Not to be outdone, he returned in February. This time, he was accompanied by the deputy county clerk, demanding that Warden Holohan produce Genevieve so that a marriage license might be issued. Holohan informed Silvey that San Quentin was no summer resort but a penitentiary, and that its inmates had no civil rights and couldn't even make a marriage contract. The doctor insisted that a recent Supreme Court decision gave inmates of penal institutions the right to marry. Holohan's retort was that "no one in San Quentin is going to wed while I'm in charge."[7]

Who was Dr. Silvey? In 1922, five years before his campaign to marry the imprisoned love of his life, the *Los Angeles Times* published a brief background of Silvey. The account coincided with Dr. Silvey's announcement of an intended building project: an extravagant dance pavilion and club on his twenty-eight-thousand-acre tract near Ensenada, Mexico.

The announced cost of construction was estimated to be a quarter of a million dollars. Dr. Silvey said, "I will personally superintend the building of the clubhouse. It will be built of native rock and be of old mission architecture. The patio, sixty feet square, will be the dance floor. I am a rich man and I am merely doing this as a hobby. When completed, the clubhouse will be open to all and the prices charged will be nominal."[8]

It turns out that Dr. F. L. R. Silvey was indeed a former friend and business associate of George Paddleford, and well acquainted with Genevieve. In 1910, he was employed as one of the surgeons serving the workers of the Mexican Petroleum Company in Tampico. He was a rich man. According to the *Times*, Dr. Silvey had made a fortune as an investor in Mexican oil:

> *While working for the Mexican Petroleum Company, he located oil land for himself near Tuxpan, state of Veracruz, which for the last several years has brought him an income of $2,000 a day, he stated yesterday. In 1911, he occupied offices in Mexico City with Clement Swain, Los Angeles capitalist. Together with Julio Madero, he designed the Madero peso, a silver coin still circulating in Mexico. In 1914 and just previous to Pancho Villa's raid on Columbus, and while he was still at Madera, State of Coahulla, Dr. Silvey gave surgical treatment to Pancho Villa, who at that time was suffering from a gunshot wound in the right leg.*[9]

Genevieve readily initiated a prison correspondence with Dr. Silvey. Their friendship had probably blossomed as far back as when both resided at Camp Ebano in 1917. Genevieve, the consummate flirt, would have drawn the sparkle of Dr. Silvey, as well as that of other capitalistic, rough-and-ready oilmen in the company.

Dr. Silvey was well acquainted with George Paddleford. He even went so far as to announce to his friend by telegram that he intended to marry Genevieve in prison. Paddleford's response was to forward the telegram to his attorney, "for whatever action he considers it merits." When reporters confronted Dr. Silvey, he replied, "We love each other, and we have both been married and divorced often enough to be credited with knowing what we want."[10]

But Silvey turned out to be a no-show. When Genevieve walked out of San Quentin on May 19, 1928, he was nowhere to be found. She was greeted instead by the deputy sheriff from Salinas, who held out a second warrant for her arrest, this one for defrauding another shopkeeper, who claimed to have been swindled of clothing valued at $600. But the charges were dropped. On May 28, Judge Treat, of Salinas County, ruled that she had been punished enough for a crime that was only slightly above a misdemeanor. "She walked out of the Salinas courtroom a free woman, wearing a silk ensemble and an expensive fur coat."[11] According to the *Los Angeles Times*, her attorney, Russell Scott, "sought every legal means of saving the woman from the penitentiary."[12]

Dr. Silvey, as a parting benevolence, it seems, helped pave her way to freedom. But what happened to him? Did the luster of his prison romance become tarnished by a deeper look into Genevieve's past? After all, from the time of Dr. Silvey's early friendship with the Paddlefords in Mexico until her incarceration at San Quentin, Genevieve had racked up nearly ten years of sordid filchery. Perhaps it was too much for him to swallow. And possibly he had not actually seen and visited Genevieve until after he had made his appeal to the warden; then, finding, to his dismay, a woman who bore little likeness to the dynamic, raging beauty of his imagination, he fled. She would have appeared portly and full-faced, with thinning hair, and teeth in need of dentistry. She would have exhibited the strain of prison life and years of practicing the art of duplicity.

Genevieve/Eleanor/Margaret McKinney/Paddleford had become a bona fide crook. Like a poker player, she measured her winnings against her losses, and, with the confidence of a talented actress, she found, more often than not, a gullible client. She was hooked on her trade. For Aunt Eleanor, in her early fifties, it was the only game in town. Until her final wager, she would willingly gamble her freedom against playing the ruse and beating the rap.

Dr. F. L. R. Silvey had walked. Three years after Genevieve's release, he was listed in the Denver, Colorado, city directory as a physician, residing there with his wife, Josephine.[13]

Chapter 24:

San Quentin Redux, 1929–30

The fascinating Mrs. Paddleford is in again—less than a year after she got out.
              —Ogden Standard Examiner, *June 16, 1929[1]*

Mrs. Paddleford walked out of San Quentin, only to find herself back in the Salinas County courtroom. Thankfully, the secondary charges were dropped, and on May 28, 1928, Genevieve took flight. Throwing caution to the wind, she moved quickly to restore her prowess and status. At first she must have seen herself as haggard, flaccid, and in poor health. And, worse, she may have noticed a lump on her breast. But her first concern was not for her health; rather, it was to stage a notable comeback. She was well on her way when, grudgingly, the show had to be interrupted. In September, four months from her release, she checked herself into the Dante Hospital in San Francisco to face a mastectomy. A tumor was removed from her right breast. Again, she was graced with good fortune: the cancer had not spread. However, it wasn't long before she found herself back in court, and for some time, her health and recovery remained an issue.

Just six months after her operation and only eleven months out of San Quentin, she faced Santa Barbara County Supreme Court for passing fictitious checks under an alias. She had languished in a jail cell there for weeks, again as Grace Potter. Then, vending her name not as Genevieve but as Eleanor M. Paddleford, she was called before the Santa Barbara court on April 7, 1929.

Her story is told from the court transcripts and reports from various newspapers. After eleven months of hectic homeless travel involving hospitals and her usual transient obliquities, she was picked up at El Encanto hotel in Santa Barbara. The court called several witnesses in the case of *The People vs. Eleanor M. Paddleford.*[2]

First, a doctor testified as to her health. The court wanted to know if she had been malingering in regard to her present physical condition. In part:

Q. What is your name, Doctor?
A. Harold R. Schwalenberg.

Q. Did you have occasion yesterday to examine Mrs. Paddleford?
A. I did.

Q. Will you state to His Honor what your findings were with reference to her general condition?
A. Her general condition seemed to be quite good. She had a few bad teeth and a mild increase in her blood pressure. She had evidences of an operation on the right breast, which, from the type of scar and findings in that region, was probably done for cancer. She had no gross evidence of extension from the mastitis to other parts of the body.

Q. Was there an operation?
A. Probably within the last six months. It was for the removal of the right breast.

Q. Doctor, you noticed the appearance of the witness on the stand this morning?
A. Yes, sir.

Q. Do you think she was malingering at all during her time at the county jail?
A. I think there is a tendency to malinger.

Q. Did you think so yesterday when you were talking to her?
A. I was of that impression yesterday.

Q. You do not think it was a true physical condition?
A. I don't think so.

Eleanor's practice of malingering had been well honed, probably from the time she was first incarcerated at New York's Blackwell's Island prison, way back in 1909. Her theatrics yielded the relative comfort of a hospital bed over that of a cold cell. According to the testimony of her current prison matrons, she complained daily about the food, about sleep, about stomach pain. She complained of nausea and could vomit on command.

When Eleanor was called to the witness stand, she gave an account of the months following her parole from San Quentin. She had checked herself into three different hospitals:

Q. State your name, please.
A. Eleanor McKinney Paddleford. McKinney is my maiden name.

Q. Will you tell His Honor the events leading up from last June until you arrived in Santa Barbara?
A. In September, I was in the Dante Hospital [San Francisco] for an operation by Dr. Collin. After I left there, I went east to my home [?], at which time I was taken ill again. I was taken to Rochester to Dr. Mayo for a second operation in November. At the end of November, I left St. Mary's Hospital at Rochester and came out to California. I arrived early in December. I have been with friends. I was taken sickly again and went back to Rochester. From there I went to Johns Hopkins in Baltimore, and I was in Johns Hopkins for two weeks, then to New York. I arrived in California the seventeenth of February, in Pasadena, at the Maryland Hotel.

I remained at the Maryland until the following Saturday, then came over to Los Angeles and was at the Roosevelt Hotel. Then I had some friends coming out from Chicago and I motored up to Santa Barbara. I arrived about eight thirty in the evening at the El Encanto hotel.

Newspapers ran their own stories of Eleanor's travels and trespasses. A human-interest story noted that "Genevieve Eleanor McKinney Paddleford created a furor in Pacific Coast circles when she reappeared in her old familiar and popular role as a society matron."[3] Her first prompt out of San Quentin was to cloak her identity. The name Genevieve Paddleford was too well known. She entered the city of San Francisco as Mrs. Lois Millicent Wilson, millionaire woman from New York, and, when it suited her, she referred back to herself as Mrs. Ben Teal, also a millionaire woman from New York. She checked into San Francisco's most elegant hotel, the Mark Hopkins, as Lois Millicent Wilson. The clever ruse she used to crash the fashionable hotel was described as follows: "In a dramatic and efficient manner, she strolled up the hotel steps and collapsed, thus gaining a temporary suite at a private hospital clinic, then a suite in the hotel. After answering some 'bothersome questions' at the clinic, she was welcomed as a guest at the Mark Hopkins."[4]

As per her modus operandi, she scanned the society pages, tapped into her memory bank, and began making contacts. For a brief period, while exhibiting her acquired social poise and apparent breeding, Lois Millicent Wilson moved easily into San Francisco's upper stratum.

Her social engagements and appearances, for a time, were frequent and receptive. But Genevieve fell victim again to her own sticky fingers. Two nurses from the private clinic where she had been briefly treated and dismissed complained to the State Labor Commission that "Mrs. Lois Millicent Wilson had decamped a watch, uniform, [and] surgical instruments, and had not paid her clinician charge of $438."[5]

The nurses, Miss Freda A. Plath and Miss Freda A. Glindamann, were presented with a rogues' gallery of photographs from the San Francisco Police Department. It didn't take long for them to pick out Mrs. Genevieve Paddleford. The police then searched for Lois Millicent Wilson. The search fizzled. Genevieve knew she'd have to make a run for it, and she did. The nurses' case lagged and was allowed to lapse.

In February, months later, according to her own testimony, Eleanor returned to California following hospitalization at Johns Hopkins in Baltimore. Her stated travel itinerary, from hospital to hospital, from California to the East and back again, seemed too hectic to be believed.

The *Los Angeles Times* reported that she popped up in Los Angeles in early February, purchased an expensive car, and ran up a large bill at the Biltmore in Santa Barbara. From the Biltmore, she moved into the luxurious El Encanto. The manager of El Encanto testified that Eleanor drove up in an eight-cylinder Packard sedan that she had recently purchased in Pasadena. El Encanto, located in the lush hills of Santa Barbara, overlooks the Pacific and to this day is billed as an icon of the 1920s. The manager, Mr. A. K. Bennet, described in his testimony how Eleanor passed a spurious check on a fictitious Chicago bank. Then, with $150 cash in hand, she drove off in her new car. He became suspicious when he noticed her entering the car with a little dog.[6]

This, in part, is his testimony:

Q. On or about the twenty-sixth of February, was Mrs. Paddleford a guest at your hotel?
A. She was.

Q. On that night, did you cash a check in the sum of $150 for her?
A. Yes.

Q. State for the court the circumstances surrounding the passing of that check.
A. Mrs. Paddleford came to the lobby in the morning and asked to see me after she had her breakfast. When I sat with her, she said she was on her way to San Francisco to meet her family. She asked me to make reservations at the Fairmont in San Francisco. She made very fine reservations for her family for the following Monday. She also made reservations for some very prominent people from Chicago. In fact, exceptionally good reservations.

Q. Did she make reservations for a party named McKinney?

A. McKinney—those were her own relatives.

Q. She registered at the hotel as Mrs. McKinney?

A. Yes. After we had this conversation about the reservations, she said that the day before she had been in Pasadena and had left her purse at a friend's home, possibly on a couch, and she was rather short of funds. She was afraid she might have a blowout on the way up to San Francisco, and she only had a few dollars, $13 or $14.

I knew Mr. McKinney from Cleveland, Ohio, and I thought this was his daughter. They were very wealthy people. I said it would not be wise to continue on her way with a small amount of money. It was some $300 to $400 that she had left in her pocketbook on the couch at Pasadena. I said that we would be very glad to accommodate her with sufficient funds to see her through. The sum agreed upon was $150, for which she gave me a check. In writing out the check, she did not have her glasses. She had left them in her pocketbook. She asked the clerk to make out the check. I stood directly by the clerk, and she said, "Illinois Trust Company." She signed the check, and $150 was handed over to her. I thought she then left for San Francisco.

She had not been away more than ten or fifteen minutes when I remembered the little dog she had in her arms, a very pretty Japanese poodle or whatever you might call it. We have in the California Hotel Men's Association the secretary who sends out notices of people who have defrauded hotels in several ways, and I went and got this notice and compared it, thinking in my own mind it must be the same party.

Then the phone rang, and Mr. Wilson at the Santa Barbara Biltmore called me and asked if a certain lady had been there. He described her without mentioning her name. I said she got from me $150. He said, she [had] just passed a check for $75 but [he had gotten] his money back. I called the sheriff and described what happened. Then I went right down to the County National Bank and asked them if there was an Illinois Trust Company. There was not. There was an Illinois Merchants Trust Company but no account there in the name of McKinney.

Testimony of Charles D. Wilson, Santa Barbara Biltmore Hotel:

Q. Your full name?
A. Charles D. Wilson

Q. On the twenty-sixth of February, did you see Mrs. Paddleford at your hotel?
A. Yes.

Q. Was there a transaction at that time in which she passed a check for $75?
A. Yes.

Q. State the circumstances.
A. Mrs. Paddleford came in, apparently asking [for] accommodations for her parents, who expected to arrive the following Monday. I came into the office just at that time, and in some manner she recognized me and called me by name, claiming previous acquaintance, which I did not dispute.

I showed the accommodations, and they were satisfactory. Five trunks were supposedly coming through by express. As we were returning to the office, she commented on the soiled condition of her gown and said that she was staying at the Los Angeles Biltmore. She thought she had better get a new gown before she went back. She found she did not have enough money to make the purchase and asked if I would cash a check. She asked an unusual question, which was, "How much I thought she ought to have?" I suggested $50. She said $75 would be nearer, that she might have trouble on the way to Los Angeles with her machine.

We stepped to the cashier's desk, and I asked her if she had a check, and she said, "No, will you furnish me a blank check?" I filled in the check for her at her direction, as she did not have her glasses. She signed it and received $75 cash. She immediately went to Magnin's to make a purchase. I followed her.

When she came out, I questioned her acquaintanceship and asked her for further identification. Immediately she said, "I don't believe I will get the gown. I don't think I need the money. I will give back the cash and take my check." Which I said would be all right with me, but I still asked for identification. She said, "I haven't any with me, but you can call the Biltmore in Los Angeles, and they will tell you all about me." She refunded the $75, took the check, and tore it up. That closed the incident.

By the Court:

> *The information charges that you, Eleanor McKinney Pad-dleford, are accused by the district attorney of the County of Santa Barbara of the crime of making, passing, and uttering and publishing a fictitious check—a felony. Upon this infor-mation you were arraigned and entered a plea of not guilty. Subsequently, you came into the Court with your attorney, and in open Court asked permission of the Court to with-draw your plea of not guilty and enter a plea of guilty. Per-mission was granted to this charge. Your attorney thereupon applied to the Court for probation in your behalf, the time for hearing set for this morning. The time for pronouncing judgment was also set for this morning, to be pronounced in the event your application for probation was denied. The application for probation has been denied. It now becomes the duty of the Court to pronounce its judgment upon you for the commission of this crime. Have you any legal reason to cause to assign why the judgment of the Court should not be pronounced against you?*

The Defendant [*a long, rambling prevarication*]:

> *Your Honor, I did no wrong. I have money, and if you ask my attorney right here—I need not state where—but he knows there is some money in existence waiting to be paid over to him. I have done no wrong, and all I can do is to ask your leniency. I was told to plead guilty, that it would be best, and that I had a better chance, so I did it. That is all.*
>
> *But I still say I did not do any wrong when I gave the check on the Guarantee Trust Company. I have had an account there since 1917, and I gave this check to Mr. Bennett. It was his own offer to hold the check until I returned.*

I have lived in Los Angeles since I married Mr. Paddl-eford. I have an account at the Ambassador Hotel and differ-ent places. I have owned two Pierce Arrows. They have been paid for. I don't owe any money. I have accounts all over. I have accounts all over Los Angeles, and I have accounts at Altman's and different places in New York. I have money standing waiting to be paid over to me; even some came by telegram the other day.

I meant no wrong, and, so far as my reputation is con-cerned, for every bit of money in my life, I can account. If given a chance, I can assure you that you will find that I have never done any wrong. You may say my affair of some few months ago—I can only refer you to the federal government— when they came to me and told me that all my sorrows and troubles had been brought onto me by Mr. Paddleford.

There is nothing against me. I have never had a conviction; I have never been arrested and paid any fine, and any money I owe I will be glad to pay. I only ask to be given a chance.

My health broke down. My little boy was kidnapped and taken to Mexico by Mr. Paddleford. I don't know whether he is alive or dead. It is a nervous condition? You may say it is a nervous condition only. It is not. My only child, all I had in the world, was taken from me in 1923. Sheriff Treager, I am quite sure, will tell you he did everything to find him. He was taken to Mexico, since then, and my health broke down.

I had some trouble in Salinas. It was brought on and found that Mr. Paddleford with his lawyer—who has been before the Bar Association—were responsible. I appealed to the appellate court. They went into it and found I was not guilty, Your Honor. And in the same thing, I had no wrong intention of defrauding Mr. Bennett, or to defraud anyone. At Long Beach I asked them to send money. The money came. I paid Mr. Bennett. I owe nothing. I only ask Your Honor's leniency to give me a chance, and I will prove that I will do my part.

Statement of the defendant by the Court:

Q. What is your full name?
A. Genevieve Eleanor Margaret McKinney. I have been married three times.

Q. Have you ever been convicted of a crime before?
A. Never.

Q. Were you not convicted of a crime at Salinas and sent to the penitentiary?
A. The Appellate Court reversed the decision.

Q. During that time, were you not in the penitentiary?
A. I was there for sixty-two days.

Q. How long?
A. From the first day of November, I believe, until the first day of March—I was held four weeks on account of quarantine.

Q. What was the charge against you?
A. The charge was a dressmaker's bill. The charge was $120. And when they arrested me, they found on me $1,240.

Q. Were you ever convicted of any other offense?
A. I never served a sentence in my life.

Q. Where were you born?
A. Hamilton, Ohio.

Q. What is your age? Do you care to give it?
A. I will give it to you written down. I don't want the newspapers to have it.

Q. Have you any children?
A. The little boy that was kidnapped is all.

Q. Where is he?
A. Mr. Paddleford kidnapped him. I don't know.

Q. What degree of education did you receive?
A. I graduated from the Girls' Convent in Oakland, California. I then went to Berlin for my music education.

Q. Have you ever sustained any serious personal injuries—broken arm or anything of the kind?
A. I was thrown out of an automobile in Los Angeles.

Q. Have you ever had any sicknesses outside of what the doctors testified about this morning?
A. Mr. Paddleford kicked me in the breast and in the head, and I lay unconscious for two weeks in Long Beach, New York.

Q. Have you been addicted to the use of liquor?
A. I never drank.

Q. Or drugs?
A. Never.

Q. Have you ever had any occupation other than housewife?
A. In a literary way, I have written a great deal.

Q. How long have you lived in California?
A. I was married in 1917, and I came to California with Mr. Paddleford at the end of 1917, and I lived there until 1923.

The Court:

> *Mrs. Paddleford, it is the judgment of this Court that you be punished for the commission of this crime of making, uttering, passing, and publishing a fictitious check, a felony, by*

being imprisoned in the state prison at San Quentin, in the
state of California, for the term presented by law as the pun-
ishment for the commission of this crime. The sheriff of this
county, Mr. James Ross, is ordered and directed to deliver you
to that state prison for the execution of this judgment.

The *Los Angeles Times* reported:

It was a broken, feeble woman who was assisted into the
courtroom by sheriff's deputies. Once a famous beauty whose
escapades have startled high-society circles on the continent
as well as in the United States, Mrs. Paddleford now would
not be recognized by those she once knew as friends.

Dressed in the same simple yellow jersey she wore when
arrested, Mrs. Paddleford was accompanied into the courtroom
by her attorney, W. Lindley Abbott. The attorney entered a plea.
Then Mrs. Paddleford was called upon, first by Judge Crow and
then by the court clerk, to confirm the lawyer's statement.

She was forced to hold on to the massive table in front of
the judge's bench for support as she arose to answer questions.
Her voice, hardly audible, affirmed the plea of guilty.[6]

Judge S. E. Crow sentenced Mrs. Paddleford to four more years at San Quentin. Eleanor's flash of freedom and fancy had collapsed once again.

The distance from the luxurious El Encanto to the Santa Barbara county prison where Aunt Eleanor languished for weeks was all but ten miles. From the Santa Barbara county prison to San Quentin was 340 miles. It would have been a long, hot, forlorn ride on a prison bus. But there was a glimmer of optimism. The *Los Angeles Times*, in reporting her court sentence, also announced, "Mrs. Genevieve Paddleford has signed a contract with a newspaper syndicate to write the story of her escapades. She is to receive $10,000 for publishing rights."[7]

Could Eleanor have been found in her San Quentin cell bent over a writing pad? Perhaps. The prospect of a $10,000 advance for publishing her memoirs, combined with time on her hands, might have given her enough incentive to put to paper her scorching life story. Somewhere, an unfinished memoir may lie fallow, yet to be discovered. One thing is certain: she did not give up. Of her many letters of appeal, one found its mark. She was again thrown a lifeline, and again, true to form, another release from prison came her way, only eighteen months hence, on November 9, 1930.

Chapter 25:

Mr. Fisher and Mr. Whyte, 1930–31

The career of the beautiful international adventuress is one of the most astounding ever brought to the attention of the police. Psychologists are eagerly analyzing the compulsion that apparently forces Mrs. Paddleford to possess luxuries at any cost.[1]

Genevieve, now identified in the San Quentin State Prison record as Eleanor Paddleford, relentlessly pursued her parole. After ten months into her stint, the parole board received a very favorable letter of recommendation. The letter came from Mr. John B. Fisher, attorney at law, New Orleans, Louisiana, February 3, 1930, and indicated that Mrs. Paddleford, as the wife of George Paddleford, had been both a close friend and, at one time, employed in the legal department of the Mexican Petroleum Company. Eleanor apparently had located and recruited Mr. Fisher as her confidant and benefactor. This might have raised some eyebrows, as Mr. Fisher, at this time, was serving as a municipal judge in New Orleans. The parole board included his letter and "several others from this party" in a brief that would set the board's recommendations.

Fisher wrote:

I have known the lady many years. I know her to be a devoted and affectionate mother to her young son, and from my observation, made every effort to give him a good Christian education at the De La Salle Institute in New York. While with us she lived a very quiet life, and had the usual refinement of one of her station. She did not drink, smoke, or care to indulge in the usual dissipations of what is commonly known as a "night life." Her acquaintances appeared to be persons of the best standing. She seemed to be haunted with the idea that Mr. Paddleford was trying to do all the harm he could. She had means, and did not want for anything. Her habits were simple. Do not believe that she had any criminal intent. I presided on the Criminal Bench here for many years, and in such cases no prosecution was ever had.

She informed me that she was advised to plead guilty, which should never have been advised. I AM WILLING TO ACCEPT HER PAROLE, and my family will welcome her with us in our home, as soon as she is able to come to us, and she is anxious to come. She is in a precarious state of health and ought to undergo an operation without delay, for a very serious malady.[2]

The words attributed to Judge Fisher should have leaped suspiciously as coming from the cunning hand of Eleanor McKinney. It was a voice much too loud! Was there a New Orleans postmark on the envelope? Had the board investigated? Or were there just too many cases to be heard? How could Eleanor have slipped letters into her file? Had she co-opted an insider? She was that clever.

Judge John Fisher and his wife were indeed listed in the New Orleans directory in 1930. From the board's perspective, all appeared to be in order. Eleanor's lawyer, Mr. W. Lindley Abbot, was quoted in the parole brief in regard to her letters of recommendation: "If the story she tells is true, she has been subjected to persecution unduly. I recommend that she be paroled."[3] The parole board recommended a delayed parole. Eleanor would first have to serve out half of her four-year sentence. The parole date was set for October 25, 1930.

That day finally came. The board met. Then, as had happened before, there was a snag. On the eve of Eleanor's release, Miss Freda Plath, the nurse from San Francisco who had not forgotten Mrs. Millicent Lois Wilson, submitted a charge of grand theft over a missing gold watch and $280 in lost wages.

Eleanor, accompanied by a prison matron, had to appear before San Francisco municipal judge George Schonfeld to answer the charge. Lo and behold, someone had already worked out a reimbursement with Miss Plath behind the scene, and Miss Plath refused to prosecute. Eleanor had "friends," some on the inside and some on the outside. Judge Schonfeld dismissed the case. She returned to her cell and waited for the gates to open. Three weeks later, she was granted her parole and accorded a charity ticket to New Orleans on November 19, 1930. Again, the locks had sprung. But was Judge Fisher the benefactor? The board seemed to have found sufficient weight and credibility in the letters appropriated to him. The terms were that Eleanor would reside in New Orleans under his watch.

Two newspapers made brief reference to Mr. Fisher in regard to her parole. On October 16, a month before her release, the *Oakland Tribune* said, "Her benefactor, it is learned, was John B. Fisher, New Orleans attorney and friend of her family, into whose care she is to be paroled. Had he not come to her rescue, and had a conviction resulted in the case of Miss Plath, Mrs. Paddleford would have served another prison term, since failure to pay wages is classed as a felony under California law."[4]

Months later, after her release, the *Los Angeles Times* reported that Eleanor had again violated her parole and had been passing fraudulent checks once again, this time in Alameda, New Orleans, and several unnamed cities. "Officers said that if she is rearrested and convicted, she will face a life term. When paroled last November 19, 1930, to Judge Fisher of New Orleans, Mrs. Paddleford said she was 'going back to my music studies.'"[5]

If Judge Fisher was assigned as overseer, he seemed not aware of it. Was he ever aware of anything? Was he aware that an "old friend" had purloined his name to procure an advantage? He was never directly quoted in any newspaper, and his name in regard to Eleanor never appeared again. Her parole seemed steeped in foolery. Eleanor seems to have pulled off another slick one.

California state parole officer Ed Whyte was assigned her case. For six years he tracked Eleanor Paddleford in an attempt to bring her in, but she was always just one or two towns or cities beyond his grasp. Two months after her release from San Quentin, Mr. Whyte received a jolting investigative report from the Volunteer Prison League in San Francisco concerning Eleanor's parole and subsequent movements:

Mr. Ed H. Whyte
January 17, 1931
State Parole Officer
San Francisco, California

My dear Mr. Whyte:
At the time of Mrs. Paddleford's hearing in the Public Court here in San Francisco, the money sent in her behalf and disbursed at her request came from a woman named Clara Lehman and was sent via Western Union from Los Angeles, but we have been unable to locate such a person, so it is evidently a fictitious name.

Mrs. Paddleford arrived at New Orleans on January 3 (46 days after her departure from San Quentin), and, from the investigation that was made for us, it seems that she registered at the Roosevelt Hotel. She told the management a long story about an automobile accident in Mississippi, which she was obliged to settle in the sum of $350 and asked the hotel to give her $150 to supplement her present funds in order to settle the claim. It would further seem that she gave Judge Fisher as reference and the hotel advanced her this money on the strength that she would receive funds from New York.

It would further seem that she was under arrest in Meridian, Mississippi, for passing bad checks, also in Houston, Texas. Our information further states that the attorney, who obtained her release in Meridian, because he too tried to be a Good Samaritan, unwittingly aided her.

This will, no doubt, answer your query and explain how she has been chaining money. She evidently is not cured and is still up to her old tricks. As she lied about me, she would lie about anyone. She is not to be trusted. She should have been told to ride on the charity rate ticket which was obtained for her as she came under that classification. There is no doubt, but what she will be picked up by the authorities sooner or later. We regret that she fooled us, but conclude that she is an expert in misrepresentation and connivance.

Sincerely yours,
H. J. Kleefish, Adjutant [6]

Eleanor was again on the run, leaving a murky trail and along the way raking cutpurse swindles over gullible hoteliers. Complaints were being lodged, but authorities seemed always too slow to engage in hot pursuit. Her first stop out of San Quentin was the swank island of Alameda, across the San Francisco Bay. There, she plied her trade, but, knowing that California was "hot," she took to the road and headed south, arriving in New Orleans in early January 1931. Soon after that, she left for Havana, Cuba, and by the end of the month landed in the Bahamas. It was in Nassau, Bahamas, where she made one of her more dramatic moves.

Chapter 26:

Mr. Fawcett, 1931

Woe betides the gullible and bighearted folk who cross her path.[1]
—Lewis L. Fawcett, justice, Supreme Court,
State of New York

T he Graycliff Hotel in Nassau was a popular, swank watering hole
for wealthy New Yorkers on holiday during the 1920s and '30s. Mr.
John Fawcett, a dental equipment manufacturer and dealer from Brooklyn, was a frequent visitor. An attractive newcomer caught his attention
one evening in mid-January 1931. She introduced herself as Eleanor Roberts, the widowed wife of Mr. Heath Wilson Roberts, an Egyptian shipbuilder who had recently perished when his automobile, a Rolls-Royce,
had careened over a cliff near Alexandria. John found her charming,
engaging, and extraordinarily attentive. And she was about his same age.

John Fawcett was a member of a prominent Brooklyn, New York,
family. He had three brothers and three sisters. He and his brother Albert
Fawcett founded Fawcett & Fawcett, Inc., a very prosperous dental supply
company. His other two brothers, Lewis L. Fawcett and James M. Fawcett, both served as justices of the New York Supreme Court. The brothers
were members of prestigious civic clubs and organizations.

Nassau was a favorite destination for the Fawcett family. Passenger
lists from the Port of New York show John Fawcett returning from Nassau

to New York at least seven times beginning in 1922.[2] He would have been well known at the Graycliff Hotel.

The hotel had a long and storied past, going back to the pirate days of the eighteenth century. "By 1844, Graycliff became Nassau's first inn ready to provide the traveler with genuine Caribbean hospitality. During the American Civil War, it became a refuge for rum and cotton runners. During the Prohibition days of the 1920s, Graycliff was owned by Polly Leach, a friend of Al Capone. Needless to say, Graycliff was the most sophisticated gathering spot for the rich and famous."[3]

A romance developed very quickly between the longtime bachelor and the newly arrived widow Roberts. John Fawcett was a plain-appearing man with no distinguishing features. It is unlikely that he was accustomed to such intimate attention. Suddenly, he was swept off his feet and mention of marriage was almost immediate. John had met an unfamiliar happiness, and he readily succumbed to her charm. They were married within the month. John appealed directly to the island governor for a special license to marry in the Commonwealth of the Bahamas. It was granted. The announcement of the wedding ran in the *Brooklyn Daily Eagle* on January 30, 1931:

> *Announcement is made of the marriage at Nassau, Bahamas, on Wednesday, of Mrs. Heath Wilson Roberts of Mentone, France, and John C. Fawcett of 1347 Dean Street. The ceremony was performed in Christ Church Cathedral, Nassau, in a private ceremony. The dean of Nassau presided under the special license of the Governor. Mr. Fawcett is well known in Brooklyn and in Wading River, L.I., where he spends much of his time. He is a brother of Lewis L. Fawcett of the Supreme Court, Second Department; of Margaret Fawcett of Dean Street, and of Alfred Fawcett of Union Street. Mr. Fawcett and his bride will probably make their home in Brooklyn.[4]*

John and Eleanor spent their honeymoon in Germany. They returned to New York two weeks later on the liner *Vulcania* on February 13, 1931, arriving from Husum, Germany. Mrs. Heath Wilson Fawcett was listed on the passenger list as a native of St. Paul, Minnesota, age thirty-eight, and her new husband from Brooklyn, age fifty-four.[5]

A writer for *True* magazine, in a story entitled "Queen of the Gold Diggers," published in 1941, described the newlyweds' arrival in New York:

> *A large group of society friends, newspaper photographers, and reporters met the couple when they docked in New York. Everyone was eager to see the bride, for Mr. Fawcett had been considered to be a confirmed bachelor. Genevieve held her breath as their boat sailed up New York Bay. But no one in the crowd waiting for them recognized her as the notorious and much married swindler.*[6]

The newlyweds checked into the Ambassador Hotel. A week later, they hosted a reception in the Green Room of the Ambassador for the Fawcett family. There were fifteen guests, including Judge Lewis L. Fawcett, justice of the New York Supreme Court. A society page notice of the Fawcett gathering concluded, "Mr. and Mrs. John Fawcett, who were married last month at Nassau in the Bahamas, will stay at the Ambassador until spring, when they will go to their place, Villa Mimosa, on the Riviera, France."[7]

Eleanor had hit the jackpot: a bachelor with a bankroll, a hotel suite, a villa on the Riviera, a fine, prominent, wealthy New York family. How long would she be able to keep up a front? February passed into March, and, as with all couples who have known each other only briefly, probing questions began to arise. Some of the answers were conflicting. More questions arose along with increasing doubt and insecurity. As the husband looked for reasons to trust his wife, his pressing questions became more intense, the answers more worrisome. There were arguments and disagreements. Then these persistent questions: Why are you shopping so much? Why do you spend so much money on clothing and jewels!

The breakup came quickly. In mid-March, there was a domestic verbal showdown and Mrs. Fawcett booked a voyage to Europe. Several weeks later, the *Los Angeles Times* placed her in Rome. She was quoted as saying, "While dining one night in Rome with friends, including none other than Benito Mussolini, a sleek footman brought to my plate a silver tray on which lay a cablegram. Opening the message, I read these words: 'Genevieve Paddleford unmasked.' That was the end. I had not told Mr. Fawcett of serving in San Quentin. I considered that a closed book, but apparently he found out. He had our marriage annulled. But my attorney in New York is trying to reopen the case on the ground that it was fraudulently obtained. Many innocent persons have served time in prison and none more innocent than I."[8]

The annulment had been filed on May 11, 1931. The King's County clerk of court summons and complaint, together with an affidavit of publication for the annulment of the marriage of John C. Fawcett, was officially ordered sealed.[9]

Eleanor's sojourn in Rome with new, influential acquaintances was but a brief interlude. New adventures beckoned. She claimed to have received a marriage settlement from Mr. Fawcett of $75,000. That was false. However, she would likely have had a small cache of Fawcett money. In a letter to a colleague in California, Judge Lewis Fawcett wrote that "she has cost Jack more than ten thousand dollars, as he made good the checks she forged on shopkeepers and other bills she incurred at different stores."[10]

Whatever money she ran off with very shortly ran its course. On May 22, Eleanor checked into the Imperial Hotel in Vienna and then took a train four hundred miles away to Carlsbad, Czechoslovakia, a busy tourist town famous for its hot springs—the purpose of which was a brief shopping spree. Having had no success in Carlsbad, she returned to Vienna, where she attempted to "purchase" leather goods and underclothes from two Vienna stores. But she had not left Carlsbad without making waves. Carlsbad police had put the Vienna police on alert. A Carlsbad firm notified police that an American woman was attempting to obtain goods by fraud. Eleanor was stopped and detained by Vienna police, who returned her to Carlsbad for questioning. She was not held long. Again, she talked herself out of a predicament. But authorities were not entirely sympathetic. She was released but promptly and efficiently deported to the United States. Nothing more was heard from Eleanor for eight months.[11]

Parole officer Ed Whyte had long ago lost track of Eleanor McKinney Paddleford. From town to town and city to city, Eleanor kept one or two steps ahead of him. The American Hotel Association, responding to a long string of complaints, hired the William J. Burns International Detective Agency to find her, while at the same time pressuring the parole board to do its job. In a letter to the San Quentin parole board, the detective agency wrote, "We have received several claims against Mrs. Genevieve Paddleford for defrauding hotels with checks and obtaining of fraudulent cash advances. The amounts in which she has defrauded hotels are of such that in some cases they are not extraditable, but, as you know from her record, she is a menace to society."[12] The American Hotel Association wanted her behind bars.

In December 1931, Eleanor surprised everybody and showed up in San Francisco to defend her parole violation. True to form, she made a satisfactory account of herself and the parole violation was momentarily dismissed. However, she failed to mention her brief marriage to Mr. John C. Fawcett. When the board was informed, presumably by the investigative efforts of Officer Whyte, she was charged with "a technical violation of her parole." Mr. Whyte informed Genevieve Paddleford that she must remain in the vicinity of San Francisco while on parole from San Quentin or face imprisonment.[13]

When reporters from the *Los Angeles Times* caught up with her, they questioned her about the "Genevieve Paddleford unmasked" cablegram she had received in Rome from Mr. Fawcett, and about reports from abroad that she had been arrested in Carlsbad after her ill-fated banquet in Rome. She confidently replied, "A mere nothing, boys. Don't worry about it."[14]

Did she stay in San Francisco? On the day she received the order to remain, reporters asked what she was going to do. Her reply was, "I plan to visit my only son, a twenty-two-year-old boy, in Pasadena."[15]

Her son, Ben Teal Jr., was known by this time as Jack Teal Paddleford. He had just turned twenty-four in October. The last time he'd seen Eleanor had been when they were in New York City, just after the Paddleford breakup in 1922. Ten years had gone by, and he had no intention of seeing her again. It is very unlikely that he ever did.

Jack Teal Paddleford's record is sketchy. When he testified at the divorce hearing in Los Angeles in 1923, he was fifteen. He said he had been "hiding out" on a ranch, working in the fields. When asked by the judge what he was going to do, the boy said,

"I don't know. I like Dr. Paddleford, but she broke him. I wish I might have a guardian who would give me a happy home and educate me."[16]

Dr. Paddleford had come through. Jack, it seems, moved into the Paddleford home. He attended Burbank High School and graduated in 1926. During the summers, he worked in the Tampico oil fields with his stepbrother, George S. Paddleford. A photo taken of the two boys looking

George S. Paddleford with Ben "Jack" Teal at Huasteca oil seep. 1927

at an oil seep was taken on July 9, 1925. Obviously, they had developed a companionship. Passenger lists on two separate vessels arriving eight months apart in New York from France in 1930 identify each of them as passengers. George S. arrived home in January and Jack in September. If George S. and Jack had become close, they, at some point, parted ways. They may have maintained a relationship, but no further record of an association surfaced.

Jack went on to college. He graduated from the Colorado School of Mines in 1933, enjoyed membership in the Colorado Delta Fraternity, and pursued a career in the oil industry. While in college, he listed his address as Tampico, Mexico. City directories show him residing in Wichita and Oklahoma City, listed as a geologist scout. He married three times. His first marriage, right out of college, in May 1933, was to Mary "Gwendolyn" Martindale. They had no children and divorced in about 1939. He appears to have lived alone in Oklahoma City for a number of years. In 1954, he is listed in the Oklahoma City directory with his spouse Rebecca Paddleford. In 1959, his spouse is listed as Dagmar Paddleford. The public record of Jack Paddleford ends with a notice of his passing in 1981 at the age of seventy-three. At that time, he was residing in Albuquerque, New Mexico. He was interred at Resthaven Gardens Cemetery in Oklahoma City. There are no recorded children. One wonders if he ever tried to contact his adopted sister, Cynthia Teal, who once declared that she loved him. Perhaps somewhere there are letters.

Eleanor did not sit still in San Francisco, as ordered. How could she have? She had no shelter, no money, and no source of income. Her only resource was her scam, and San Francisco was too "hot." She fled once again. If she tried to find her son in Pasadena, she very likely failed. Jack may have been in the LA area on break from college at the time. Would he have acknowledged her if she'd made an appearance? Quite unlikely.

Eleanor went on the run again. Curiously, knowledge of her whereabouts in the early months of 1932 came from Judge Lewis Fawcett. The Fawcetts were still smarting from the fast one Eleanor had pulled on John when he'd fallen for her in Nassau. The Fawcett brothers wanted her behind bars. In letters that Judge Lewis wrote to his colleague Judge Foelker in Oakland, California, he expressed gratitude for assistance provided in the matter and lamented having learned that "the woman" had fled the jurisdiction of California and again violated her parole. His letter reads:

Supreme Court of the State of New York
Honorable Otto Foelker
January 14, 1932
1540 San Pablo Avenue
Oakland, California

Dear Otto:
This is to gratefully acknowledge receipt of your two very kind letters freighted with information. Your last communication dated January 11, arrived this very hour. In making reply, I shall first proceed to answer your inquiries. Jack did not agree to pay the woman in question $75,000 or any other sum, nor has he seen her or made or promised to make any remittances to her since she sailed for Europe last March. The canard is in line with many of her other monumental lies. She causes Baron Munchausen's, Grimm's, and Andersen's fairy tales to pale into insignificance by comparison.

I do hope the Chicago Tribune story can be stopped and all other publicity. This awful creature has already plunged the family into a deluge of most distasteful articles and a mass of unwelcome notoriety. However, since she has again fled the jurisdiction of California and again violated her parole, it is highly probable she will not again loom up here or in San Francisco.

She is most likely now traveling under another alias. During her stay in New York after returning from Europe and before going west, she was living at the Savoy-Plaza Hotel under the name of McCormack. It would not surprise me to hear she "broke the bank at Caliente, Mexico"!

Thank you for the two pictures you enclosed. I will turn them over to Jack for his rogues' gallery. In addition, I will keep

on the watch for your good friend the Honorable Earl Warren
and show him some entertainment in and out of court.

Each member of the family joins me in warmhearted sen-
timents and greetings.

Affectionately yours,
Lew[17]

The judge's letter was written in January 1932. He would write another letter to his friend in March. The Fawcetts were seemingly becoming the principal players in trying to keep track of Eleanor. It was winter, so Eleanor was again making her way south, just as she had done the year before when paroled out of San Quentin, at that time arriving in New Orleans. It is interesting that Judge Fawcett should have mentioned Earl Warren in his letter. Justice Warren was the district attorney of Alameda County, where Eleanor had briefly plied her trade. He was tough on crime and in a 1931 survey was listed as the best district attorney in the country. In 1953, he would begin serving his distinguished sixteen-year career as the chief justice of the United States. The Fawcetts were certainly well connected. Eleanor was on thin ice.

In Judge Fawcett's second letter to Judge Foelker, he told of the Fawcett family's unlikely encounter with Eleanor in Havana, Cuba:

Supreme Court of the State of New York
March 6, 1932

Dear Otto:
The information you furnish relative to the gold-digger is
appreciated and notes carefully made. You have certainly
gone to an endless amount of trouble, but be assured the Faw-
cetts are all truly grateful.

It occurs to me that the person who told Mr. Whyte that
the adventuress was in Shepheard Hotel, Cairo, where she
planned to remain until the end of summer, may have been
right about her having been there, but she is not there now.

Recently, Dean, Sade, Marion, Alfred, and his wife were in Havana, Cuba, and they all saw her on two occasions the same day. First while shopping, and later on they chanced across her again at a restaurant. She was there with a short, dark-complexioned man. Realizing she was recognized, she spoke to the man. He quickly left the table and went to the toilet. Alfred followed him, but when he got to the room he found that the man had exited by way of the kitchen through a rear door. The "bird of prey" left by the front door.

Dean got his guide and interpreter to follow her. He reported the next morning that she joined the man a few blocks away from the restaurant, and they went from place to place until after midnight, when they went to the Montserrat Hotel at no. 87 Belgia Avenue. He also stated that the hotel clerk told him the man and woman had arrived on a steamer from New York on February 16 and registered as Mr. and Mrs. Theodasin and [had been] assigned to room 402. He said they [had] booked passage for Florida, leaving that morning and could not extend their stay. Hence, he learned no more about the "woman in the case."

The Fawcett family returned home with this story last evening and I am hurrying this word on to you, in case you wish to convey it to Mr. Whyte. Since she sailed from New York to Cuba, it may be that she sailed direct from Egypt to New York. It occurs to me, she has to keep on the move, doubling on her tracks and looking both ways, and dodging in order to avoid the police.

Last week, I received a letter from a man in Philadelphia, seeking information as to her whereabouts, as he had cashed a fake check for $250 for her, and his wife had lent her $150! This took place in Carlsbad last summer. Woe betides the gullible and bighearted folk who cross her path!

It is a coincidence, but on the afternoon of February 16, the day the "vampire" landed in Havana, thieves entered the room of Dean and Sade at the Boulevard Hotel in Miami

Beach, Florida, and stole $23,000 worth of jewelry. It has not been recovered. Dean has offered a $5,000 reward for the return of the jewelry and an extra $5,000 for the arrest and conviction of the thieves.

    Please convey to Mr. Whyte assurance of my deep appreciation for his kind and valuable assistance in endeavoring to secure our family photographs.

    Keep well. Be happy.

Always affectionately,
Your friend,
Lew[18]

In May, John and Lewis Fawcett visited Nova Scotia. Their names were on a manifest of the *Gripsholn*, sailing from Halifax on May 22, 1932. Perhaps they had enjoyed a fishing trip together, or could they have been chasing a lead on Eleanor, hoping to bring her in? The ship's manifest was the last record found of Mr. John Fawcett until his obituary was published in 1943. He died of a heart attack while seated in a beach chair at Delray Beach, Florida, while visiting his brother Lewis.

Chapter 27:

Stakeout, 1932

With a flourish of the pen, Genevieve signed for the room under her newly assigned name, no doubt still considering how easy it was to fool men.[1]
—*"The Jade of Diamonds," by Horace Heffern*

Eleanor knew the world. She knew geography. Ocean liners and trains, timetables, maps, depots, piers, cities, towns, hotels, and shops were her stepping-stones, the rigging for her life on the lam. She was an agile and erudite traveler, and her moveable scam propelled her across two continents. She claimed to have fluency in French, Russian, Italian, and German. It seems plausible.[2] Her easy way with language, her cunning, her knowledge, her confidence and poise, had made her a formidable artist of the con. She had a wardrobe of aliases: Millicent Lois Wilson in San Francisco, Grace Potter in California, Mrs. Heath Wilson Roberts, and many others.

Since her divorce from Paddleford, she lived precipitously for ten years on the fat of the land, parading as Genevieve Paddleford with fine clothes and a regal manner. She was irresistible to the shopkeepers in New York, California, and Europe. She knew, of course, that she was a marked woman. In 1932 and thereafter, she had to move quickly, changing her name often, checking into the best hotels, and writing her fraudulent checks. After a day or two in one place, she would scoot down the road. Months would go by before reporters or authorities would catch her trail.

The Fawcetts and the detectives working for the American Hotel Association kept the heat on. In his letter to a colleague in California, Judge Lewis Fawcett wrote that $25,000 worth of jewelry had been stolen from his sister's room at the Boulevard Hotel in Miami, and that the theft had occurred on the same day the "vampire" landed in Havana.[3] This was a curious and remarkable assertion. Was this theft a bizarre coincidence or had Eleanor actually followed the Fawcetts, colluding with an accomplice in grand larceny? The Fawcetts were obviously suspicious.

Accounting for Eleanor's moves during 1932 came almost entirely through the letters posted by Judge Fawcett. According to one of his letters, she had been seen at the Shepheard Hotel in Cairo, Egypt. The Shepheard was the grandest hotel in Egypt and one of the grandest in the world. In the same letter, the judge reported that members of the Fawcett family had witnessed her presence in Havana as early as February. The judge also noted that "this awful creature" was armed with photographs of the Fawcett family and using them to ply her way into confidences.[4] Then, in the fall of that year, another of Eleanor's stops was accounted for, not by a Fawcett letter or newspaper but by members of her own, nearly forgotten family living in Havre, Montana.

The Montana stopover, sometime in late summer or early fall of 1932, was Eleanor's second visit to see the family of her half brother, Gilman McKinnie. She arrived at the age of fifty-seven, unannounced and alone. The McKinnie family had long since moved out of the little farmhouse outside of Chinook, where Eleanor, her unnamed traveling companion, and Ben Jr. had visited sixteen years earlier. She stepped off the train in Chinook but learned that Gilman had been killed in a car accident years ago and that her sister-in-law, Florence, was living in the nearby town of Havre. There, she found Florence and Florence's son, Ben, running a candy-and-tobacco shop. The visit was brief, not even overnight.

The death of Gilman McKinnie, on June 26, 1920, was a terrible blow to the family and a shock to the community. He had just turned thirty-seven and was at the height of his career as a well-known businessman. Florence was thirty-four. The children were eight, nine, thirteen, and fifteen years old. The car, a Ford Model T, rolled off the gravel road south of Chinook. The driver, a wool buyer from Boston, was killed instantly. Gilman crawled away and was picked up by a passing traveler. He died that night in the home he just finished building on the corner of Indiana and Tenth Street. One by one, he bade farewell to his children. Florence was inconsolable for weeks afterward. At the cemetery, she had to be held back from the grave. No one could doubt that they had been very much in love. Folks arrived from around the county to pay their respects.

Florence became the family's safe harbor. For three generations thereafter, she was the family matriarch, and, as far as anyone could tell, she never expressed defeat. It was a role she played with enthusiasm, and although she must have had her private moments, her children, her grandchildren, and her great-grandchildren were the focus of her life.

Eleanor and Florence must have had an interesting visit in Havre twelve years after Gilman's passing. Ben recalled that he drove Aunt Eleanor to the bus station, but later that day, he saw her attempting to hoof a ride west on Highway 2. Hitchhiking had probably become an accustomed means for Eleanor to get from place to place.

When Eleanor had visited the little farmhouse years earlier, in 1916, she had been a fancy young woman—beautiful, vivacious, charismatic, very self-assured, and well adapted to a modus vivendi of self-importance. But fifteen years had taken a toll, and Ben recalled a tired and drawn older woman. Nevertheless, she presented a ready charm and boastful independence. A lot had happened to her in those intervening years, events that should certainly have challenged her confidence. She was now dead broke and on the run from creditors and the law. She had married her third and fourth husbands, she'd been in and out of prisons in both America and Europe, and her children had abandoned her. Such was the cruel twist of fate that, for a second time in her life since childhood, she was left wanting a family.

A year after Eleanor's visit, Florence received two letters from her. Eleanor wrote that she had landed another husband. His name was Mr. Hall Thompson. She claimed to have found new security and "happiness," though a melancholy lingered between the lines. The letters were addressed to Florence, but Eleanor greeted her deceased half brother, Gilman, as well.

She had blocked his passing from her memory. The first letter was, curiously, postmarked from St. Moritz, Engadine, Switzerland:

July 13, 1933

My Dear Gilman and Florence,
I never intended to write you again, but after thinking it over I feel life is too short. After all the unhappiness that I have had, there must be a good God, as I am happily married with a lovely home, so why should I worry? I owe all my unhappiness to my father, but I guess he received his punishment all right. No father could treat his own children as he did and get away with it. However, I am happy. So I do not care. I always loved you, Gilman, and that is why I can condescend to write you.

A few evenings ago, my daughter told me a girl who had been attending the same school as she, was leaving for Chinook, so I thought I would write. My own child is most happy, a wonderful father, and he has a brother and sister, so the three children are wonderful and happy.

My husband made his money in the oil business and is a very fine man. So you see, God was good to me. I must have deserved it. I will not write any more this time. If you care to write me, you can address here:
Mrs. G. M. Thompson
Care/Hollywood Hotel
Hollywood, Los Angeles, Cal.

My love to you all and the children,
Eleanor

PS: Just mark the letter "hold." Our home is out about ten miles, but I motor in nearly every day.*

Florence must have read that letter with some astonishment. How could Eleanor not have remembered hearing about the fatal accident that killed her half brother, especially after she had visited only the year before? And to claim that she had so soon remarried a man with money! Was that a testament to her uncanny pursuit of rich men, or was it, more likely, another fabrication? Florence certainly had a handle on Eleanor's mendacity. The regret expressed in the letter, however, is heavy as it relates to her father and the hand she was dealt. From the time she was abandoned as a child, Eleanor's life was characterized by a deep longing for security and, at the same time, by a firm tethering to reckless temptation. These burdens drove her to practice a mastery of deceit and self-aggrandizement that would lift her at once to corridors of wealth and influence and then drop her mercilessly to the lowest possible defeats and most severe despairs.

Eleanor, at a young age, had found within her a rare talent for deceit that lured rich men into lairs, ensuring her survival and satisfying her avarice for glamour. Florence recognized this and over the years quietly stowed away bits and pieces of information chronicling her sister-in-law's extravagant, sad, and sordid life, including these letters.

Eleanor's second letter again greeted her deceased half brother, which seemed to reveal both an emotional attachment to him and a selective sense of reality. She openly expressed love for Gilman. Quite probably, he was the only man she ever genuinely cared about. Eleanor wrote that she wanted to repair her connection with her brother and his family, for whom she expressed great affection. Sadly, her attempt to mend past differences was woefully late. And her claim of a newfound security in her Mr. Thompson would, if true, have been but a tenuous anchor, as she was soon back in jail. The letter was written not long after the first, sometime in 1933, and this time mailed from Hollywood, California:

> *My Dear Gilman and Florence,*
> *I wrote you some time ago. But do not know whether you received my letter, so I will write again. And if you are still in Chinook, write me; also let me know what small amount of money that you seem to have been so upset over. You know,*

Gilman, I was very much offended at your conduct in writ-
ing me the letter that you once did. I am quite sure that you
forgot the fact that I had to return the money to Aunt Alice
(Mrs. Moline) in Chicago that your father borrowed. Also the
money he borrowed of Mr. Toomey. Don't forget some things,
Gilman. I am happy and successful now with a lovely hus-
band and all that I wish.

Regarding your father, it is needless for me to express my
feeling regarding him, but I always loved you and Laura, and
you are all that I have living now. In every letter I receive from
Aunt Alice, she asks after you and yours. She is still in Chicago.

How are the children and Florence? We are all fine. And
how is everything with you. You know I am always interested
so write me.

With love to you and all,
Lovingly,
Eleanor

Eleanor mentioned, unexpectedly, her half sister, the child Laura who died in the Portland orphanage. If she had known Laura, Eleanor would have been a teenager living in Portland with her father, Albert, and his Portland family in the 1890s, and would have been a witness to the tragic events that occurred there. There is no way of knowing whether she was ever aware of Laura's death. Her letter then mentioned Aunt Alice (Mrs. Moline), who lived in Chicago and who apparently corresponded from time to time with Florence. Had Eleanor spent part of her youth in Chicago? Was Aunt Alice her mother's sister? The letter begs these questions.

Eleanor's letters to Florence were written a year after her visit. She did not mention, of course, that, all along, a parole officer had been nipping at her heels.

On November 10, 1932, not long after Eleanor had thumbed her way out of Havre, Montana, Parole Officer Whyte received a letter from his assistant, Deputy Parole Officer Lewis, in which he reported, "A Mr. W. F. Roberts, insurance company investigator, who drove her from Winslow, Arizona, in September, was in today. He has a $20 bum check she gave him on a New York bank."[5] In the same week, Mr. Whyte got word from the San Francisco Police Department that Eleanor had paired up with a former San Quentin inmate, Ora Nye, and that together they were working a bunco game (an outlawed dice game) in Hollywood. "The Paddleford woman was going under the name of Mrs. Wilson Roberts."[6]

A clever bunco operator could set up a confidence trap and fleece a player. Eleanor would have been perfect for the part.

Mr. Whyte and Deputy Lewis then staged a stakeout, the sole purpose of which was to capture Eleanor McKinney Paddleford as she exited a bunco game at an address discovered on Hollywood Boulevard. It was a storefront for a form-fitting shop. Ora Nye's son-in-law, Richard Van der Beets, "a very crafty individual, 'ran' the shop." Ora and Richard were seen coming and going in a newly purchased Packard Coupe. A check on the license plate found the car registered to Van der Beets at a fake address. A follow-up search found the correct address entered on a chattel loan. Both locations went under surveillance, but the stakeouts were a bust. The quarries had somehow gotten wind. Having failed once again to nab Eleanor, Officer Lewis concluded, "Will leave no stone uncovered to apprehend her."[7]

Eleanor's whereabouts were not uncovered again in any way until a year later, in 1933, when the William Burns Detective Agency reported in a letter to the warden at San Quentin that "the above subject (Genevieve Paddleford, aliases) defrauded a hotel in Italy while carrying an English passport. As you no doubt are aware, the American Hotel Association is very much interested in this woman for having defrauded hotels all over the United States. We would appreciate being advised whether you would be interested in having this woman extradited to the United States."[8]

Chapter 28:

Banished, 1936

All countries reserve the right to deport foreigners. Foreigners who have committed serious crimes, enter the country illegally, overstayed and/or broken the conditions of their visa, or otherwise lost their legal status to remain in the country may be deported.

—*Encyclopedia of Human Rights*[1]

In 1932–33, crime in America was at a peak. The FBI under J. Edgar Hoover was just getting organized. Fingerprinting, crime statistics, and crime labs used to catch the guilty were in their infancy. Law enforcement at every level in America was overwhelmed by crime.

The early days of Prohibition unleashed a crime phenomenon unforeseen and unimaginable across the country. The bootlegging profiteers and gangs became legendary and unimpeded. Tommy guns were rattling murder in city after city.

The "war to end all wars" was over, but a new one was just beginning—on the streets of America.

On one side was a rising tide of professional criminals, made richer and bolder by Prohibition, which turned the nation "dry" in 1920. In one big city alone—Chicago—an estimated 1,300 gangs had spread like a deadly virus by the mid-1920s. There was no easy cure. With wallets bursting from bootlegging profits, gangs outfitted themselves with "Tommy" guns and operated with impunity by paying off politicians and police alike. Rival gangs led by the powerful Al "Scarface" Capone and hot-headed George "Bugs" Moran turned the city streets into a virtual war zone with gangland clashes. By 1926, more than 12,000 murders were taking place every year across America.

On the other side was law enforcement, which was outgunned (literally) and ill-prepared at this point in history to take on the surging national crime wave. Dealing with the bootlegging and speakeasies was challenging enough, but the Roaring Twenties also saw bank robbery, kidnapping, auto theft, gambling, and drug trafficking become increasingly common crimes. More often than not, local police forces were hobbled by the lack of modern tools and training. And their jurisdictions stopped abruptly at their borders.[2]

The front-page headlines were captured by the lords of crime: Al Capone, Bugs Moran, Lucky Luciano, John Dillinger, Homer Van Meter, Clyde and Bonnie Parker, Baby Face Nelson, Doc Barker, Ma Barker, Pretty Boy Floyd, and others.

Eleanor McKinney Paddleford Fawcett, by comparison, became more of a back-page public nuisance. Only the American Hotel Association agitated to get her back into prison. Only California state parole officer Ed Whyte and the association's hired detective agency were on her tail. No nationwide dragnet was set out to catch the hotel con artist. Her profile was broadcast to association members, but the slow processes of printing and mailing flyers was hit and miss.

Eleanor had escaped the stakeout that teamed her up with Ora Nye and her son-in-law in the Hollywood bunco scam. At that time, the *Los Angeles Times* reported that she was registered at an unnamed hotel on Wilshire Boulevard as Mrs. Wilson Roberts. The hotel advanced her "several hundred dollars, which she used to make a $100 down payment on an automobile and $300 for facial and hirsute transformations at a beauty parlor." She then hit the road, leaving on the table a $200 hotel bill as well.[3]

Again, it was winter, sometime in early December 1932, when Eleanor motored out of California. Only guesswork can frame how far she might have gone and how many souls she might have conned along the way. She may have kept to a familiar southern route to New Orleans. Or this time she might have taken Route 66 from Los Angeles to Chicago. Route 66 offered accommodations and ready service stations. In Chicago, she may have contacted Aunt Alice Moline, who could have offered temporary refuge. With help from relatives, she may have ditched her car for cash. What is certain is that she found enough cash to reach a port, and that, with a wardrobe and an alias, she boarded an ocean liner for her fourth trip to Europe.

The passage of time from one continental visit to another allowed her to present a new face and a new name without drawing attention. She would have employed a dozen aliases along the way. None of her familiar names showed up on any passenger lists in 1933–34.

It took another year and a half before Genevieve McKinney Teal Paddleford Fawcett's name would again turn up in the newspapers. *The San Bernardino County Sun* reported on May 4, 1934, that she appeared before a court in Paris, France, as Marion Fawcett. She stood before the Sixteenth Court, on her own behalf, to appeal the imposition of double prison sentences, one for five years on charges of passing false checks in Paris, the other for a year for defrauding fashionable dressmakers in the French town of Chambéry. Both sentences were imposed at the same time. Her story was carried in several UP syndicated newspapers.

Previous to her stop at Chambéry, news reports had her in Milan, Italy. There she'd been stopped for carrying a false passport. The American consul at Milan seized it. Then, without delay, she went to the British consul, where she "charmed a youthful British official and obtained a British passport in the name of Elaine Robinson."[4] She carried the fake passport to Chambéry. From Chambéry, she crossed back into Italy, where she was caught and arrested. The fake passport was found in her possession.

For over a year, from her fourth arrival on the continent to her appearance before the court in Paris, Eleanor had worked her way through France, Switzerland, and Italy. She was extradited from Italy to answer charges of fraud committed in Chambéry and sentenced to a year in Chambéry prison. But she was held only a month before appearing before the court in Paris to appeal the dual sentences.

By now, Eleanor was quite adept at legal proceedings and at representing herself. She appealed on the basis that she could not be sentenced concurrently for crimes committed in two different places. While poised confidently before the court, she insisted that she was a member of a prominent New York family. Eleanor beat the five-year rap. However, she was returned to serve out a year at Chambéry.

The beautiful, ancient city of Chambéry, in the foothills of the Alps, held a small prison embraced by a rock wall and shade trees. It is completely understandable why Eleanor fought so hard to be retained at Chambéry, rather than Paris. In Paris, she would have been incarcerated in the Prison at de la Santé, often cited as one of the worst in the world.

Eleanor, now in her late fifties, served her year. Then, near the time of her scheduled release, she found herself facing a new charge pending from the French city of Nice. The Nice officials had caught up with her as she was serving her time. She was slammed with a charge of writing false checks against a hotel to pay a bar bill in the amount of 35,000 francs (about $2,300 at the time). Eight more months in Chambéry prison were tacked onto her current sentence. Then the Swiss, appearing in line for prosecution, presented extradition papers on swindling charges from the town of Neuchâtel. France was only too willing to turn her over to the Swiss.

Newspaper accounts at this time reported her as having been in Switzerland in the summer of 1933, parading there as Helen Thompson. One of the letters she wrote to Florence and Gilman McKinnie was mailed from the beautiful Alpine resort town of St. Moritz, Switzerland, about four hundred miles east and south of Neuchâtel and minutes from the Italian border. Her stay at the St. Moritz Hotel had occurred just before she was caught with the fake passport in Milan and extradited to Chambéry.

Following her release from Chambéry, the Swiss held her in Neuchâtel for six months. She was then moved to a Swiss detention center, where she was processed for deportation. The American consulate arranged Eleanor's last crossing. She was deported in steerage class on a ship to New York in February 1936.

In April 1936, after three years of trekking across America and Europe, she registered at the Olympic Hotel in Seattle, Washington, as Helen Thompson. It would be her last hotel suite.

Chapter 29:

Ming Toy, 1936

Eleanor slouched back into the United States. The Great Depression was well into its sixth year. In every city, hundreds of former wage earners stood in bread lines, and legions of hobos were jumping freights, looking for day jobs, and getting by on handouts. America's new norm was "we have to make do." The hungry returned to hunting, fishing, gathering, and gardens. Housewives sewed feed sacks into towels and curtains and dresses. The dust bowl and grasshopper swarms had turned farmland to desolation. Tens of thousands had lost their homes, businesses, and farms. It was early spring 1936.

Not everyone was down and out. Some had money. Those who remained well off carried on as if nothing happened. There were still hotels operating and autos on the road. Gasoline fluctuated around fifteen cents per gallon. Trains were moving. Eleanor's familiar world had grown thinner but was still intact. Three years had passed since her scramble off to Europe. The passage of time, the scourge of the Depression, and the sweep of crime worked to her advantage as a kind of shield. Traveling now as Helen Thompson, she reentered the country under a temporary cloak of anonymity. US customs missed an alert that a warrant for her arrest was still active.

A fascinating short story entitled "The Jade of Diamonds," published by a pulp magazine in 1941, sensationalized the villainous journey of a showgirl first known as Margaret Busby, "a beautiful brunette girl in her middle twenties who had all that it took to get by on the stage in that mauve decade known as the Gay Nineties. Her eyes were dark and flashing and her hair was luxuriant brown; any burlesque director would have welcomed her curves in his stable."[1]

The short story was written by Horace Heffern, a writer whose name does not appear with any other published writing or in any public record. The article colorfully captured the language style of the time. It was written, curiously, as if the writer knew Eleanor personally or as if she had written it herself under a clever pen name.

In this story, the writer told us that in April 1936, Helen Thompson was found working the shops of Seattle and that she had checked into a suite at the Olympic Hotel with a red Pekingese dog named Ming Toy. She had come up to Seattle from Los Angeles, where, having leaned on old friends, she acquired a suitable wardrobe, a little cash, and the Pekingese. Perhaps she thought the dog gave her an added flair. A Pekingese dog had been part of her retinue many years earlier, when she had appeared as a visitor to her relatives in Chinook, Montana. At that time, the McKinnie children thought it a monkey.

Helen Thompson's Seattle visit was brief. According to the story and newspaper reports, she first raided a few shops to refine her wardrobe. Then, dressed in the haute couture of the day, she entered the Seattle Bon Marché department store, carrying Ming Toy and her handheld eye glass, a lorgnette. She selected and had delivered many gowns and fur pieces to her suite at the Olympic, then quietly checked out and disappeared.

The Seattle police, of course, were called. The modus operandi was recognized immediately by Captain of Detectives Ernie Yoris as that of the world-renowned Genevieve Paddleford. His office sent out a dragnet circular calling for her arrest.

Days later, on June 11, 1936, using the name Mrs. Lucille Chandler, a woman registered at the Pueblo Hotel in Pueblo, Colorado, and informed the clerk that her mother would be coming along on the following day, having paused to get some repairs done on their automobile. The alert hotel clerk was not fooled. He had seen Captain Yoris's circular. The hotel guest was holding a Pekingese dog. It was Ming Toy, prominently displayed on the circular.

Two weeks later, Genevieve Paddleford was sitting in a Seattle jail. She was indignant and brazen, but her practiced facade no longer beguiled her captors. Here, at last, was a rap she could not beat. She was charged with defrauding a Seattle clothing shop of $200, but the judge held before him a rap sheet that included the recent passing of two bad checks in France on a 35,000-franc bar bill. It was time to put Mrs. Genevieve McKinney Toomey Teal Paddleford Fawcett away for good. At the approximate age of fifty-eight, she was sentenced to fifteen years in Washington State Prison at Walla Walla for grand larceny. She entered the prison gates identified as Mrs. J. R. Thompson, as well as by numerous other aliases, on October 2, 1936. The record also identified her nearest friend as Countess Micsini of Rome, Italy. The fate of Ming Toy is unknown.

Chapter 30:

Earl, 1938

Everything is all right with me and it will be easier for you in the future. Lovingly, Earl[1]

As is often said, there is no honor among thieves. Eleanor McKinney, after nearly two years of incarceration in Washington State Prison, was moved into a cell with Mary Ellen Smith, fifteen years her senior. Mrs. Smith, like Eleanor, had been convicted of grand larceny. Naturally, they came to share each other's pasts. Eleanor, after a time, heard something from Mrs. Smith that piqued her interest and caused her to mine for more. It wasn't long until Eleanor wrested a dark secret from Mrs. Smith and unraveled one of the Northwest's most notorious murder mysteries.

Mrs. Smith and her cryptic son, Decasto Earl Mayer, had been in the murdering business. Although Mother didn't wield the knife, she was a willing accomplice. Mrs. Smith spilled out her son's murders. There were three in Montana, a fourth in Seattle, and possibly others. The Seattle murder was the one that had captured the headlines up and down the coast.

The *Los Angeles Times* reported on November 28, 1929, that a sheriff's posse searched the Bothell area of Seattle for the body of missing former naval officer, Lieutenant James Eugene Bassett, a graduate of the Naval Academy and son of a respected Annapolis family.[2] Murder was suspected, but his body was never found.

A week later, two suspects, Decasto Earl Mayer and his mother, were picked up in Oakland, California, in possession of Bassett's car, a distinctive Chrysler roadster. Because the search failed to find a body, they were charged only for the theft of the car and of personal items, which included the victim's watch and important papers. Also found in Earl's possession was a poison-gas pistol that held a discharged cartridge. "The shotgun-like shell could expel a lethal poisonous gas, leaving no telltale mark. In addition, police found a shoebox full of newspaper clippings about unusual murders and clippings from detective magazines."[3]

Decasto Earl Mayer was sentenced to life in prison as a habitual criminal. His mother was sentenced from five to eight years for grand larceny. Then, ten years after Lieutenant Bassett went missing, Mrs. Smith confessed to the young lieutenant's murder and other murders committed in Montana. The motive for the murder of Lieutenant Bassett, Mrs. Smith said in her confession, was simply robbery. "My son never allowed his victims to suffer. He killed Bassett because he needed the car to start a new life."[4]

In September 1928, the victim, Lieutenant Bassett, placed a classified ad in the newspaper for the sale of his roadster. As an envoy of the US Navy, he was scheduled to take a position at the naval station in Manila as secretary to a naval commandant. He needed to sell his car. Mayer answered the ad. In the course of the transaction, at a lonely house north of Seattle, Earl Mayer bludgeoned Bassett to death as Mrs. Smith looked on. They dismembered the body and buried it in various locations in that area.

The Montana murders had been committed five years earlier, in 1922 and 1923. One victim was a woman; two were men. As Mrs. Smith's confessor, Eleanor nudged out the sketchy details:

> Mrs. La Casse, a schoolteacher and Earl's sweetheart, took a ride with Earl and disappeared. Earl couldn't get rid of Dorothy La Casse, other than to kill her. Her body was dumped in a ditch near Warm Springs, Montana. Earl then killed his own stepfather, Ole Larson, dissected his body, and we dumped it in the same ditch near where we dumped Mrs. La Crosse. A friend, Dave Randall, was buried in a stone quarry near Pocatello, Idaho.[5]

At the murder trial, months after Mrs. Smith's confession and ten years after the murder of Bassett, the prosecutor for the state, Mr. B. Gray Warner, according to an AP wire, revealed evidence that Decasto Mayer had also received $2,000 for murdering a mother and her illegitimate child, paid for by the father of the child.[6]

Mrs. Smith's pursed lips were pried open just in time, near her release from prison. This feat was accomplished by the guile and wit of the notorious con artist recorded officially in Washington State Prison as Helen Fawcett Thompson. It could have been that she was a plant by the authorities, who gambled that she, like no one else, might crack one of Seattle's most acerbic cases. Was she offered an incentive? The newspapers gave no hint of a deal. To the reporters, Eleanor insisted, "All I wanted is justice for the young man."[7]

Surely, at least some hint of consideration had been dangled in front of Eleanor as a reward for taking on the role as Mrs. Smith's confessor. The matchup between the two hard-bitten adversaries would have been a gamble worth taking. The outcome, though, was never in doubt. Eleanor, so talented a con, thoroughly convinced Mrs. Smith that "the prods of conscience would cease scourging her soul if she confessed and told all concerning the horrible crime her son committed with her acquiescence and assistance."[8]

Only months after her cell placement with Mrs. Smith, Eleanor, armed with Mrs. Smith's confidential revelations, notified the prison warden, J. M. McCauley. Her contact with the warden was through her prison matron, Mrs. L. E. Nixdorff. In Eleanor's mind, though, the case seemed to lag. Was the warden sitting on it? A push was needed. Foolishly, Mrs. Nixdorff, at Eleanor's prodding, went to a private investigator with the goods. But the case had not been shelved and the warden was not amused. Mrs. Nixdorff was fired for taking information outside an ongoing investigation.[9]

The investigation, conducted by State Police Chief William Cole, was methodical in shaping an airtight, long-sought conviction of Decasto Earl Mayer and Mrs. Smith, whom investigators referred to as the Wolf Mother, for her fierce protection of her son, and whom police called Shoebox Annie, for a shoebox she kept filled with various news clippings of committed murders found in Bassett's car. Eleanor had loosened Mrs. Smith's tongue, but a confession extracted from one convict by another would not hold up in court. Nevertheless, Eleanor's work had set the stage for the introduction of a more reliable witness.

Thus was hatched a scheme wherein a detective dressed as a clergyman would receive Mrs. Smith's anguished confession, further breaking the Wolf Mother's silence. They had to act before she again tightened up like a clam. The scheme, though legally inadmissible, worked, and Mrs. Smith sang to the "clergyman," further confirming her and her son's guilt.

The case solidified when Eleanor, while gaining Mrs. Smith's confidence, goaded her into writing secret letters to Earl, which, Eleanor promised, could be smuggled easily to his cell. Mrs. Smith could then tell her son about how she had relieved her own conscience and how she wished that he, for the sake of his own soul, would do the same. The letters, of course, passed by the eyes of the investigators and provided them with even more information. An AP wire reported a statement from prosecutor B. Gray Warner:

> We have evidence, from Mrs. Smith's letters, which she hoped would be smuggled to her son, of nine other murders. There is no question but that she was the moving force.[10]

Police Chief Cole employed one more tactic. He arranged to have Mrs. Smith meet and confess to her son, face-to-face.

"I think you're crazy!" burst Earl when he heard from his mother's lips the secrets they had kept for more than ten years. But when he was told that she had taken investigators to the spots where body parts and been buried and that she had answered minute questions about the killings, he agreed to a meeting with the warden. The warden later disclosed Earl Mayer's statement:

> After a discussion with Warden J. M. McCauley and after seriously considering the situation, I have decided to plead guilty to the murder of Bassett. I will disclose the details to the proper authorities. Signed, D. E. Mayer.[11]

The trial opened on November 28, 1938.

"The state has summoned fifty witnesses, chief among whom is Mrs. Millicent Paddleford Fawcett, who, as a cellmate of Mrs. Smith in the state penitentiary at Walla Walla, was credited with inducing the aged woman to confess that her son killed Bassett. Admissibility of this confession, obtained by a state patrolman masquerading as a clergyman, was expected to be one of the points to be argued early in the trial."[12]

Eleanor had a lot to say on the witness stand. She, as the star witness, was in her glory. Her dramatic testimony was reported in the *Daily Capital Journal*, Salem, Oregon, on December 8, 1938:

Appearing more like a dowager than a woman convict, Mrs. Fawcett, who gave her age as 48, used her tortoiseshell spectacle in the manner of a lorgnette as she parried questions by the defense. She switched often from direct quotation of what she said Mrs. Smith told her into a third-person recital and engaged in several verbal give-and-takes with defense counsel.

As per her testimony:

"Mrs. Smith told me that she and Mayer had killed Bassett. On the day of the slaying, Earl told her to get some water boiling on the stove and he'd bring Bassett out to the house. They talked about Mayer's contemplated purchase of Bassett's robin's-egg-blue sports roadster.

"Mr. Mayer had a hammer on the mantel. He motioned to his mother to get out of the room, and she did. She overheard Earl say, 'I'm going to have your car and I'm not going to pay you a so-and-so cent. I want you to write this telegram.

"As he took the telegram from Bassett, he picked up the hammer and hit him on the back of the head. Mrs. Smith said she came into the room and said, 'Earl, he's gurgling.

*He's not dead yet. You'd better give him another whack'—
and he was dead.*

"They put him in the bathtub and took off his clothing and
got a galvanized pail and washtub. Mrs. Smith assisted—she
brought in the pail and washtub while her son dismembered
the body. They put the head and hands in the pail and the rest
of the body in the tub. Mrs. Smith said that the boy worked so
hard to keep his strength that she made him an eggnog.

"She then said the pair took pieces of Bassett's body in
gunny sacks and hid them in the woods north of Seattle.

"Mayer had also removed Bassett's scalp, and they
burned it in the stove with the clothes. They removed the teeth,
and Mrs. Smith said they scattered them along the road where
they never could be found.

"Mrs. Smith said she sat in the car while Mayer took parts
of the body into the woods. She had the lights off but turned
them on occasionally to let him know where she was. She said
Mayer was wearing Bassett's overcoat.

"The head and hands still were in the pail in the cellar.
The next morning, they burned Bassett's BVDs in the fireplace.

"From then on I listened to everything Mrs. Smith told
me about all the other murders. She told me about the murder
of Ole Larson and Dorothy LaCasse and Dave Randall."[13]

The court reconvened on Monday, December 12, opening the third
week of the trial.

The jurors, who had been sequestered over the weekend, glanced in
astonishment at Mayer's vacant chair when Judge Batchelor announced,
"The defendant, Decasto Earl Mayer, has died during progress of the
trial."[14]

Judge Batchelor did not tell the jurors it was a suicide. Decasto, age
forty-four, had killed himself Sunday in the county jail by strangling on
wads of paper. He'd lashed his mouth shut with his belt strap and tied his
hands so that he could not ward off death. He had left his mother a note,
which read:

Dearest Mother:
Words are sometimes meaningless. I am tired and wish to
depart from a place wherein is oppression, and leave the
house to tell its builders' fate. And for the place I leavest, I
shall find another land. Everything is all right with me and it
will be easier for you in the future.

Lovingly,
Earl[14]

The parents of Lieutenant Bassett had, naturally, been distraught over their son's disappearance when first notified of it, ten years earlier. The young man was visiting his sister and his brother-in-law, a US naval commander, in Bremerton, Washington, before his intended journey to Manila. He left their home to sell his car and never returned. Mr. and Mrs. Bassett left immediately for the West Coast to prosecute the search. Mr. Bassett offered a $1,500 reward from their modest savings for any news of their son. None was forthcoming. He returned again and again to chase down rumors that his son's body had been found. Finally, worn out by waiting, he died of a broken heart in 1932, four years after his son's disappearance.[15]

Marion Bassett, Lieutenant Bassett's mother, attended the murder trial in 1938 and took the stand. She pleaded for Mrs. Smith not to be executed. The jury was impressed with Mrs. Bassett's plea for this mother, MaryEllen Smith, who had been described as "a macabre crone, as eerie and repulsive as any figure that sprang from the fertile mind of Edgar Allan Poe."[16]

Mrs. Smith was sentenced to life in prison. Fifteen years later, on May 13, 1953, a local newspaper announced that the aging woman was to be released, due to frailty and blindness, and placed in a state nursing home. The newspaper said that until her blindness, she had read the Bible daily and had been baptized into the Seventh-Day Adventist Church. She kept a photo of her son on her cell wall. She was eighty-six.[17]

Chapter 31:

Helen Fawcett Thompson, 1941

Eleanor McKinney was registered at Washington State Penitentiary on October 2, 1936, as Mrs. J. R. Thompson. She died on September 19, 1941. Her vital statistics report entered her name as Helen Fawcett Thompson and her age as fifty-two years, ten months, and nine days, which, if true, meant that she had married her first husband, William Toomey, in St. Paul at the age of twelve. Her vanity always tended toward clipping ten years off her age. A closer estimate would have placed her age at the time of death at sixty-six or sixty-seven.

Eleanor entered Washington State Prison at Walla Walla with a sentence of ten to fifteen years. Her maximum sentence would have allowed for a release date in 1950, at which time she would have reached the age of about seventy-five. In late 1940, two years after the Bassett murder trial, Eleanor retained a lawyer for the purpose of appealing to Governor Clarence Martin for an early release. The governor called the matter of her parole to the attention of the parole board. The board's response was encouraging: with good behavior, she could earn three years and four months off her minimum, ten-year sentence and expect a release in May 1943:

Memo to the Governor
November 22, 1940
RE: Mrs. J. R. Thompson, WSP #16701

The members of this Board do not care to make any favorable recommendation in this case until this subject has earned her good time credits. We will then have jurisdiction to grant a parole to this subject.

Mrs. Thompson is privileged to earn three years and four months off her ten-year minimum term. Her good time expiration minimum is May 27, 1943.

If the Governor desires to have our reasons, we have reports in our office which prevents us to make any favorable recommendation in this case.

Respectfully submitted,
Board of Prison Terms and Paroles

Eleanor was desperate to get out of Washington State Prison. An eruption of gossip and recriminations on the prison grapevine had occurred following Mary Smith's surprising confession. Eleanor had broken a cardinal prison rule: one must not sing to the warden. Shortly after Eleanor contacted Warden McCauley, she was transferred to the King County jail for her protection, as other female convicts had threatened her life. She remained there throughout the trial, a period of about four months. When she returned to Walla Walla, her fellow inmates scorned her. Eleanor submitted two appeals for release, one in November 1940, the other in March 1941. Both failed, and she became deathly ill. Her prison death certificate stated that she suffered from nephritis, a chronic kidney disease. She died alone without family or friends.

Eleanor's release from prison came by way of death, twenty months before the term prescribed by the parole board, based on credits earned for good behavior.

Eleanor's sister-in-law in Chinook, Montana, Florence McKinnie Elsner, received a newspaper clipping reporting her death. In November 1941, she wrote to Superintendent P. E. Maloney, of Washington State Prison, in regard to Eleanor's personal effects.

He replied on November 24, 1941:

Mrs. Florence McKinney Elsner
Chinook, Montana

Dear Madam:
I have your letter of November 20 in which you make inquiry concerning the personal effects of Mrs. Eleanor Paddleford Fawcett.

The only personal belongings Mrs. Fawcett had at the time of her death were those which she had with her when she was arrested. They were very few in number and of no value.

We got in touch with her son, but he disclaimed any interest in her.

She did not leave any word for her friends or relatives in Chinook.

Yours truly,
P. E. Maloney, Acting Superintendent

Helen Fawcett Thompson was buried in the Catholic cemetery at Walla Walla State Prison. The grave was marked only with her WSP number: 16701.

BOOK TWO:
Cynthia Tells Her Story

Introduction to
Cynthia's *Confessions*

I first heard that I had a notorious great-aunt Eleanor as a youngster. Much later in life, after my retirement, on one of my visits to my aging mother in my home town of Chinook, Montana, I learned that Aunt Eleanor had played a significant role in my grandfather's destiny, and thus in the destinies of those who followed. My interest was piqued, and, as mentioned, I took an exploratory road trip across the country. Then I began searching the Internet.

Late one night, while browsing old newspapers online, I was startled to learn that Aunt Eleanor's adopted daughter, Cynthia, who had been only marginally cited in those earlier news clippings that were found in a sequestered manila envelope, was a really a very beguiling young woman. Her name began to leap out again and again from archived issues of various newspapers, in particular, the *Indianapolis Star*. Surprisingly, Cynthia Teal had written her own remarkable, heart wrenching life story entitled, *The Amazing Confessions of a Trained Swindler*. Fourteen chapters of her story, over fourteen weeks, were published serially and syndicated in the *Indianapolis Star* and various other newspapers from October 1, 1922 until December 31, 1922, by the International Feature Service, Inc., Great Britain. It told of her harrowing life as the adopted daughter of a world swindler.

A ship's passenger list shows that on July 18, 1922, at age seventeen, Cynthia disembarked from the SS *President Van Buren* at the Port of New York. Alone on that ship, while crossing from London to New York, she chronicled her life over a ten-year period, from the time she was adopted in New York City by the Teals in 1912 until July 4, 1922, when she left her foster mother, Genevieve Paddleford, languishing in a Vienna prison. Her story was published only three months after her arrival in New York.

After the last chapter of her story appeared, Cynthia was not heard from again for two years. Presumably, during that time, she lived and worked in or near New York City. Then, amazingly, on October 20 and 21, 1924, several news articles reported that Genevieve Paddleford and her daughter were together again and back to Eleanor's old tricks of defrauding merchants. In Zurich, Switzerland, they were both arrested and held on suspicion of swindling. Cynthia remained with Eleanor for a time after that but mysteriously disappeared in 1926.

The first installment of Cynthia Teal's *Confessions* was published with an introduction in the Sunday edition of the *Indianapolis Star* on October 1, 1922:

> *A beautiful, wistful girl came quietly into a New York court-room recently and asked the court to relieve her from the guardianship of a woman who was incarcerated in a prison in Vienna. The judge asked her many questions, and she gave him a series of answers the like of which for dramatic "punch" had not been heard in a courtroom since Evelyn Nesbit Thaw left the stand in the memorable trial of her maniac husband.*
>
> *The girl was Agnes Cynthia Fitzgerald-Teal-Paddleford-Naughton, foundling, foster daughter of the former wife of the illustrious Ben Teal, who is now the wife of the millionaire oil magnate George Paddleford. Mrs. Paddleford is the woman in the Vienna prison from whose hold this girl begged her release and relief.*
>
> *She told the story of Mrs. Teal-Paddleford's career, into which she had been cajoled, dragged, driven, lashed, and luxuried. She had been forced into a sensational secret marriage; she had been made to "cat's paw" high-powered blackmailing plots; she had been schooled and compelled to "vamp" the rich and the mighty in almost every metropolis on Earth.*

And, there she stood, seventeen, diffident and fragile, the wife of a fugitive gambler, the ward of an amazing adventuress in a European jail, asking to be given into custody of a self-respecting woman who might help her to redeem the years of her wrecked youth.

The judge granted the girl's plea.

She now tells her story—honestly and without either concealment or bravado—as the next step toward wiping out the past by revealing how she was victimized and virtually enslaved into participation as a principal in the wild series of episodes which came to a climax in her guardian's arrest and exposure.

—V.E. Palm

Cynthia Teal's story, in her own words . . .

Chapter 1:

Three Girls

Dear Reader,

I have just turned eighteen years old. My clothes are the latest Paris cut. I have five trunks filled with French lingerie. I love pearls, ermine, perfumed baths, breast of squab, and certain brands of champagne. I, who was born in a charity hospital and left a foundling in a pubic orphan asylum, never rode in a taxicab until a few months ago. From the age of ten I had my own motor, my own maid, my own governess. All of my tastes and inclinations are those of an avenue debutante bundled in a cradle of luxury. And yet the woman who showered me with [such things] craved luxury so passionately that she would lie, cheat, bulldoze, blackmail, conspire, and even steal to get it. I face life today no more fit to grapple with it than a baby.

The last time I saw Mrs. "Margaret" Genevieve Paddleford, renounced wife of the oil multimillionaire Dr. George Paddleford and widow of the famous Broadway producer Ben Teal, she was crouched in a Vienna jail—a broken, hounded woman, who came at last to the end of her gilt-edged tether, awaiting trial in a foreign court.

I have only pity for her in my heart, where once I loved her and later hated her. Yet pity does not blink the fact that her irrepressible money mania left me stranded at eighteen with nothing to stack up against the world except some finery and a voice, plus the added responsibility of caring for her little boy, who clung to me in the final crash.

Because she made me a princess, I am all but helpless to help myself. Because she made me her tool—trying to force me to swindle the opulent society in which we moved, to meet hospitality with cunning and return kindness with knavery—and because she was a silk-shod, cruel "Fagin" and I a helpless, beaten, protesting girl "Oliver Twist," I am branded as "a pretty little crook" by those who do not know my story.

That is why I shall write these confessions without restraint and without apology—to clear myself insofar as [is] possible in the eyes of those millionaires, social leaders, stage celebrities, rich merchants, hotel magnates, wealthy girl chums, sportsmen, artists, and literati who were the spectators and, not infrequently, the victims in the amazing web of trickery and flimflam that Margaret Paddleford wove.

I shall tell, for the first time, the true story of Margaret Teal Paddleford, the woman who bluffed her way from millions into jail, back to millions, through fortunes, back into jail again—all through greed for gaudy clothes that often she never wore after she got them.

I do not believe there is a character in fiction stranger than this luxury-crazed woman, or a career more spectacular than hers. Before she was thirty she was married and divorced, the plaintiff in a $25,000 breach-of-promise suit in which the defendant charged blackmail, and married to the foremost theatrical producer of his day.

I came into that household after Margie Teal, as Broadway knew her, had been imprisoned for a year on Blackwell's Island for her unsavory connection with the Frank Gould–Helen Gould divorce case, after Ben Teal had spent thousands trying to save his wife from prison.

I saw behind the scenes of that tragedy, blacker than any Ben Teal ever staged, when the woman for whose sake he had gone bankrupt returned his fidelity by getting into a scandal with a headwaiter. I know the inside story. I was there when "Daddy" Teal died—of a broken heart, I say.

I shall tell how and why Margie Teal suddenly disappeared from Broadway after that; how deliberate was her plot to snare a rich new husband in the booming oil fields of the Southwest; how incredibly she succeeded in marrying Dr. Paddleford when the poor man did not even know her real name, to say nothing of her prison and divorce record.

My own story is in reality a tale of three. Three girls—Agnes Fitzgerald, the orphan; Cynthia Teal, the child who grew up in the glitter and glare of the footlights; Marie Paddleford, who lived a double life, in which she was one minute the gay society flapper and the next a frightened, cringing little creature, fighting to escape from the machinations of an unscrupulous adventuress.

I was Baby Agnes. I was Cynthia Teal. I was Marie Paddleford. I feel today as though I were still another girl—a happy, a freer girl than any of those three—who stands aside and watches them, and hates them sometimes, but most often intensely pities them.

I am sorry for Baby Agnes and for her mother, the little Irish colleen who loved too well. My father deserted my mother. For that I do not hate him. He is too shadowy a figure to hate. I never saw him. I do not know what he looked like, whether he was handsome or plain, debonair or brute. He is just a name to me. I will be content if he is always that.

But my mother, my little Irish mother—she is different. I know she loved me, for she struggled to keep herself beside me after she was forced by want and hunger to put me in an institution.

Until a month ago, I never knew who my mother was. And yet I love her.

Sometimes I think I can remember her—the ghost of a smile, the memory of a laughing blue eye. Someday, perhaps, I will have her again. Wherever and whatever she may be, I pray, should she read this, she will come to me.

I know of her only what the sisters told me when I returned a few weeks ago from Europe, delivered at last from the grip of the foster mother who had trotted me over half the continent just one jump ahead of gendarmes, lawyers, a swindled society man in London, defrauded Swiss merchants, American process servers, and all the high-low and in-between that Mrs. Margaret Teal Paddleford had plucked in this metropolis and in that.

I got it from Sister Therese at the orphanage. She told me my mother loved me so dearly she sacrificed three years of her life to be near me. Tears rushed into my eyes.

Through them I looked out the window at the little boys and girls playing in the yard where I once played, at the tiny iron cradle nestled near the gateway in the tall iron fence around the home. I had a mother who was mine for three years, and who came, perhaps, at night to stand beside my crib and look at me while I was asleep.

She took me to the New York Foundling Hospital because she could not support us both. And there, until I was eight years old, I was one blue-frocked, freckle-faced nonentity among a hundred other blue-frocked, freckle-faced nonentities.

And so I might have grown up as Agnes Fitzgerald; I might have reached my teens and gone out to work and become a nursemaid or a waitress and eventually married some hardworking laborer and never known either the happiness or the misery of millions, if fate hadn't chosen Mrs. Ben Teal as the instrument to make Agnes Fitzgerald into Cynthia Teal.

I call myself Cynthia Teal today because it is the name, among the dozen aliases my foster mother made me bear to promote some shady enterprise she had on foot, I love the best. It represents the happiest period of my life, when I went from the orphanage to what seemed to me a home like a palace, Ben Teal's.

If Ben Teal had lived, Cynthia Teal might have kept her identity and her happiness.

But Ben Teal died, and Marie Thompson sprang into Cynthia Teal's place—Marie Thompson, forced to masquerade with her foster mother in the adventure of plucking a millionaire out of the oil-booming West.

And so when my foster mother got her man, I got another name. As Marie Paddleford, I began that incredible adventure in which a seventeen-year-old foundling was tossed as the beauty bait into a whirlpool of millions and told to decoy men of wealth or else suffer the consequences—a flogging.

Marie Paddleford had a wonderful and woeful time. She was given the wardrobe of a king's daughter. She was groomed like a follies beauty. She was instructed in French, voice, piano, dancing, and painting. She had three motors at her disposal. She rode thoroughbreds. She hunted in deluxe Colorado camps. She went yachting. She traveled in a private car. She learned to scorn diamonds as cheap and to discard a $50 pair of slippers after she had worn them once.

She was the pet of opera singers, artists, and composers. She toured Europe. She played around with the daughters of the New York 400.* She lived at the Plaza and the Ritz. She thought taxicabs were common.

And yet Marie Paddleford suffered miserably. She was beaten until she was black and blue. She was yanked out of a fashionable school and put to scrubbing floors with criminals—for a pure whim. She had the humiliation of discovering a secret romance flourishing under her nose between her foster mother and her own tutor. She was lashed into becoming the unwilling instrumentality in an attempted blackmail plot. She was duped into a farcical wedding. She was forced to dodge bill collectors and deputy sheriffs.

While she swaggered through the Ritz, she was haunted by the knowledge that she must visit a pawnshop to raise enough money to pay a hotel bill. When she finally rebelled, after fleeing over half of Europe, just one jump ahead of the law, it was because her girl's shoulders could no longer carry the load of deceit, treachery, fear, and cruelty that would have driven mad a woman twice her age.

This is but the sketchiest outline of Marie Paddleford's story—and mine. I propose to tell it courageously and frankly, not as Marie Paddleford, the rich little poor girl, nor as Marie Paddleford, tool of a fortune hunter, but as Cynthia Teal, flying under her own colors and asking from the world only what she deserves.

---

*Refers to the 400 Club of New York City's Gilded Age. It was not an official club but a designation offered by social arbiter Ward McAllister, who felt that "there were only 400 people who could be counted as members of Fashionable Society. He did not, as is commonly written, arrive at this number based on the limitations of Mrs. Caroline Astor's New York City ballroom." (Wikipedia, "Caroline Schermerhorn Astor"; Terrence Gavan, *The Barons of Newport: A Guide to the Gilded Age* (Newport, RI: Pineapple Publications, 1998), 27.)

Chapter 2:

"He's Rich"

Dear Reader,
I have a heaping pile of bills before me as I write. Some of the envelopes have never been opened. Most of them are accompanied by duns. Several threaten immediate prosecution. Filtered among the bills are court summonses. The names on the envelopes range from Fifth Avenue to New Bond Street and the rue de la Paix. There is one for $2,250 from a New York modiste. There is another for twenty-five cents from a Los Angeles laundress. Mrs. Paddleford played no favorites.

I marvel at the ingenuity of the woman who could run up such debts and "get away with it." Her life for the past five years must have been a nightmare of collectors, deputies, process servers, and lawyers. Yet she could keep on bluffing and buying in spite of it. There are letters here of recent date from a Fifth Avenue firm soliciting her patronage!

I marvel more, glancing at the items, over Mrs. Paddleford's insatiable shopping hunger. I call it that because it was in the buying more than in the wearing of clothes that she was greedy. Here, for example, are the purchases of a day:

"Fur coat, $650; black satin hat, $39; jersey dress taupe, $25; rose jersey suit, $135; one set of lingerie, $85; one pillow, $100; one slip of rose pompom, $85; one robe Pierrette, $375; one corset, $55."

I recall most of the articles listed. The fur coat Mrs. Paddleford wore only once. Then she made me go to a Sixth Avenue pawnbroker's and raise on it less than half what she paid. She gave away the black satin hat to a friend without even trying it on after it came home from the shop. Most of the other pretties hung in her closet, undisturbed.

As a matter of fact, she dressed like a dowd. She had one or two favorite gowns, which she wore threadbare while her room was piled high with fresh frocks and squads of bellboys knocked at her door with more purchases. When she wanted to, she could put up a stunning appearance, as I shall show when I relate in this chapter how she captured the rich Dr. Paddleford. But generally she was content to go slipshod and buy extravagantly.

I dare say she had what the psychoanalysts describe as "an inferiority complex." Snubbed by so many people because of her escapades during her life with Ben Teal, risking similar slights from Los Angeles and New York society when she became the wealthy Mrs. Paddleford, yet thirsting for recognition and admiration, she sallied forth to find it somewhere.

She got it in the shops. To step out of a limousine before some exclusive salon, sweep by the obsequious doorman, turn a haughty lorgnette on Madame and the salesgirls and proceed to "buy out the place"—that was a splendid sop to Margaret's vanity; that must have given her the kowtowing "kick" she wanted to get, but couldn't, out of the 400.

I have seen her finger a piece of exquisite silk with diamond-flashing hands, and I have heard her warble, "Only a hundred dollars? Really, it's ridiculously cheap! Oh, well, I'll take it if you haven't something better." And the chances were she never wore it—and never paid for it.

I shall describe later some of the methods Margaret Paddleford used to get so much stuff on credit. It was amazing how she outwitted hardheaded merchants in almost every part of the globe. What I wish to show now is the peculiar kink in the character of this woman—the lust for power, which manifested itself in astonishing extravagance, which in turn manifested itself in the driving desire for scads of money.

Money, because of the "superiority sense" it brought, was the breath of life to Margaret Paddleford. That insight into her nature was made clearer to me as I grubbed through the mass of unpaid bills she left. It explains, hitherto, the cloudy details of her great husband-hunting campaign after Ben Teal's death in 1917, which had left her an all-but-penniless widow.

Consider the situation she had been in as Mrs. Ben Teal. Spending extravagantly always, she had exhausted Ben Teal's fortune fighting for her legal battles when she was indicted for subornation of perjury in the Gould divorce case. When he died, praying with his last breath that heaven would protect little Ben and me from "that woman," his widow had nothing but a few thousand in insurance. And she owed on every side.

It was typical of her—a sort of final flourish—that she gave Ben Teal an expensive funeral. Solemn Mass was celebrated at the Church of the Holy Sacrament. Flowers completely covered the chancel. She had a magnificent headstone erected over Ben Teal's grave at Woodlawn Cemetery. And she paid not a penny of this cost until many months later, when she got the money—as I shall show—by a trick.

Little Ben and I, red-eyed with weeping, came home from the services to a house of misery. Not only had we lost "Daddy" Teal, but we found our only refuge in the world was a woman who had suddenly become so hard-eyed, so bitter, so coldly scheming that we shrank from her in terror.

"Fool!" she burst out at me when I timidly asked her what we were going to do now. "We are going to starve—unless we get money. Don't you know your father left us nothing?" I crouched on the sofa in our hotel suite, little Ben next to me, and watched her with a frightened heart.

I can imagine only today what her thoughts were back then when I experienced the extraordinary lengths of which Mrs. Paddleford would go to get what she wanted. Would she lose her beautiful clothes, jewels, fine wine, expensive dishes, a motorcar, a summer home, all the pocket money she wanted? No, these were as much a part of her existence as her right. Give them up? Sell her jewels and furs to pay her debts? Retire to some fourth-rate boardinghouse? Seek work? Ride the tramways? Trump through snow, sleet, and rain on threadbare soles? Eat prunes and hash? To contemplate this future and accept it gracefully was no more possible for Mrs. Teal than to tear out her heart. Yet she had scarcely any other alternative. The Gould scandal, and on top of it Ben Teal's suit charging her with consorting with a headwaiter, had made her somewhat persona non grata on Broadway. Many of Ben's friends were bitter, and rumors were being bruited about that we were poverty stricken. Ben Teal had not been buried a week before suave gentlemen were knocking on our door and leaving this bill and that, long overdue.

Margaret Teal probably realized that fortune was about to turn thumbs down on her. Already I had seen her get the cut direct from more than one woman who had been glad to know her when Ben Teal was in his glory as America's foremost producer.

"Money is everything," she told little Ben and me that night. "We must get money. And the only place to get money is where money is. I am going to that place."

This remark was pure Sanskrit to me then. But I believe I understand her philosophy now—and see her plot as clear as daylight. I am not posing any "counselor and advisor to fortune hunters," nor would I emulate Margaret's example myself for all the wealth of the Indies. Yet if a woman were unscrupulous and cold-blooded enough to do it, I believe she could get a millionaire via Margaret's method, just as Margaret did.

She went out prospecting for a rich husband like a forty-niner prospecting for gold. She plucked him as neatly as a miner would pluck a nugget from a gulch. Her technique was perfect. And her success was complete.

"The only place to get money is where the money is." And the best way Margaret knew to get money was to find a man who had it and then marry him. She married Toomey. He was wealthy. She sued Dr. Bettingen for breach of promise after he refused to marry her—and she lost. She married Ben Teal. He was no millionaire, but he was rich as riches went twenty years ago.

Ergo, "the place where money is," in Margaret's mind, was the place where millionaires are. Where do millionaires grow in America? In New York. But New York knew Mrs. Ben Teal a little too embarrassingly. In Chicago and the Middle West? But she had a past there. In some parts of the Southeast—notably Florida? But Florida swarms with New Yorkers in the millionaire season. There was one happy hunting ground left—the Southwest: Texas, Mexico, Southern California.

The newspapers that year were full of stories and gossip about the oil millions being made suddenly in Oklahoma, in Mexico, and in the boom-towns along the Texas border. Not only would Mrs. Ben Teal be absolutely unknown there, but she would find a "new richer" raw to the ways of the world, a gilded fly who would be fat game for any clever spider.

There is a certain "demon process server" in New York who will read what I am about to write now with amazement, perhaps with chagrin. There is also a woman somewhere in the United States who may exclaim, "Well, I'll declare!" when she scans these lines and learns she was unwittingly responsible for changing my name from Cynthia Teal to Marie Thompson. And there are a great many people, nonplussed for years by Mrs. Ben Teal's "sudden and mysterious disappearance" from Broadway in 1917, who will learn here for the first time the truth about that disappearance.

We vanished from New York one April night—Mrs. Teal, little Ben, and I—with the demon process server waiting for us at the front door of the hotel while we slipped out the side door, bundled into a taxicab, and made for the Pennsylvania Station. We left not only the process server behind us but, as I learned later, some $20,000 in unpaid bills.

Little Ben and I had no earthly idea where we were going—only that we woke up the next morning in Washington and traveled south all that day. Mrs. Teal made the acquaintance of a woman on the train who asked her if she wasn't Mrs. Jack Thompson, the widow of a New York composer. She shook her head at the time, but the inquiry must have given her an idea, for when we registered at a hotel in a small Texas town in the oil country a few days later, we had changed our names.

"I am Mrs. Jack Thompson, do you hear?" Mrs. Teal told us two children when we were in our room. "You are Marie Thompson and Jack Thompson Jr. And if you ever give me away, if you ever mention that your name is Teal, if you ever breathe a word about Daddy Teal, I will beat you both."

We knew she meant it. I was only thirteen. Jack was nine. We accepted our new identity, cringing and helpless. What else could we do? A refusal or a slip meant one of those terrible floggings Margaret knew so expertly how to give with brush, flat, and dog whip. You can be sure we were careful enough in the weeks that followed to learn our new names.

We flitted from one Texas town to another. We would stay only a few days in each. Jack and I were locked in our room most of the time. Margaret dressed in the height of fashion. She wore all her jewels. She dined alone in the hotel dining room generally, and she would stroll about the lobby and the parlors, picking acquaintance with this person or that.

I have no means of knowing all that was going on inside her head, but I imagine she found the happy hunting ground poor picking—until we reached Galveston. The second day we were there, she rushed into the room late in the afternoon in great excitement.

"Get out my satin dress—quick, Marie!" she snapped at me. "I am going to dinner with Dr. Paddleford. He's a multimillionaire."

That was the first time I heard the name that is so familiar to Wall Street and the financial world of the West. I was to learn later not only the picturesque history of the petroleum prince but the many sterling qualities that make him, in my opinion, one of the finest men it was ever my lot to meet.

Paddleford was one of a quartet of young men who grew up with the West in the days when cowboys were still fighting Apache Indians in Arizona and the glamour of the goldfields still hung over California.

Paddleford was in Galveston on a millionaire's yacht. I did not know all these circumstances until much later—that Mrs. Teal, in her pose of Mrs. Jack Thompson, rich new York widow, met Dr. Paddleford informally in the hotel where we were staying; that he was so impressed he took her to the yacht as his guest; and that, during the week before he sailed for Mexico, he gave her a "grand rush," bombarding her with flowers, dinners, and invitations.

All I knew then was what Margaret Teal flung at me and little Ben as we cowered in the hotel room, watching her before the mirror, flinging off one set of fripperies for another, slapping on the rouge and powder, and sputtering out warnings and commands between lips pursed over hairpins. At last she was ready. She swept across the room like a queen, patting her back hair into place. She was really beautiful then, with her flashing dark-blue eyes and her haughty carriage. I am not surprised that Dr. Paddleford was fascinated by her.

"What do you think you're doing?" she snarled at me. I had slipped over to the door and stood with one hand on the knob.

"We haven't had any dinner," I said timidly.

"Get away from that door!" Margaret fairly screamed at me. "Do you think I want this man to see a brat like you? I tell you, he's rich. He's the man I've been aiming for. You and the boy stay in the room till I come back. And if you breathe a word to this man about Ben Teal, I'll break every bone in your body!"

She swept out, locking the door behind her. And so little Ben and I stayed hungry while my foster mother dined and danced with her "prospect" and practiced on him the charms that were to intrigue him—and did.

The night of the day Paddleford sailed for Mexico, we were on a train speeding for New York. There, with the last of her funds, Margaret rented an apartment in the Fifties, near Fifth Avenue. She had dodged back into New York under her Thompson alias, and she kept in close seclusion during the next two weeks.

The third week she began, twice a day, to telephone the New York office of Dr. Paddleford. Eventually, he returned from Mexico and she got him on the wire. He was at the apartment thirty minutes later. And a week of two afterward, Margaret, kinder and more smiling than she had been for years, informed me, "Get your things ready. I am going to Texas to marry Dr. Paddleford. You will stay here at a hotel till we come back."

I never knew how Margaret persuaded Dr. Paddleford not to have a New York wedding, since it might have resulted in her debtors learning she had acquired a multimillionaire husband. But she did. The ceremony was performed in Houston, Texas, December 18, 1917.

Margaret was married under her maiden name: McKinney. The bridegroom was in total ignorance of her past. She had told him her favorite story of a rich father McKinney in San Francisco and a millionaire brother McKinney in Cleveland—not a word of Mrs. Ben Teal or Mrs. Toomey.

Jack and I were too afraid of her to speak the name Teal. Dr. Paddleford thought we were the children of his wife by her "dead composer-husband, Jack Thompson." He was very kind to us. He did not know, until I wrote and told him on my return from Europe a few weeks ago, that I was the orphan Agnes Fitzgerald.

He believed everything Margaret told him, he was so blindly in love with her. For example, there was the matter of Ben Teal's funeral expenses, which I mentioned Margaret had not paid. Four weeks after her wedding to Paddleford, she got threatening letters from the undertakers. This is what she did:

Before he married her, Paddleford had been attentive to a certain Broadway beauty. Margaret knew of this. She went to him and told him this woman was threatening a $100,000 breach-of-promise suit but that she, Margaret, could "square" her for $9,500. Without question, Dr. Paddleford wrote a check for this amount. And with it Margaret paid the funeral expenses of her former husband!

I have told how Agnes Fitzgerald, orphan, became Cynthia Teal, child of mingled happiness and misery. And in this chapter I have related how Cynthia Teal in turn became Marie Thompson, forced to masquerade as a dumb witness to her foster mother's acquiring of a multimillionaire. In my next letter, I shall touch on another phase of my career—how Marie Paddleford, a new butterfly, rose from the shed cocoons of those other girls, a poor, rich little butterfly, who found a mesh of millions, intrigue, cruelty, luxury, lies, and schemes tangling her at every turn.

Chapter 3:

Los Angeles, 1918–20

Dear Reader,

I have just finished reading *Oliver Twist*, and my heart burns in sympathy for the poor little London lad driven to sneak and steal through fear of Fagin. Oliver is a very real person to me, for, though he was a slum gamin and my world a thing of silken luxury, we quailed under the same lash. Both of us were drilled, though we shrank from it, in evil. Each of us was ordered to plunder or be punished. There was only this difference—that while Fagin wanted handkerchiefs, cheap jewelry, and shillings, Mrs. Margaret Teal-Paddleford craved furs, diamonds, and millions. That while Oliver was compelled to steal, I successfully resisted my foster mother's efforts to make me a society swindler.

I have never accused Mrs. Paddleford—and I do not accuse her now—of adopting an orphan for the deliberate purpose of using her as the innocent cat's paw for her schemes. I am grateful to the woman who gave me a home instead of an institution and showed me a wider horizon than a foundling's. I am not grateful to the woman who would drag an orphan—and even her own son—through a mire of chicanery and deceit to satisfy her own vanity and her own desire.

I no longer hate or fear Mrs. Paddleford. As I write, the newspapers inform me that she is in jail in Zurich, Switzerland, awaiting trial for defrauding Swiss merchants, and I receive a telegram stating that $400 will release her. If I had $400, she should have her freedom. But that sum is a fortune to me, who saw my foster mother squander thousands. And what little I have will go toward the passage money back to America of young Jack Paddleford, my foster brother. I left him in Vienna with Joe, the single servant of Mrs. Paddleford's retinue who stuck to the son, though the mother borrowed—and never paid back—the very wages she paid.

Her original motive in adopting me was simply to get a playmate for her boy. Though she never liked me, though she made me the football for her rages and her whims, though she began to beat me before Ben Teal died and kept it up to the day I left her, I dare say it never entered her head until I was fifteen that the thin, pale face, frightened atom she flung about the room could ever be of any use to her except as a caretaker for her son and a convenient punching bag for her.

There were moments, let me say, when she was generous if she was not kind. If she locked us in a hotel room one night to go supperless to bed, she might shoo us into the Ritz the next and allow us to gorge on everything we wanted, from the clam cocktail to Nesselrode pudding. She was as greedy for pretty clothes for me as she was for herself, with the result that, after she began spending the Paddleford oil millions, my gowns were the envy of some of the richest girls in California.

Many an old friend of Margaret Paddleford's will testify to this generous streak in her erratic nature. Valeska Suratt, Edna Wallace Hopper, Marie Doro—I could name a score—have been guests in her home and will confirm my statement. I am sure that Margaret Paddleford was as reckless in lavishing presents on her friends as she was ruthless toward her enemies.

Margaret kept "open house" at the million-dollar Paddleford villa in Los Angeles after her sudden marriage to Dr. Paddleford in Houston, Texas, in December 1917. Visitors from Broadway she welcomed, but before she acknowledged them or admitted them to her home, she swore them to silence on the secrets of her past.

"Why, Mrs. Ben Teal!" exclaimed a certain notorious soubrette and divorcee one day when she bumped into Mrs. Paddleford in the Ambassador Hotel. Margaret "sh-sh-ed" her hastily, drew her aside, and told her that Mrs. Ben Teal was "dead" as far as Los Angeles was concerned. This woman happened to have several skeletons of her own she didn't want rattling in California and made a mutual "hush" agreement. And so it was with her old acquaintances whom Margaret encountered. Those who might not have been so agreeable, she "cut on sight." Thus, she kept from Dr. Paddleford her scandalous past. He believed she was Mrs. Jack Thompson, the widow of the composer, when he married her, and that Ben was Jack Thompson Jr. and I was Marie Thompson. And, naturally, as Margaret waved threats at us, little Ben and I never revealed the truth.

Dr. Paddleford's friends believed, of course, what he told them. And so did his little boy by a former marriage to Dr. Paddleford. When we arrived in Los Angeles after the honeymoon in the East, the Paddleford villa was strewn with wedding presents and the hall table was piled with telegrams of congratulation from the directors of the Mexican oil company in which Dr. Paddleford was associated, and from others.

Margaret seemed to achieve at the outset what she so ardently desired: to break into California society. She was accepted by everyone save the Stetsons, the family of Dr. Paddleford's first wife. They snubbed her, and Margaret responded by giving a lavish reception and leaving them out of a list that included practically everyone in the "who's who" of Southern California.

If anybody doubts how imposingly Mrs. Teal-Paddleford established her place in California society, he has only to turn to the society section of the Los Angeles newspapers of 1919 and 1920. I have clippings before me that show, better than any words of my own, how the woman with a career that included divorce, a blackmail plot, and Blackwell's Island penitentiary hoodwinked the Los Angeles elite into receiving her as the most charming hostess of the season. I quote:

> *Miss Rita Weiman, playwright, and Daniel Froiland share honors this evening at a brilliant affair to be hosted by Mrs. George Paddleford and Mrs. Florence Pierce at the home of Mrs. George Paddleford in Hollywood. A late musical concert will be followed by a midnight supper and dance. Among those bidden are: Sir Gilbert Parker, Elinor Glyn, Mrs. Tyrone Vincent Duffy, Florence Bosard Lawrence, Lady Marin Landsdowne, Rosemary Theby, Miss Venita Godowsky, Gaston*

Glass, Charles Wakefield Cadman, Keith McLeod, Edward Knoblock, Raymond Harmon, etc., etc.

Dr. and Mrs. George Paddleford have recently been seen at the picturesque home of former Lieutenant-Governor Albert Wallace at Sunset Boulevard, and Laurel Canyon, Hollywood. Dr. Paddleford is one of the officials of the Mexican Petroleum Company, and both he and Mrs. Paddleford are well known socially throughout the West, abroad, and in Mexico and the East.

Here is Cholly Angelino's account of the Los Angeles opera week:

Many noted men and women will entertain groups of friends in the loges and boxes. A number of dinner parties will precede the performance, and an equal number of suppers will follow. One of the smartest parties will be that given by Dr. and Mrs. George Paddleford. Mr. and Mrs. Richard Jewett Scheppe are to entertain with several box parties during the week.

And so on:

Mrs. George Paddleford entertained Tuesday evening at a handsomely appointed dinner party in her Hollywood home at Laurel Avenue and Sunset Boulevard, in honor of Miss Anna Fitsiu. There were twenty-five guests, and Mrs. Paddleford plans to entertain again within a few days for the prima donna, the affair to be a tea.

I could cite reams of stuff, for I have a bale of these society clippings. As I glance at them, they bring back colorful memories of the Paddleford home transformed into a shimmering garden of flowers and music and wine and dancing, with the wit and beauty of Los Angeles bowing and smiling before a handsome woman in a low-cut evening gown, her coal-black hair rippling beneath a diamond tiara.

Will there be a gasp, I wonder, when I tell them that the woman, only a few months before, had been biting her fingernails in a hotel in Galveston because she wasn't sure whether she would be a millionaire's wife or be washing her own dishes in a New York flat? Golden days—these in Los Angeles—for the former Mrs. Ben Teal.

Shuffling the clippings before me, I come again and again across references to "Miss Marie Paddleford, the beautiful New York girl, who recently made her debut and now looks forward to a glittering career in opera."

The inspiration for those clippings was my foster mother more than it was I. They bring me back to the subject on which I started this chapter—Mrs. Paddleford's sudden discovery that her ugly-duckling orphan might turn out to be a gold mine.

I was thirteen when my foster mother married Dr. Paddleford. For two years I was sent away to a convent. There, my closest chums were Marie and Anne Cudahy, daughters of Mr. and Mrs. "Jack" Cudahy, of the millionaire packing company. Their father and mother had been separated for years but had been reconciled shortly before I met the girls. I was a frequent guest in their home and came to love the entire family.

My own home was not an unpleasant place in those days. I had my own maid and my own motor, all the clothes and spending money I wanted. Even so, I would have been unhappy had it not been for Dr. Paddleford, for Margaret was as cruel as ever. I was getting to be a "big girl," but that made no difference in the case of whip or hairbrush.

I bear on my body today a scar left by a mirror Margaret hurled across the room at me. She would have killed me, I believe, if Dr. Paddleford had not taken my part. He was as kind to little Jack Paddleford (Ben Teal Jr.) and to me as he was to his own little son, Georgie.

The climax of Margaret's ill treatment came when she took me to the Home of the Good Shepherd, a reformatory, on a mere whim. I had just returned from the convent and made some timid reference to visiting the Cudahy girls. "You and your fine friends," sneered Margaret. "I'll give you a vacation!" And for three days I, foster daughter of a millionaire, was forced to scrub and wash dishes in the company of thieves, degraded women, and all manner of riffraff.

Finally, Dr. Paddleford, who had wormed my whereabouts out of Margaret, sent the governess for me in a car. His face was stern and his jaw set as he marched me into Margaret's presence, and told her, "If you do not treat Marie better hereafter, I'm through with you!"

That must have been a bitter pill for Margaret to swallow from the man who had proclaimed the adoration of her again and again. For the first time, Dr. Paddleford suspected that his wife was not the unselfish, bighearted woman he supposed her to be when he married her. The episode began the series of his disillusions, which eventually resulted in Mrs. Paddleford's exposure.

Mrs. Paddleford was kinder to me after that. She was afraid of Dr. Paddleford, for one thing, and for another, she was looking at me with new eyes. I was growing up. From the ugly duckling was emerging a swan. From the freckle-faced orphan Agnes Fitzgerald and the browbeaten slavey Cynthia Teal, there arose Marie Paddleford, who was not only pretty, but—wonder of wonders—talented.

I have a soprano voice, which, in all modesty I say it, competent critics have praised enthusiastically. One of these is Mary Gordon. She gave me a hearing in Los Angeles and advised me to go in for opera seriously. Another is Lorillard, the famous London producer. He thought well enough of my looks and voice to give me a star role in musical comedy. I will tell later how I never got to make my stage debut in that production because Mrs. Paddleford yanked me off to Brussels, fleeing from her creditors.

I thank Margaret for one thing—that she gave me the opportunity to cultivate my voice under the best teachers California afforded. If I am eventually a success in light opera, I owe to Mrs. Paddleford—and, more than her, to Dr. Paddleford—some very fine early training.

The nuns at the convent told Margaret she should have my voice cultivated. The suggestion must have startled her. For several days after that, she watched me curiously. She forgot, for once, to taint me about being an orphan or to hit me with the hairbrush. Finally, she told me I was to have a new outfit of clothes—and vocal lessons.

I was overjoyed, for I yearned, like most girls, for a stage career. It never occurred to me then that motive more sinister than mere kindness might have been lurking in Mrs. Paddleford's mind; that she might have seen, in the person of a young and pretty girl with a glorious voice, a rich, potential resource in the event Dr. Paddleford should ever discover the facts about her past and quit her—as did happen only a few years later.

I had scarcely begun to sing before she induced the California newspapers to "write me up" as a great artist. She did not scruple to give them plenty of lies for material. I was heralded as Geraldine Farrar's protégée. This was true only in respect that my foster mother knew Miss Farrar and her mother quite well. The papers stated that I had sung in London and Paris—pure bunk! They said I had a sister with the Metropolitan Opera Company—simply Mrs. Paddleford's imagination.

In spite of all this fuss and feathers—and not because of it, in my humble opinion—I did appear in concert in Los Angeles, and I was a success. I sang for the exclusive Wa-Wan Club. I sang at the benefits of the Ambassador. I sang before the Philanthropy and Civics Club. Charles Wakefield Cadman, the famous American composer, played my accompaniment on one occasion. Pasadena, Los Angeles, and Hollywood hailed me as a daughter who was to make California famous in opera.

Mrs. Paddleford zealously whipped along this sort of froth. She gave it out that I was to make my debut in the East. She harped on the mythical "sister" with the Metropolitan. Here is a sample of the sort of mixed-up truth and fiction she caused to be published:

If you were an heiress in your own right, and your parents owned a country home in England, a townhouse in London, a château in the south of France, a New York mansion, and a lovely winter home in Hollywood, would you devote from three to six hours a day to musical training?

And would you give up all the social diversions of motoring and balls, and state and diplomatic affairs in the world's capitals, in order to create a role in a new opera—and turn your income therefrom to charity?

It sounds like a fairy tale, but it is a true story, and its heroine is Miss Marie Paddleford, the debutante daughter of Mr. and Mrs. George Paddleford, who are in their Hollywood home on Laurel Avenue for the season.

> *Miss Paddleford, who is just seventeen, has a soprano voice that has brought her an offer to create a role in the new Franz Lehar opera that is to open in London in October. She is a close friend of Geraldine Farrar, who has always urged her to adopt an operatic career, and her sister, Elaine Paddleford, who is only twenty, is already a member of the Metropolitan Opera Company.*
>
> *She is the granddaughter of A. H. McKinney, formerly of San Francisco, and well known in Los Angeles, who is now residing in London, and it is to him she will go when she leaves here in July to rehearse her new venture.*

Readers of these confessions will not have much difficulty in weeding out the lies from such a screed. The truth was that Mrs. Paddleford had only heard of Franz Lehar and invented the fairy tale of his offer. Later, by sheer coincidence, I was to meet Mr. Lehar and be the beneficiary of his kindness.

As for "studying from three to six hours a day," the fact is, I was too busy trying to keep out of Mrs. Paddleford's hot-tempered way to do much studying. For my success, though, it went to her head and never touched her heart. Though I may have looked to the outside world like a girl with a serene and gilded future, I was beginning to realize more miserably every day that my life as Margaret Teal-Paddleford's adopted daughter was only just entering on its hardest phase.

She was quarreling more fiercely than ever with Dr. Paddleford. He was beginning to get suspicious. Some New York tradesmen she owed had discovered her whereabouts. They were threatening trouble. Added to that was a new complication—a secret romance that Mrs. Paddleford began to carry on, in defiance of discovery.

All of these elements were verging swiftly toward a climax of exposure, bitterness, desperation, and high-handed swindling. I shall leave that for my next letter.

Chapter 4:

The Breakup

Dear Reader,

My foster mother's relations with Dr. Paddleford suddenly reached a crisis. He found out the truth about her—that she was never Mrs. Jack Thompson, as he had believed ever since he married her, but that, as he phrases it in his divorce suit, she was "the notorious Eleanor McKinney Toomey, of St. Paul, Minnesota, and later was known as Mrs. Ben Teal, of New York, who, in 1907 and 1908, was for ten months in prison on Blackwell's Island for subornation of perjury." And the truth, when he taxed Mrs. Paddleford with it, caused such a cyclone in the beautiful Paddleford home on Laurel Avenue, Los Angeles, as I have never seen before or since.

The events of that night are as vivid to me as though they had happened only yesterday.

I see Dr. Paddleford called to the telephone, and Mrs. Paddleford glancing up from a magazine with a frown as he passed through the room, putting on his hat and overcoat and stating briefly he was "off to the club."

I see my foster mother fidgeting after his departure, until finally she flung her magazine to the floor and told me to order the car. All the way to the club, she was biting her fingernails. While we waited at the curb for Dr. Paddleford to come out, she tapped her foot impatiently and cut me off with a snarl—"Shut up!"—when I ventured some timorous remark.

I see again the face of Dr. Paddleford under the glare of the arc light—white, drawn—suddenly become the face of a man of sixty, and Mrs. Paddleford's face, distorted with desperation, as she came close and peered at him and demanded to know what was the matter. She knew well enough. Her instinct told her.

"Margaret, are you Mrs. Ben Teal, and did you spend ten months on Blackwell's Island!" the doctor asked her huskily. "That is what a friend has just told me."

She denied it. She began to whip out a torrent of imprecations against whoever informed him. Dr. Paddleford could say nothing. He just stood there, his head bowed, until she whirled about and rushed down the street, declaring she would ride home, for the first time in her life, on a trolley car.

"Go and get her, Marie," said the doctor quietly.

The scene changes. We are at home now, in the conservatory. Dr. Paddleford stands beside a big palm, repeating in a monotonous voice what he has been told. I huddle at his side, staring at Margaret. She faces us with her dress torn open at the throat by her own hands. Her eyes glitter. Her fingers clench and unclench. She seems struck speechless by the indictment the doctor brings against her. Of a sudden, without any further effort at denial, she seizes the thing nearest to her—a huge potted hydrangea. With one sweep of her arm, it topples to the marble floor. She lifts above her head the small table on which the hydrangea stood and brings in down like a battle-ax on a bowl of goldfinches.

This is but the opening volley. While Dr. Paddleford gapes at her and I tremble and put my hands to my ears to keep out the percussion of shattering brick and glass and china, Mrs. Paddleford proceeds to wreck the conservatory. When she is done, the "loveliest grotto in Hollywood," as one society reporter called it, is a shell of ruins.

I remember I had a favorite flower in the conservatory, a little blue jar of marigolds, and the most vivid picture I have of that night is of the jar, smashed to myriad pieces, crunched under Mrs. Paddleford's heel, one of the marigolds trailing forlornly across the dirt-stained marble. I wanted to pick it up, to put it in water, but I stood shivering and silent. Dr. Paddleford, with a hopeless gesture, strode from the room.

Joe, the butler, came running in. He stopped, aghast. Mrs. Paddleford turned on him, and it was then she made an accusation against Dr. Paddleford, which later she forced me to report by bruising me almost unconscious.

"Clean up this trash, Joe! Do you know what your employer has done to Marie? He—"

I cried out in horror at the words that fell from her lips, "It isn't true, Joe! It isn't true!"

Margaret went into another flare-up, and I ran out of the room to locate Ben and Georgie, the latter Dr. Paddleford's own boy, and to offer them the comfort I could not find in these bitter grown people.

Dr. and Mrs. Paddleford patched up enough of a facade as to put on a brave front before Los Angeles society, but the revealed truth marked the end of things. Margaret knew it. She arranged for all of us to go East. Jack, her son, and Georgie were to enter an elite school. Dr. Paddleford drove them across the continent in his car. My foster mother and I went on the train. In New York, we took a suite at the Plaza. Dr. Paddleford was with us there for a while, but Margaret was aware he was seeking to confirm the things he had heard about her. A complete break was inevitable unless Margaret could achieve some coup to keep him.

She had done this before. As afore mentioned, soon after their marriage, that famous "demon process server" whom Mrs. Ben Teal left sitting at one door of a hotel while she slipped out the other and fled west saw her sweep out of a Fifth Avenue shop. He recognized her. He hailed a taxi and trailed her motor downtown to Dr. Paddleford's office, back to dinner, to a performance of *Friendly Enemies*, and finally to the fashionable uptown apartment in which we were living then. There he learned from the doorman that the woman he had recognized as Mrs. Ben Teal was now Mrs. George E. Paddleford, a multimillionaire's wife.

He wrote to Mrs. Paddleford, demanding payment for old bills. She did not answer his letter. He took out a summons. One morning, as Mrs. Paddleford was about to step into her car, she was served. She asked the process server what he was being paid. He said $100. She offered him $200 if he would tear up the summons. The man laughed in her face. And still she refused to pay.

The process server informed his chief, who wrote to Dr. Paddleford a letter stating that his wife was Mrs. Ben Teal and owed bills aggregating several thousands. Dr. Paddleford showed the letter to Margaret. She was furious. Declaring he did not love her if he allowed such scandal for a moment, she swore she would leave him if he took any notice of it. Because he deeply loved and trusted her then, Dr. Paddleford sat down and replied to the process server that he knew all about his wife's past and was quite sure there was an error about the bills. He did not, however, commit himself to the statement that he knew she was Mrs. Ben Teal.

That, so far as I know, is something of which he was in complete ignorance when he married. He is correct, to the best of my knowledge, when he states in his divorce suit that he did not know her real identity until shortly before they separated in November 1921, when he was "tipped off" by friends and made an investigation that convinced him of facts he had hitherto only suspected.

Back in New York again, Margaret would set out to disprove her past. She would do her utmost to hold him. Throughout the late autumn of 1921, Mrs. Paddleford and I were at the Plaza, just waiting for what she knew was going to happen. It came on the night she instructed Louise, my French governess, to telephone the school where Jack and Georgie were students. I heard Margaret shriek. The boys, Louise had been informed, were not there. Dr. Paddleford had called a few days before and taken them away.

Mrs. Paddleford went into hysterics. I pitied her then. I tried to console her. I told her I would go out and hunt for Dr. Paddleford. I went to the hotel where he usually stayed, the Belleclaire. He was there. So were Jack and Georgie. At first Dr. Paddleford was cold and hard to me. Finally he seemed to melt. He told me to sit down.

"Marie," he said, "I want to tell you something. You may know it already. You may not. The woman who bears my name is the notorious Mrs. Teal. She served a stretch on Blackwell's Island. I am told the verdict against her later was reversed, but that does not alter the feeling in my mind that the woman I married was a prisoner for ten months. And I never knew it until a few weeks ago!"

He was a broken man. I could see that. And little Jack, Margaret's own son, stood beside him, trembling and crying and whimpering that he loved "Daddy" better than he did Mrs. Paddleford, that he wanted to stay where he was and not go back to her.

But Dr. Paddleford made Jack go back to Mrs. Paddleford. After all, we were not his children but hers. He had never legally adopted us. He had no right to keep us, even if he was compassionately sorry for us.

There was a scene when I returned to Margaret. I gave her the doctor's message—he was "through." She went into hysterics again. Then she began to brood. This lasted for days. The upshot of her morose silence was an incident that will always be burned in my memory. It is the one thing that still rankles when I try to forgive Mrs. Paddleford. It has left a mark—on my heart as well as my body—that I cannot seem to blot out when I am sorry for Margaret, when I honestly pity her plight, a prisoner in a foreign city.

"Copy this and sign it!" she commanded.

We were in our room at the Plaza. Mrs. Paddleford had been seated at the desk for more than an hour, staring for minutes at the wall in front of her, then scratching away with a pencil. I walked over and began to read what she had written. It was a letter to Dr. Paddleford, purporting to be written by me. At the third or fourth paragraph, I gave a little gasp and pushed the letter away from me.

"I won't!" I pleaded, for there, cleverly woven into the body of the letter, was the old lie that Margaret had flung at Dr. Paddleford on the night she smashed the conservatory. She wanted me to accuse him, in black and white, of a monstrous thing. "I won't!" I cried again. "It isn't true! You know it isn't true!"

"You will," announced Mrs. Paddleford grimly.

I dashed for the door, for I knew what was coming. She was before me. Twisting the key in the lock, she seized me as I tried to dodge past. Her right hand locked itself in my hair, and she dragged me across the room. As she passed a table, she yanked off a mahogany lamp stand a long, heavy, thick piece of wood.

"Will you do what I say?"

I shook my head—and the beating began. It was the worst she ever gave me. She would stop every now and then and ask me if I was ready to write the letter, and when I shook my head and sobbed to her for mercy, she would swing the lamp stand again—across my face, my head, my neck and shoulders. She broke one lamp stand, only to take another. I couldn't hold out. My head burning, my back aching, the blood spurting out of a dozen cuts, I groveled on the floor and gasped, "I'll sign! I'll sign!"

I wrote the letter. I signed it, my hand shaking, my eyes a blur. And so it went to Dr. Paddleford. What he thought then, I do not know. I can only thank Providence that the day came when I did what I could to undo the injury, when I returned from Europe, freed at last from Mrs. Paddleford, and in the office of a New York lawyer, with my new guardian at my side, took the first opportunity to make affidavits exonerating Dr. Paddleford from that false charge and explaining how it came to be made.

I am glad to know that, according to his divorce petition and his letter to me, he has absolute proof, other than my own word for it, that my foster mother flogged me into writing that letter. He knows to what straits I was put. He has forgiven me. And that thought removes much of the sting of this episode left in my heart.

The Los Angeles newspapers say that besides the divorce suit, there is much other litigation to be decided in the smashup of Dr. Paddleford's romance. One suit, says the *Examiner*, is pending in the matter of the sale of Dr. Paddleford's Hollywood villa, which is valued at $150,000. Though I am not familiar with all the legal twists and turns involved in the case, I can throw some light on how the property came to be tied up in court. It was Mrs. Paddleford's final desperate move to jockey what she could out of her husband when she saw there was no hope of reconciliation.

Chapter 5:

Edward and Raymond, 1921

Dear Reader,

When two suave and good-looking young Englishmen slid into New York society last winter, and a few months later slid hurriedly out again after the police raided the roulette game in their fashionable Fifty-Fifth Street apartment, there was very little in the newspapers about their sudden disappearance. But among the Manhattan 400 are certain bloods and beauties who, with rueful remembrance of thousands dropped on the wheel, would give a good deal to know the present whereabouts of Messrs. Raymond Brownlow and Edward Jeffries Naughton, the gentlemen who flitted.

I, too, would like to know where Mr. Naughton is, for, though I sincerely trust I never see him again, he happens to be my husband. Any girl may be pardoned a natural curiosity as to what becomes of her husband, even if he is a husband in name only—even if she was literally shanghaied into marrying him, as I was, because two grafters thought they were trimming each other out of millions of dollars.

In all my adventures in American and European society, when Mrs. Margaret Teal Paddleford pitched me at this rich man, and that in a desperate attempt to feather her own nest, there is none more tragic—and none more ludicrous—than the way I was kidnapped and doped into matrimony.

I say tragic, because it is a tragic thing for a girl of seventeen to wake out of a stupor to find herself the bride of a man she scarcely knows. And I say ludicrous, because this, the prize plot of Mrs. Paddleford to use her adopted daughter as the innocent means for replenishing her own purse, rebounded on her own head and actually cost her money.

Ask some not particularly wise member of New York society who Edward Jeffries Naughton is, and he will tell you he remembers Naughton as a very charming chap of thirty-two or three, who flitted about the clubs and dances for a while last season. "The fellow was rich, an Australian cattle king," you will be told. "A dandy tennis player, too."

Ask any Australian about Naughton, and you will get a different answer. It may be only a stare. It may be a shrug. If he knows his Melbourne and Sydney sporting world, however, he will very likely say the only Naughton he recalls was racetrack gambler of more than spotty reputation. That, at any rate, is what responsible Australians tell me.

I know very little about Naughton myself, considering the fact that I bear his name—or would bear it if I had not chosen to face the world simply as Cynthia Teal in the new life I am trying to carve out of the hash Mrs. Paddleford made. What I do know, however, will startle not a few Fifth Avenue hostesses whose hearts went pit-a-pat to the Naughton smile. I saw him first at the Plaza Hotel. We had come east from California with a train of servants, trunks, and motorcars befitting the family of a Mexican oil magnate. Mrs. George E. Paddleford, of Los Angeles, fresh from social triumphs in the exclusive Pasadena colony, was a far different person from Mrs. Ben Teal, who had scurried out of New York only a few years before under a cloud of debt.

Now she was back to swagger where once she had skulked. She was betting that none of Mrs. Ben Teal's creditors would recognize her in the rich Mrs. Paddleford. Or that none of the people who knew Agnes Fitzgerald, orphan, or Cynthia Teal, adopted daughter of Ben Teal, would spot her in Marie Paddleford, "the beautiful California girl who is in New York to study for the operatic stage."

I did not know then what I was to learn very shortly and very rudely—that Mrs. Paddleford had another reason than vanity for her New York invasion. Someone had informed Dr. Paddleford of his wife's past. They were at the breaking point. It was imperative that if Mrs. Paddleford lost her multimillionaire husband, she find a substitute. I was to provide the substitute. By hook or crook, no matter how I protested or rebelled, I was to be the innocent, unwilling magnet she would use to attract the dollars. That, I realize today, was her plan. That, I know, was why she chose the Plaza, a favorite rendezvous of the New York younger set. That is why she let up on the rein she had kept on me and encouraged me to renew old acquaintances. One of these was Constance Bennett, daughter of Richard Bennett, the actor. Connie was, and is, a beautiful girl, who at that time was the sparkling leader of the most ritzy flapper crowd. It was she who so breezily introduced me to Lord Victor Paget at a Plaza tea dance one afternoon, and it was Lord Paget who casually waved me on to Edward Jeffries Naughton.

Let me be fair to both Connie Bennett and Lord Victor Paget in disclaiming any responsibility on their part for Jeffries Naughton. New York's younger set is not the close corporation that older society is in Manhattan. The free and easy, adventure-seeking, convention-scorning temperament of the New York society girl of seventeen or eighteen makes her circle about as difficult to penetrate as tissue paper.

"Why, all you need to get in is a shave and a dinner coat!" I heard one Harvard junior tell another who didn't have a "bid" to the coming-out dance of one of America's richest heiresses. That is deplorably true of about nine-tenths of the parties given for and by the younger set in New York when the season is in full swing, especially in the smart hotels. Among certain boys, down for the weekend, it is considered a sport to "crash" a function uninvited. Youths far less presentable than Edward Naughton—and not nearly so well connected than he appeared to be—can boast of having trotted the night clubs and ballrooms with the "best people."

Lord Paget presented Jeffries Naughton for what he appeared to be—a smiling, easy-mannered young man who "belonged" simply because he was there and looked the part. I would like to know, however, in just what way Edward Naughton and Raymond Brownlow first edged into society, and how the illusion got abroad that Naughton was an Australian cattle king and Brownlow a London broker who was chummy with the notables in England.

Mrs. Paddleford was pleased when she saw me dancing with Naughton. She had made inquiries. She was satisfied that he was as rich and eligible as gossip said he was. Naughton, on his part, was delighted when I introduced him to my "mother." They struck up a great friendship then and there. Mrs. Paddleford beamed on him. He hovered about Mrs. Paddleford. Brownlow joined the group. He informed us they were also stopping at the Plaza. A dinner invitation was broached and accepted. A party was suggested by Brownlow. Mrs. Paddleford agreed graciously. I sat quiet—a spectator, as usual—in my foster mother's presence. From then on, she seized the reins in this affair. She drove, and I was as helpless as any pony under the whip.

"I like your friends," she told me when we went to dress for dinner. "See that you are nice to them." Then, when I responded apathetically, for neither Naughton nor Brownlow meant anything to me, she said, "You'd better be, or . . ." A glance at the riding crop in a corner of the room finished the sentence.

Thus began the strangest game that was ever played out over a young girl's destiny—my foster mother maneuvering to keep Naughton and Brownlow dancing attendance on us, and trying to egg me on to do the same, while they, not at all reluctant at this sign of favor from the wealthy Mrs. Paddleford, bombarded us with invitations for drives and theater parties, which gave Naughton the chance to make love to me.

Naughton and Brownlow, I have learned, went to a well-known New York lawyer soon after we met and had him investigate Mrs. Paddleford's financial standing. The lawyer, who was under no illusions about the former Mrs. Ben Teal, did not give them a glowing report. But did that sheer them off? Not at all. They had seen photographs of the Hollywood home and the millionaire's yacht. They had read the clippings from the California papers in Mrs. Paddleford's scrapbook. They knew Dr. Paddleford was worth millions—though they didn't know that he was about to split with his wife. They preferred the evidence of their own eyes to any cautious legal report. And all the evidence went to show that here was a rich, doting mother, eager to wed her daughter to the first eligible man, such, for example, as a polished Britisher with acres of sheep and cattle ranches in Australia and money to throw away.

None of this jockeying and plotting and counterplotting was as transparent to me then as it is now. I only know that, for some reason of her own, Mrs. Paddleford desired to placate these men in every way possible. I knew that I must call Brownlow Uncle Ray if I wanted to please her. I knew I must submit to Naughton's caresses, in her very presence, if I did not want her to slap me as soon as he was out of the room.

I was terribly unhappy. I did not dislike Naughton, but I was far from loving him. I enjoyed going to theaters and restaurants, but these people treated me with indifference, almost contempt. They discussed things I did not understand. All the conversation was between Mrs. Paddleford and the men. When I spoke, they drowned me out. After a while I learned to maintain a dreary silence. After all, I was only a seventeen-year-old girl who wanted to play with her own kind and not be bored to exhaustion night after night of champagne suppers, where I had to choke down fizzy stuff that tasted queer and gave me a splitting headache the next day.

At one of these dinner foursomes, the strain was too much for me. I became quite ill and had to go back to the hotel to my room. Mrs. Paddleford followed me there soon afterward. She reproached me, but not unkindly, for leaving the party. She combed out my hair and made me put on my prettiest negligee.

"I've told them," she said, "it's your birthday." (A falsehood.) "Now, spruce up and look your best. I think Mr. Brownlow's coming up."

He did come up. He patted me on the cheek and said he was so sorry they hadn't known it was my birthday; Jeffries, he declared, was simply brokenhearted. To have a little girl ill on her birthday!

A moment later, Jeffries bounced into the room, carrying a great bunch of American beauty roses. He fussed about the bed, as contrite as though I had been his best friend about to die. And, Mrs. Paddleford, with a mechanical smile frozen on her face, watched him triumphantly and kept saying, "Poor little Marie—my only daughter!"

Never had I had so much attention. If I hadn't been so dazed and sick with headache, I would have been more astonished than I was. I dimly remember Jeffries leaving with the declaration that I must go to a belated birthday lunch with him next day and my moaning that I felt too sick to go anywhere. I might have known that this flurry was but the prelude to the real drama. That began the next morning. Jeffries telephoned me about the luncheon engagement. I asked him if "Mama" was included. He said no. I told him I never went anywhere without her. Mrs. Paddleford immediately was at my side. "Oh, go along with him!" she whispered. And so I went.

Jeffries called for me at once. We went to a fashionable restaurant on upper Fifth Avenue. A friend of Jeffries met us there. The men ordered cocktails. I insisted that I didn't want one, but Jeffries said, "Oh, come on, drink it! You need a pickup!"

I raised the glass to my lips and gulped it down. Then I began to feel sleepy. The world was going gray. I heard a voice say, "Help her in!" The next thing I knew, I was stumbling into a taxicab and we were whirled away. Then there is just a succession of dim pictures: stone steps leading upward; a swarm of people waiting in an office; a pen poked into my hand and a voice telling me to sign my name; somebody mumbling something while I leaned heavily on Jeffries' arm; his whisper "Say, 'I do'!"

My head began to clear when we reached the air again. I was sobbing and crying. "Jeffries, what have you done to me? I'm sick! Where have we been? What's happened?"

"Don't take on so," he told me fiercely. "We're married." Then, to a friend, "I guess we put one over the old lady there, eh?"

They left me at the Plaza door. With my last strength, I stumbled into my room. All I could think of in that moment was that I had a dinner engagement with Rudolph Friml, the composer, and I must break it. I was in no condition to meet anybody. Mrs. Paddleford flew into the room just in time to hear my conversation with Mr. Friml.

"What are you breaking your engagement for?" she demanded, as I hung up the receiver and turned to her, my hair down and my eyes wild.

"Because I'm married to Jeffries Naughton," I said stupidly.

She began to scream at the top of her voice. She called me an ingrate, a guttersnipe, everything she could think of. She swore she would throw me into the streets. She swore she would kill Naughton on sight. But she swore too loudly and too long. Even in the swooning, hysterical state I was in, I could detect the ring of hypocrisy in every word she uttered. She overacted her part, and I saw she did.

"Lies! Lies!" I screamed back at her. "Everything you say is lies! You let him marry me! You helped him do it! You knew Dr. Paddleford wouldn't stand for it if he thought you allowed it! Oh, you terrible woman!"

My guess was borne out a few hours later when Naughton called. She received him in another room. I do not know what they said to one another. But after that, Mrs. Paddleford was all smiles. She referred to Jeffries as "the dear boy." She asked me if I knew how much he was worth. "He is very rich," she told me confidently.

What a surprise to her—and what a surprise to Naughton—it must have been when the dénouement came a few days later. It began when Naughton took me to his lawyer's office and demanded $25,000. I laughed in his face. I told him the truth. And it ended when Mrs. Paddleford, in turn, went to Naughton and demanded $25,000, and he laughed in her face and told her the truth—he was worth practically nothing; the "Australian cattle king" story was bunk.

Such was the climax to Mrs. Paddleford's plot to marry me to a millionaire—tragic to me, who found myself unwanted by a man I did not want and yet was tied to by unbreakable bonds; ludicrous, perhaps, to anyone who knows what hopes Margaret had staked on this alliance.

They patched up a piece. Naughton and Brownlow must have decided Mrs. Paddleford was worth whatever they could get out of her, for they continued to take us out to dinner and the theater—and borrowed $1,000 from her. As for Mrs. Paddleford, she must have liked those men for their own sake. She never got her $1,000 back. It is the one and only occasion I know of where she, the grasper, lost money to a grasper cleverer than she.

I have no idea where Jeffries Naughton is today. I saw him scarcely a dozen times after our marriage. I would not realize him to be my lawfully wedded husband did I not have the marriage certificate testifying to the fact.

A few weeks after the ending of the "cheating cheaters" farce between Mrs. Paddleford and the pair she had picked to "fake," and while we were still on friendly terms with them, Naughton got into a fight at the Rendezvous, a popular café in the Forties. He was with a British lord, who took his part. Their trouble was with Louis Slowden, the professional dancer. He was at the Rendezvous with Mrs. George Unne, a beauty and an old acquaintance of Naughton's.

Slowden resented Naughton's attitude toward Mrs. Unne, and a few minutes later there was a free-for-all scuffle on the sidewalk in front of the café. Slowden bloodied the lord's nose and mussed up Naughton considerably, I understand.

Influential friends hushed up the incident as much as possible, but they couldn't stop gossip. People began to ask who Edward Jeffries Naughton was. A week later, they got the answer in a way some of the society friends of Naughton and Brownlow hadn't expected.

When we moved from the Plaza to the Ritz, as we did shortly before this, Naughton and Brownlow took an apartment at No. 105 West Fifty-Fifth Street. They set up a roulette wheel—for their friends, they said. For a while, this private gambling den—for it was nothing more—flourished fruitfully. I have seen the room crowded with gallants and beauties from society and the stage. If a poll had been taken of those present on a big night, it might have passed as a roster of "who's who" in the upper bohemian circles of New York.

A man named Nathan Goldfinger, rich and prominent in the manufacturing world, was a guest at the Naughton-Brownlow apartment one night. Brownlow had invited him to a party. I am told that the "party" resulted in Goldfinger's losing several hundred dollars, and the result of that was that Goldfinger went to the police.

The roulette game was raided. Brownlow was arrested, spent the night in jail, and got out on bond. Naughton was not taken into custody, but the district attorney began an investigation of his record.

We knew nothing of this until the next night, when Brownlow telephoned us to invite us to dinner at the flat. We alighted from the elevator to find the English lord mounting guard at the door. A crowd of people was inside. So was a policeman, but he was comfortably intoxicated and bothered nobody. Jeffries sat in a chair, laughing and talking with sympathizing friends. But Brownlow, completely unnerved, sat at one side of the room, while a prominent society woman hung over him and patted his cheek and called him "poor little Brownie!"

It was a gloomy dinner party. We left early. I never saw Brownlow again. He skipped the country, although on bail signed by the lord. I saw Jeffries Naughton only once, when he came to say good-bye. He knocked on my bedroom door. I refused to come out.

"Be a sport, Marie," he said. "It may be the last time."

I opened the door. "Is it that serious?" I asked.

"Well, your husband and your 'uncle Ray' have decided to go on a vacation until things blow over. Our first stop may be Spain—it may be Africa. Anyway, it's good-bye, Marie. Luck to you—poor little kid!"

And that was the last word from the man I married.

Chapter 6:

Flight

Dear Reader,

Margaret's troubles now were assuming cyclonic proportions. She informed little Jack (Ben Teal Jr.) and me that there was only one thing for her to do—get out of the country. In my next chapter, I shall describe Mrs. Paddleford's remarkable flight from New York via three different hotels and two different aliases, and how we found ourselves well-nigh penniless aboard an ocean liner, en route for Paris and a rumble-tumble tour over half of Europe.

Of the tens of thousands of Americans who went abroad this year in a giant junketing invasion unequaled in the history of ocean travel, I believe I stand alone as the only one in that vast pleasuring army who was literally yanked to Europe in luxury when she didn't want to go, and who came back penniless with a gladder heart than the most homesick dough boy seeing the Statue of Liberty again after a three-year billet on the Rhine.

To you who want to travel but haven't the money, to you who read enviously how school teachers cross steerage on their savings and how college boys work their way over on cattle boats—to Americans who yearn to visit Europe, though broke—I can outline a method that will get you there, put you up at the best hotels, take you everywhere, give you the cream of the shops, and yet cost you practically nothing.

But I advise you not to try the method. It might bring you, as it brought Mrs. Margaret Teal-Paddleford, to a hard and disagreeable fin-ish in a jail in an alien and unsympathetic country, where you might lan-guish, as she has languished, until evidence piles up against you from dozens of people fleeced in dozens of different cities.

Though Mrs. Paddleford's method ended inevitably in arrest, her "grand tour" will stand as a record—until some super adventuress comes along to surpass it—of deluxe globe-trotting on nothing but a few hun-dred dollars, a swagger "front," plausible stories that deluded the most suspicious, unfulfilled promises that are still gulling some who put faith in them, and blind luck in flitting from one place before warnings reached there from places previously visited and hastily quitted.

There are a number of New York society people who doubtless won-der what happened to the motorcar, the country home, the town apart-ment, and other possessions Mrs. Paddleford so graciously offered them when they gave her letters of introduction to friends abroad.

Other New Yorkers, guilty of the same kindness, have heard from these friends—sorrowful, delicately reproachful letters about worthless checks and loans never paid. And now the New Yorkers are writing other friends to disregard the letters of introduction so trustingly written only a few months ago.

There are transatlantic voyagers who still tell the pathetic story of "the lady who lost her purse overboard" from the steamship *Paris*. There is a certain French viscount who wishes he had never heard that yarn. And throughout Europe—in Paris, Brussels, London, and other conti-nental capitals—there are many Americans and foreigners, from mem-bers of the nobility to untipped maids and waiters, who can say ruefully, "I, too, was stung."

Particularly is there a firm of New York lawyers who have never fath-omed the mystery of how Mrs. Paddleford slipped her baggage past the vigil they maintained at her hotel and successfully strolled up the gang-plank of a liner in the face of process servers armed with summonses and orders not to let her get aboard.

I can clear up that mystery—and many others. For I was the unwill-ing eyewitness—and generally the protesting, begging, even battling eye-

witness—to every little nick Mrs. Paddleford blazed along her flimflamming trail. She dragged me with her as she dragged her small son, until
the day when I could stick it no longer and cut loose little Jack and myself
from her control.

From the first, I strove to keep Mrs. Paddleford from embarking on
this European adventure. Our plight was bad enough in America, with
Dr. Paddleford planning to sue for divorce, with my ill-starred marriage
to Edward Jeffries Naughton changed from a fiasco into a desertion, and
with bill collectors dogging Margaret at every turn. Yet I felt it was infi-
nitely better to come to the crash in the United States—if crash there was
to be—than to be stranded three thousand miles from Fifth Avenue. And
I knew, too, that a trip abroad could mean only one thing—fresh fields
for Margaret to conquer, new victims for her to dupe, more trouble and
shame in the long run. I did not know, however, that she wove a web of
deception about our journey from the beginning.

Since my return, I have learned what she never let slip to me then,
that she used me as the decoy for getting these letters of introduction. She
told her friends I was going to Europe, not she; that I had an engagement
to sing in a Franz Lehar operetta to be produced in London; and that I
was to be coached by Jeritza, the famous Viennese prima donna.

It was the old story she gave the California newspapers when she first
began to groom me as a singing prodigy. I only smiled at it then, for it
seemed a harmless fairy tale at the worst. But I would never have submitted to its revival had I known Margaret was employing it to wiggle favors
from people who did not trust her but were sorry for me. She kept this
little game from me till we were abroad. She was beginning to be afraid
of me. I was developing a mind and will of my own. I was standing up
against some of her trickeries, refusing to connive at the frauds she was
trying to force on me.

I have also learned, back in America, that she added other inventions
to the story of my London offer. She promised one friend, an Englishman,
her "summer home in Greenwich" while we were away. I dare say, without that, he was willing enough to give her letters to his London brokers.
To another friend she offered the use of her "Park Avenue apartment"
during our absence. It existed only in her dreams. To a third she prom-

ised to "send her motor and chauffeur every day." To a fourth she "gave her limousine" outright.

Not long after Margaret was on her way, beneficiaries got together and compared notes and discovered that Margaret had duplicated her promises time and again, and that not one of her mythical homes had materialized into reality. They discovered likewise, somewhat to their dismay, that each had acted on Margaret's hints and gifted letters of introduction to friends whose trust they would regret to have violated.

Thus, Mrs. Paddleford laid the groundwork for her European adventure. When we boarded the steamer, she had assembled an excellent batch of recommendations and testimonials. They were to stand her in good stead in London, Paris, and Vienna.

She had currency, too, of course—to pay our bill at the Ritz-Carlton, for one thing; to buy our steamship tickets and get us started, at least, in the direction of Europe. She raised the money by selling her furs and jewels. There was a notable collection. Some of them were lavished on her by Dr. Paddleford. Her emeralds, I have heard experts say, were among the finest in the United States. She owned several strings of pearls and some gorgeous rings. A Fifth Avenue jeweler estimated the total value of her jewelry at not less than $100,000. She sold them for peanuts. It would have taken five times what she got in return to have met her outstanding cash obligations in New York and to have sent her away with a clean slate behind her. But the sum was sufficient to pay passage for herself, me, little Ben, and one servant. That, and a few hundred left over, was enough to launch Margaret's adventure.

On the last night at the Ritz, I made a final plea to Margaret, though she had reiterated her determination to go abroad too many times for me to doubt that anything I could say would be heard.

"Please, please!" I begged her. "Don't do such a foolhardy thing! Ask Dr. Paddleford to forgive you! He is kind!"

"Will you keep still?" snapped Margaret. "We are going to Europe because it is the thing to go to Europe. Everybody is going. Do you really intend to stay in New York this summer?"

It occurs to me, remembering this remark of Margaret's, that I may do her an injustice when I plead to refute her European foray, only to the fact that her New York creditors were pressing her and she saw opportunities for "gentle grafting" on the other side. It was just as much in keeping with her character that her incentive was also vanity; though the world was breaking up around her, though she was reduced to the extremity of pawning furs for champagne, though another month might see her on the verge of the poorhouse, she had to keep up with her social pace. It was "the thing" to go to Europe. Mrs. Margaret Teal-Paddleford, of the Ritz and California, would go!

There was nothing for it but for me to go, too. I would have run away, but there was an additional reason for staying, other than Margaret's watchfulness of my every movement. I could not leave Jack Paddleford. To me he will always be Ben Teal Jr., a chip off that dear old block; the little lad had smiled at me in the orphanage and clutched my hand and said, "Mama, I want this one!"

Our trip abroad was a hurry-scurry nightmare from first to last. It began with a rush. It went on with a rush. And, save for breathing spells such as the crossing, there was not a moment when, bewildered and breathless, I did not feel I was being whirled around the world just ahead of some grim destiny forever about to pounce upon me.

Our movements during the two weeks before we sailed were almost laughably like those of the villain in a moving picture, pussyfooting from place to place to sneaky music led by the orchestra. Take a map of New York and its environs. Star the Ritz, the Hotel Chatham, the Pennsylvania Station, Atlantic City, and the pier of the French line. Then picture a fashionably dressed woman dashing from stat to star, dragging a girl by one hand and a little boy by another, trailed by one panting servant, and followed at intervals of miles and minutes by threatening creditors, lawyers, and deputies—there you have us leaving for Europe with the rest of the wealthy and fashionables!

We paid our bill at the Ritz and departed in state in a limousine, followed by two taxicabs piled high with trunks. Some of the baggage Margaret checked at the Grand Central. The rest we took to the Hotel Chatham. There, Margaret got a suite under her maiden name of McKinney.

She planned to stay there a week, slipping out possessions bundle by bundle to the trunks at the Grand Central. Joe was in charge of this job. He hated it. "I feel like a horse thief!" he would whisper to me as he dodged out of the room with a bundle under each arm. But Mrs. Paddleford's orders were ironclad.

Her scheme worked beautifully insofar as getting out most of our belongings was concerned. But the management of the hotel eventually became suspicious. Mrs. Paddleford's real identity was discovered. Some of the eagle-eyed process servers also had trailed her. They were camping around the hotel again, just as they had done at the Ritz. It was time, to put into slang, for Margaret to "blow."

And "blow" she did. She informed the manager she had been called to Philadelphia for a conference with her husband's lawyers and would pay her bill immediately on her return. One trunk she left as security. It was half empty, but the manager didn't know that. He was reluctant to yield to Margaret, but she talked him down. She left, taking us children with her, and the trunk stayed. For all I know it—and the unpaid bill— may be there yet.

Margaret had decided to get out of town, pending the few days before the *Paris* was to sail. She already had her passports. She only had to keep out of the way of creditors till she was safely aboard. We went to Atlantic City. The first night, after registering at the Ambassador Hotel, Margaret took me strolling on the boardwalk. We were about to hire a wheelchair when Margaret suddenly turned pale and gripped my arm.

"What . . . ," I began.

"Get out of here!" she whispered. "We'll go back to the hotel!"

But it was too late. A man standing a few feet away, lighting a cigar, turned around, threw away his match, and saw Margaret. He started. He looked surprised; then his face flushed with anger. He took a step forward. He called her name.

But Margaret was gone—literally running toward the Ambassador. I scampered after her, panting and puzzled. We were back in our room. Margaret was dragging a suitcase from beneath the bed, snatching feverishly at scattered clothes. In the midst of her excitement, the telephone rang.

"Answer it, Marie," she ordered me. "Tell that man I'm not here. Tell him it's not my room. Tell him . . . anything!"

I told him, too amazed to oppose her. And back came his answer in an angry, shaking voice: "You can't fool me! You're Marie, aren't you? You tell your mother I'm onto her. You tell her I know she lied to me. You tell her I'll get her."

Not until months later did I learn the answer to all this mysterious business. I know today that Margaret, according to her victim, had maneuvered this man out of $10,000 by telling him Dr. Paddleford had hired detectives to watch the two of them on a certain weekend party months before, and that a scandal was inevitable unless she had this money to bribe the detectives. He found out later that her tale was false, he said. The meeting at Atlantic City was the first time he had seen her since then. According to his story, he would have made trouble for Margaret there if she hadn't been too quick for him.

We were out of the Ambassador and aboard a train in record time. Back in New York, we registered at the Pennsylvania under the name of "Mrs. Gilman and children." Margaret was afraid not only of her creditors now but of the man in Atlantic City. Yet she could afford to be optimistic, for the *Paris* sailed in three days.

We "made" the boat. Nothing happened to interfere with Margaret's plans.

Photographers took pictures of Jack, while Joe, acting under Margaret's orders, said his name was McKenstreet and he was the son of a rich Westerner. I stayed below. Margaret, heavily veiled, kept up the pose of Mrs. McKenstreet until we were at sea. She had a tilt with the ship's officers about this. The name did not jibe with our Paddleford passports. But she won out—how, I don't know, unless I attribute it to her persuasive tongue.

The voyage would have been delightful if Margaret had not immediately begun to figure and plot and deceive. She scraped acquaintances on deck. She invented the story that her purse dropped overboard, containing all her cash. It is extraordinary that she made people believe such a yarn, but she did. Before we landed, she had borrowed several hundred dollars from shipmates, promising to pay as soon as she landed and received a cable answering "the wireless I sent my husband." The French viscount was a heavy contributor. Another was a rich Montreal broker. I do not regret his loss so much because of my own unpleasant experience with him.

He was tremendously attracted to me. I disliked him heartily. The second night on deck, he seized me in his arms and began to kiss me. I broke away, slapped his face, and rushed to our stateroom. Margaret was there. When she saw my disheveled hair, my flushed face and angry eyes, she demanded the cause. I told her.

"Fool!" she screamed. She struck me. I cowered, for the old fear of her repossessed my lonely heart here in mid ocean. "Fool! He kissed you, did he? Then go back and tell him you love him! Do you think I'm taking you to Europe to insult every man who looks at you? I'll teach you to think better than that!"

Then I was reminded that there were men—wealthy, eligible, influential, of social standing, and eminently desirable—who were simply waiting for a chance to make love to any pretty, seventeen-year-old young lady who might happen to cross their path. All they needed was the very faintest sign of encouragement. Highly successful alliances, I was informed, were often made in that very way.

Half an hour later, my back aching from the blows she had rained on me, I crept on deck again, praying that my Montreal wooer had gone below yet desperately helpless to resist my foster mother's commands. He was gone. I flung myself into a steamer chair and wept my heart out to the stars.

"If this is the start of our trip to Europe, what will the end be?" I asked myself.

The answer was to be even more tragic than I feared.

Chapter 7:

The Grand Tour, Paris, 1922

Dear Reader,

At twilight of a gold-green April day, when all Paris seemed plea-sure bound along the boulevards, I reached the world's gayest capital with a lonely little boy clinging to my hand, with a penniless adventuress as my only chaperone, and with the knowledge gnawing my heart that her wits, which alone might keep us in luxury, likewise might land us all in jail by morning.

Paris, city of dreams! How often had I imagined its streets, its shops, its cosmopolitan crowds, its *Boul' Mich* and its Montmartre, its studios and its Seine, its every dazzling light and quaint café, its every historic stone and towering cathedral! How often, when I was training for opera in California, had I pictured my arrival there—rich, the daughter of a millionaire, in Paris to live, to study, to play, perhaps to make my debut as a singer at the opera or the *opera comique*!

I saw Paris for the first time through the window of a taxicab, rush-ing our party of four—my foster mother, Mrs. Margaret Teal Paddleford; her son, Ben Teal Jr.; the manservant, Joe; and me—from the Gare du Nord to the Hotel Crillon. I saw Paris in the dying gush of a spring sun-set, its low building rose-tinted, its parks misty, its sidewalks teeming with people and girdled with glowing lights.

Paris was never lovelier, yet it did not charm me; it stunned me, bewildered me, and frightened me. For I was not the millionaire's daughter with the gilded future; I was only a girl of seventeen, bound by fear and love for a small boy to a woman who had never been kind and was chronically cruel to me, who had dragged me hither as a tool and not as a beloved daughter, who I knew had no money except what she had borrowed aboard ship and soon frittered away, and who, events of the past week had convinced me, would go far to replenish her empty pocket.

After seeing her approach our shipmates with the fiction of a "purse lost overboard," after seeing how plausibly she inveigled them into making loans, after watching the haste with which she sped out of their sight as soon as we passed the Havre customs, after her deliberate answer "No!" to my direct question "Are you going to pay those people?" I was, no wonder, racked with fear for the future when we entered Paris. My forebodings were realized from the first. Margaret insisted on going to the Crillon, though she had little more than enough money with her to tip the taxi driver. There must have been a hundred hotels in Paris where she could have stopped with maximum comfort at no great cost. But nothing would do for her but the famous hostelry fronting the Place de la Concorde. After serving as headquarters for the American mission during the Versailles conference, it was restored to its prewar glitter and she knew that the price scale, of course, would be according.

We must have seemed a strange party to the swagger American tourists crowding the lobby as we trailed in—Margaret strutting ahead, her head high and haughty, one hand ready to raise a devastating lorgnette on the hotel clerk; at her heels me, with white and miserable face, tugging at little Jack's hand. His face was flushed and feverish. He complained of "feeling bad." He would have excited anyone's pity. Joe, at the rear, looked more like a pallbearer at a funeral than a millionaire's valet.

Had the obsequious manager taken a good look at all of us, I am not so sure we would ever have had a room at the Crillon. But he was too busy kowtowing before the regal Margaret. She insisted on the best suite he had, and, scarcely before we knew it, Jack and I were fast asleep in two featherbeds that might have served for the boudoir of an empress, while Margaret, in the sitting room, sat before a writing table, biting at her nails and ordering meals without blinking an eyelash. Her $50 she spent on taxi fare. And all day long she shopped up and down the rue de la Paix like the daughter of a Morgan or a Gould with carte blanche in purchasing a trousseau.

The old shopping urge, which was her ruin in New York, had bitten her to the core here in Paris, among the most costly feminine fineries on Earth. She went from one famous modiste to another, from milliner to milliner, into jewelers, into the wonderful lingerie salons along the Place de l'Opéra, where the chic little salesgirls "madamed" her and raved over her, and showered her with the beautiful, feathery silks and laces a woman can resist no more than a starving man can resist food on a desert island.

I gasped at the way Margaret bought and bought. She had not the price of the least of these dainty creations. Yet, with a shrug and a flourish, she would order dozens sent to her room at the Crillon. In the room I gasped aloud, "You will not be able to keep any of this."

It was, indeed, a "possessed" woman who turned on me then. She seized the nearest thing at hand, a glass decanter, and hurled it at me. It missed my head by an inch and fell unbroken to the floor. The next moment, I was being flogged with a lamp stand. It was to be very nearly the last flogging I would ever receive from Mrs. Paddleford, for the time was swiftly drawing on when I was to stage one final, successful rebellion against her. But I submitted then, shrinking under the blows, protecting my head from the storm, until her anger was spent.

My prediction that Paris merchants would not let her keep her wealth of purchases came true only as far as some of them went. Practically all were sent to the Crillon COD. But that sort of delivery was exactly the kind Mrs. Paddleford was expert in handling.

She flew into a tantrum. Of stupefied messenger boys, she demanded to know what they meant by bringing these parcels and boxes COD, when she had ordered them charged. She delivered quite a speech about herself—Mrs. Margaret Paddleford, the wife of the oil millionaire, the leader of New York and California society, the rich, the famous, and the beautiful Mrs. Paddleford! According to her, she had only to wave her hand like an Aladdin and the genii would deposit in her lap the gold of America. What did these menials mean by insulting her with a demand for a few francs for this truck? She would teach them and their impertinent masters a lesson! Back with it! Out with it! She would patronize others in the future!

The bill collectors Margaret had left mourning on the pier in New York might have smiled at this comic-tragic scene. But Margaret's French was of such impression that her purchases were left in retreat. She delighted in opening packages that included an expensive chinchilla coat, several fine furs, and a shoal of beautiful lingerie while having "done" Paris on a pittance.

Touring the shops as Margaret's horrified and squelched companion just about constituted my entire experience in Paris. I saw none of the far-famed nightlife. Neither did Margaret for several days, for she was afraid to look up any of her shipmates; and her letters of introduction she apparently was holding in reserve for emergency. She chafed at staying in the hotel before the end of the first week. Gaiety was calling to her from the bright-lit streets, and Margaret found a way to answer.

Joe, the servant, had been doing a little "seeing Paris" on his own account. On the boat he had made friends of a rich New Yorker, who assumed Joe was little Ben's tutor, not his valet. Joe is an attractive chap, I might say in passing, and true blue.

"Bring your friend around and introduce him. I'd like to have dinner with him," insisted Margaret.

Joe reluctantly introduced his friend. The rich New Yorker was impressed. He invited Mrs. Paddleford to a "party." But little Ben was sick that night. He had been feeling worse ever since we reached Paris. Finally, Margaret called the house physician. He pronounced it the flu.

Mrs. Paddleford made no effort to hide her annoyance. A little sickness, she declared, was not going to stop her chance to "see Paris." She swept out, shortly before dark, in her new coat and her other bought-and-unpaid-for trappings.

Little Ben tossed restlessly in bed. I rested on the floor beside him. As I drowsed, the last thing I heard was the faint beat of chimes from the Garden of the Tuileries, warning its closing. It was a lonely and wistful night.

Dawn was struggling through the windows when I finally woke and, cramped and cold, scrambled from the floor. There was a light in Margaret's room, but it had burned all night. She hadn't returned yet. And she didn't return until broad day, when she found Jack and me so hungry we had no heart to reproach her, no heart for anything but breakfast.

That day, the Crillon asked us for our rooms. The excuse given was that the management didn't care to have a sick boy in the house, but I have no doubt that someone on the boat had "tipped" the manager to the character of his guest, or that the continual stream of errand boys and girls, going back with the COD goods, had aroused suspicion.

Margaret faced a crisis. But she rose to it gamely. Leaving all our baggage at the Crillon, she packed the three of us into a taxicab, including little Ben, sick though he was, and ordered the driver to go to the Plaza Athénée, another exclusive Paris hotel.

We reached there at dusk. Margaret shooed us all into the lobby and told the clerk she wanted the best rooms in the house, to send for our baggage and pay our bill at the Crillon, and to put the amount on her bill at the Athénée.

Of course, the clerk sent for the manager. He was a dapper little Frenchman with a white imperial he stroked nervously and the most polite manners I ever saw in my life. For once, Margaret met her match in adroitness. Without the hint of an insult, yet he insisted on telephoning the Crillon before giving us a room. And whatever he learned from the Crillon caused him to inform Margaret that she must put up cash in advance before he could accommodate her at all.

While Margaret strode up and down the lobby, her eyes shooting fire and her tongue clacking like a millrace, trying to persuade the dapper little manager against his better judgment, little Ben sat huddled in a big chair, with Joe holding one hand and me the other.

"Have you no heart?" Margaret panted, while the manager stroked his imperial more nervously than ever. "This poor little boy is sick! Are you going to let him die on the streets? We must have a room and a doctor! I tell you, my money is all in the bank, and it is Saturday afternoon and I cannot cash a check."

It *was* Saturday afternoon. That, and more likely the pitiful face of little Ben, made the manager yield a point. Joe, he said, could take the boy to a room, but he would not admit Mrs. Paddleford and her daughter without a cash payment.

Margaret, desperate, agreed to this compromise. She ordered a taxicab. Pulling me in beside her, she gave me the address of an apartment not far from the Boulevard des Capucines. I learned later that this belonged to Joe's friend of the boat who had taken Margaret on the Montmartre party.

The taxicab stayed in front of the apartment for nearly an hour, with me in it. Finally, Margaret appeared. Her face looked as though chiseled in flint, but it also glowed in triumph. She showed me a check for 2,000 francs. It was signed by the man who lived upstairs. I do not know what happened in that upper room—what emotional plea Margaret made to her fellow American, what more sinister scheme she may have employed. But I do know that payment later was stopped on the check and that the writer of it claimed, according to a letter I have seen, he was induced to sign it while he was drugged.

This information was given me months later, long after I had broken with Mrs. Paddleford and returned to America. My only feeling then was a dull sort of bitter wonder at the amazing resources of this woman who found herself stranded in Paris and yet could raise 2,000 francs. Getting the check was one thing. Getting it cashed was another. Margaret returned to the hotel and flourished it under the dapper manager's nose. He looked politely gratified, but he just as politely refused to accept the check. Madame would have to get it cashed. Then did Margaret call on those letters of introduction she had angled out of her New York acquaintances. One of them, from a well-known American woman, was to Dr. M. Vasseur, a famous French woman surgeon whose war work won her international recognition.

Margaret telephoned Dr. Vasseur. She asked her to come to the hotel. There, in a downstairs parlor, she explained to the Frenchwoman what a terrible predicament she was in, with her little son ill and with her money sent by mistake to London, instead of Paris! It could not be rectified before Monday, declared Margaret, and meantime something must be done.

The kindly Dr. Vasseur, with the letter of introduction from one of her best friends before her, did not hesitate a moment. She vouched for Mrs. Paddleford to the hotel manager. She cashed the check herself. She not only did that but lent Margaret an additional 1,000 francs to take her to London and get the mythical "cabled" money.

Thus, the bill at the Crillon was paid. Thus, we were given rooms at the Plaza Athénée. Thus, we extended our Paris stay over the weekend, when Margaret, perhaps afraid of payment being stopped on the check Dr. Vasseur had cashed, picked us up bag and baggage and caught the boat train for a channel port and London.

One of the most regrettable memories of my life will always be of that noble, sympathetic Frenchwoman who was the victim of Mrs. Margaret Paddleford. The doctor did not lose it all. The American embassy, I am informed, reimbursed the 2,000 francs she lost on the cashed check. But the 1,000 francs she lent Margaret, because she had no receipt for them, were just that much out of her pocket—gone because she was kindhearted and generous to a woman who did not scruple to return generosity with selfishness and fraud.

Chapter 8:

The Grand Tour, London, 1922

Dear Reader,
I have written somewhere in these confessions that, had it not been for my foster mother, I might have grown to girlhood in an orphanage, hired out as a servant, married some honest fellow who worked with his hands, become the companion of his joys and sorrows, and never known either the luxury or the misery of millions.

I can write also that, had it not been for my foster mother, I might have been a stage star at seventeen. Instead of knocking at the gates of Broadway, as I knock today, I might now have Piccadilly at my feet. Instead of drifting back from Europe penniless, I might be returning this month, or the month after, with a London success behind me and an assured career ahead.

It is hard for me, just here, not to speak bitterly of Mrs. Margaret Teal-Paddleford. I would not willingly wound her or be unjust to her in any way. The harshest wish I have for her is that she does not cross my path again. I can even add to that, as one human being to another, I hope that the world will go well with her to the end.

Yet, I repeat, it is not an easy thing to forget all the scars left by the ten years I served as handmaid to her wild whims and mad ambitions. Scars of the body—they will heal. Red welts from a whip will not show nor matter five years hence. But there are other hurts—broken dreams, premature disillusions, distorted ideals, lost opportunities—nothing can restore.

Though my stage dreams still burn brightly, it hurts to know that the great opportunity to realize them at seventeen was there and is gone, snatched from me as I stood on tiptoes for fulfillment, my first part a lead in a new London production, my role rehearsed day and night for two thrilling weeks, my manager confident I was to be a hit, my debut before a brilliant first-night audience in the world's largest city only forty-eight hoursdistant.

And then to have to pitch it all away, as one would flip a newly lighted cigarette into the dark, because Mrs. Paddleford would not be content with $200 honestly earned but must chase thousands against ever increasing chances of arrest and disgrace—oh, I do not mean to be vindictive, but what I write now is too fresh in my memory for the disappointment not to bite deep. Dust has not had time to gather on the footlights that were to flare for me—and didn't because I was hustled off to Brussels on the eve of our premiere performance.

We arrived in London from Paris in early summer. It was an excellent time for contact with the stage, for managers were picking their casts for the autumn openings and the booking offices buzzed with rumors of this production and that where gilt-edged chances beckoned.

Mrs. Paddleford, who had landed in France less than a month before, with scarcely enough money to get her party to Paris, and who now was richer by some $300 as the result of $100 borrowed from an unsuspecting French woman surgeon and $200 mysteriously inveigled from a rich American businessman, had her choice of these two objectives—British blue bookers or Britain's Broadway.

Naturally, she chose to take a shot at society first. London was practically a fresh field for her talents as a climber. She knew—or thought she knew—that no one in England could spot her as the former Mrs. Ben Teal unless it served her purpose to reveal that identity. That name might go well in dealing with stage people. In society, she would carry on much further as Mrs. George Paddleford, the millionaire's wife. Her letters of introduction so described her. They were addressed to some of the most prominent men and women in England. Most of them, however, happened to be out of town.

Mrs. Paddleford had gone direct to Claridge's, and from there she immediately sent out notes and telephone calls to the persons she hoped to meet. The hotel authorities were obviously impressed by her efforts to get in touch, for example, with Lord Northcliffe, a British newspaper and publishing magnate, owner of the *Daily Mail* and the *Daily Mirror.*

The famous editor, like many others, was not in town. But two days later we received a letter bearing the Northcliffe coat of arms. Lord Northcliffe wrote that he would be happy to meet any friend of Miss So-and-So's (an American lady who had given Mrs. Paddleford nearly twenty letters to her friends abroad), and that he would be back in a few days and hoped Mrs. Paddleford would come to tea.

But we never saw Lord Northcliffe. Before the first week was out, Mrs. Paddleford had made other connections. She telephoned a number of British steel men and told them she was a sister of a certain midwestern American steel magnate. They responded with cordial invitations.

It is amazing to me, thinking it over, that Mrs. Paddleford so easily tricked these people into accepting her. Yet I suppose that it is only human nature. All of her London victims were cultured, charming people, who had no reason to suspect they would be the object of a swindle. All that was necessary was to put on a bold front, take it for granted they would believe what was told them, and receive their friendliness as a matter of course, just as they received Mrs. Paddleford's notes and telephone calls as a matter of course. After all, it must have appeared to them merely routine courtesy. An American millionaire's wife announces herself as such. She appears to be genuine. She has appropriate letters. They scarcely glance at them—a mere formality. She is received just as one millionaire's wife was last week and another the week before.

Nor was it extraordinary that Mrs. Paddleford should be in need of funds. She told them her money was delayed in cable transit. Money is frequently delayed in transit. It is common for tourists to call on London resources for loans. It is common for London bankers and businessmen to assist friends from the other side, or to assist friends' friends, such as Mrs. Paddleford.

One of the steel men Mrs. Paddleford telephoned invited her to tea. She pleaded another engagement but announced she would send her "little debutante daughter." She insisted on my going, and, truth to tell, I was not reluctant to get away for a while from the constant bickering and scheming going on in our suite, but I resolved that I would *not* ask this man for money, as my foster mother commanded.

My host was charming. The tea party was followed by an invitation to dinner. This time, Mrs. Paddleford accepted for both of us. I noticed our new friend looked puzzled when he met Mrs. Paddleford and appeared to be examining her quietly but intently. Halfway through dinner, in a pause in the conversation, he suddenly said, leaning across the table toward Margaret:

"I don't mean to be curious, but weren't you the wife of Ben Teal, who produced *Ben Hur* here years ago?"

Margaret denied, with an appearance of composure, but I could see that she was disturbed.

Naturally, our host didn't pursue his inquiry. But he knew. The next day, he asked me to tea again—alone.

"Come, now," he said, "isn't—or wasn't—your mother Mrs. Ben Teal? Aren't you Ben Teal's daughter? I ask only because Ben Teal was my dear friend. I loved and honored him. If his child is in trouble—and I think you are—I want to help you."

I told him the truth. I broke down and sobbed out the sorrows of my life as Mrs. Paddleford's daughter. He understood and gave me real sympathy. When I left, he insisted on my accepting a substantial loan— "to get you away from this woman and back to America," he said. "It's for your father's sake. You can have the rest of your life to pay it back to me."

I took the money, determined to use it for the purpose suggested. I would leave Margaret. I would fly for America. I would take little Ben Teal with me. There was enough for both of our passages—and Joe's. But I reckoned without guessing Margaret's vigilance. Jerking my purse from my hand, she pulled it open and exposed a roll of British banknotes.

"Why didn't you tell me you had this money the minute you came in the room?" she screamed. "I'll teach you to fool me!"

Again I quivered under one of her ruthless floggings. For a week, Margaret was in clover. The shops on Bond Street were the meadows where she grazed. Her shopping in Paris was piker folly compared with her extravagance in London with money in her pocket. She spent even that which was not hers, for she began opening charge accounts, giving her new-made London friends as a reference.

One of these was the honorable Mrs. Gerald Dickinson, a leader in

London society. Margaret had met her through a letter furnished by an unsuspecting British lord visiting in America. She had invited me to tea. She had been gracious, but Mrs. Paddleford did not scruple to use her name in trying to rent a London house without paying the customary fees. Mrs. Dickinson must have heard of that maneuver, for before we left London an incident happened that makes me burn yet at the memory of it.

The scene was the lounge at Claridge's. Mrs. Paddleford and I had been lunching in the dining room. To reach it, we had to pass through the lounge. A number of gentlewomen were seated at small tables, having their afternoon coffee. In one of them we recognized Gerald Dickinson. At another table was Dorothy Dickson, then playing the lead in the English production of *Sally*" She bowed and smiled, but Mrs. Dickinson did not appear to see us at all.

"Go over and speak to Mrs. Dickinson!" Margaret hissed in my ear as we paused near the exit. "Perhaps she'll invite you to tea again. She'll introduce you to those women. Be sure to get their names!"

I liked Mrs. Dickinson. I did not hesitate to parade the length of the lounge, stop at her table, hold out my hand, and smile. "How do you do, Mrs. Dickinson? We haven't seen you for some time!"

The French may be supreme in stinging repartee, the German aristocrat may achieve heights of haughtiness on occasion, and the American society leader may pride herself on her ability to register chill aloofness toward climbers—but, for the art of administering the snub devastating, commend me to your British gentlewoman in a nasty mood.

The Honorable Mrs. Dickinson raised her head and her lorgnette and remarked, icily, "No, and it will be some time before you see me again, I hope!" Then she went on conversing with her companions in the manner of one who has brushed away an annoying bit of fluff and then forgotten it. I was not so much furious at the slight as I was cut to the heart. I beat a confused retreat.

"What did she say?" demanded Margaret outside. I told her, with tears choking my voice.

And Margaret's only "comeback," as the humorists say, was to rage— far from Mrs. Dickinson's ears, by the way—"The dirty skunk! Oh, the dirty skunk!"

That experience was painful, but it was by no means rare in our travels. I understood. I was getting, in plain American, "the air." I understood what many in London were beginning to hear—the reports of Mrs. Paddleford's shaky financial standing!

The man in Paris who gave her a check for 2,000 francs—while he was drugged, he said—had stopped payment. The French woman surgeon who cashed it had complained to the police. The fingers of the law were stretching across the Channel toward Mrs. Ben Teal.

Before they reached her, however, the entire complexion of our gloomy prospect had changed. I was engaged for the London stage! More, I was engaged for a leading role in a new production by Lorilard, one of the most famous of English managers.

Mrs. Paddleford, after exhausting her society contacts, had turned to the stage. She called up several managers and told them she, the widow of Ben Teal, was at Claridge's with her daughter, Marie, "who sang *The Merry Widow* when it was revived in New York, you know?"

They didn't know. As a matter of fact, I have never even seen *The Merry Widow*.

But they called. The memory of Ben Teal, whose London production of *Ben Hur* ran there for years, ensured that. And they were sufficiently impressed to give me a hearing. I sang for them, danced for them, and postured for them.

"Did you really sing in *The Merry Widow*?" demanded Lorilard.

"No!" I cried, and "Yes!" boomed Margaret, in the same breath.

Lorilard laughed. "Never mind!" He waved at us. "I'll give you fifty pounds a week to sing the boy's part in my new show, *Love's Awakening*."

Mrs. Paddleford wanted to hold out for 100 pounds, but I refused to listen to her. I signed the contract. I had my hair bobbed. I bought costumes. I began to rehearse. Before the week was out, Mr. Lorilard told me I would "do." I was in a state of perfect bliss. In another week, I knew, I was going to succeed in the part. My future was made!

With the opening scarcely two nights away, Mrs. Paddleford suddenly stormed into our room at the Ritz, where we had moved from Claridge's, with her eyes angry and her face pale.

"Pack your bags!" she commanded. "We're going to the continent!"

"But the show—" I began.

"Never mind the show!" she interrupted savagely. "We must get out of here tonight. It's those people in Paris. They want money."

"But I'm making money!" I cried. "On fifty pounds a week, we can pay them; we can all live comfortably!"

"You little fool!" snorted Margaret. "What is fifty pounds a week? Not a drop in the bucket! Come! Pack!"

And so, despite all my plans, despite all I could protest about what Mr. Lorilard would say and what this sudden desertion might do to his play, despite the fact that I had signed a contract and this was my first great chance, I was bundled off—sobbing, fighting, begging Margaret to let me stay—to the night train for a Channel port and the boat to Calais. For weeks after that, I cried myself to sleep nightly—and dreamed of footlights guarded by ogres who sneered at me and spat at me and thrust me away with hairy arms. It was, I think, the greatest disappointment of my life.

Many weeks later, while little Ben Teal and I snoozed in the sunshine beside an alpine lake, I read in the continental edition of a British newspaper, "Lorilard, the producer, has indefinitely postponed the premiere of his new musical comedy, *Love's Awakening*."

And, still later, when I was returning to America to start my life again, I stopped over in London—to learn from his own lips that my forced desertion at the eleventh hour had "spoiled the show."

He forgave me. When I told him, with tears in my eyes, how Mrs. Paddleford snatched me off to Brussels despite all my protests and actual physical resistance, when I described to him the weeks of torture that were my lot after that, he put his hand on my shoulder and said, "That's all right, kiddie—I sized you up as the sort who would never let a chap down. It's been a puzzle to me just what happened, ever since you left. I'm glad to know the truth at last. I'm only sorry it's too late—it's too late."

Too late! Those words have rung in my ears ever since, as the memory of that lost opportunity sweeps back to me. But is it ever "too late? Now, while I study so hard for a stage debut in America, I tell myself that I will win back that vanished chance—that if opportunity knocked once and fled, I will make her knock again.

Chapter 9:

The Grand Tour, Brussels
to Venice, 1922

Dear Reader,
When Mrs. Margaret Teal Paddleford sailed for Europe at the height of the fashionable transatlantic pilgrimage, she did not go blindly and purposelessly, with no idea except to escape her dunning New York creditors and perhaps strike into riches abroad by sheer luck.

She had a definite plan. What it was, I did not know until the very eve of its collapse. I was only bewildered by her extravagant purchases in the shops, only dismayed when she charged thousands of dollars' worth of finery and bluffed merchants into accepting her account. I knew she was practically penniless. I thought she was "buying out the town" only through a passion for power and appearance and pretty clothes.

In a measure, this was true. But there was an additional and more practical incentive, which she revealed to me just before the end of our wild scamper across Europe, after the Paris police started on her trail and the menace of Scotland Yard sent us helter-skelter out of London.

She told me she was getting all the furs, laces, jewelry, and lingerie she could abroad for the fixed purpose of bringing them back to New York, claiming duty exemption on the ground most of the goods were bought in this country originally, and then selling them for enough to "square" her most pressing obligations and give her capital to fight Dr. Paddleford's divorce suit and demand a settlement of millions.

She mapped out our itinerary, she explained, in a way that would keep her several jumps ahead of outraged merchants in the cities she visited and bring her in a circle through France, Italy, Austria, Germany, and Holland to a Dutch port and a ship to Canada, whence she would cross the border to New York, the possessor of imported valuables she would sell for a profit that would be all net.

"But that is outright swindling!" I cried out in horror. She glared at me. Then and there, I decided that I would break away from this woman and her shady, brazen enterprise, and take little Ben Teal with me, no matter what the consequences might be to Margaret or to us.

I did what I resolved to do, with the result that Margaret's adventure was cut short midway. She was thrown in jail, and we children were cast penniless on the streets of Vienna. But, because I did not know her scheme, I did not act until we had dodged for weeks from North Europe to South Europe to Middle Europe in a succession of skirmishes with shopkeepers, hotel managers, train acquaintances, customs guards, flunkies, and pursuing telegrams.

When I think that, only a few months ago, I was touring the most beautiful and famous cities in the world, I am almost ashamed that my knowledge of them is so limited. My New York friends ask me about St. Mark's in Venice, the Milan cathedral, the St. Gotthard Pass, a famous Viennese restaurant, and I can only shake my head and say, "Yes, I have heard of them."

But is it to be wondered that I do not know more? During those breathless, bewildering weeks, little Ben and I were either nodding the nights away in speeding trains or strange hotels, or else seeking what amusement we could in parks and plazas that, to us, had no names, while Margaret reveled in the shops.

My memories of Europe are not of museums and galleries and gay theaters and famous restaurants, but of stuffy train compartments, flashes of fields and mountains that might have been Switzerland or might have been Alsace, for all I knew; of gabbling porters and bustling bellboys; of the suspicious eyes of gendarmes and customs inspectors; of little Ben's tear-stained face; of Margaret's anger.

When we left London, we went directly to Brussels via Dover and Calais. I was heartbroken and rebellious over my forced desertion of Mr. Lorilard's new production. To appease me, Mrs. Paddleford said she had met at lunch in Brussels the popular American composer and producer Irving Berlin, who had promised her to give me a part in *The Music Box Revue*. I only half believed her. Later I learned she made up the invention out of the clear blue sky—but I optimistically agreed to keep up my music on the chance of this engagement when I returned home.

We were in Brussels only a few days. Perhaps Margaret feared to stay longer, though she had registered under an assumed name. At times she was "Mrs. Thompson and family," at other times "Mrs. Gilman and family." In Venice, I recall, she registered the party as "Cynthia Teal, mother and family." Thus, she did stave off investigators from Paris to London.

We left Brussels at seven o'clock one morning and traveled all day to the south. I had no idea where we were going. Margaret was morose and uncommunicative. At last we reached a little border town. It was Basel. I was told we were going into Switzerland. The next morning we were in Lucerne, where we stayed for a week.

Here, Margaret plunged into a new shopping orgy, leaving little Ben and me to amuse ourselves as best we could. We sought the lakes. We would row and dream all day beneath the blue Swiss skies, dreading to go back to the hotel—and Margaret's quarreling—at night.

Again, as in Paris, streams of errand boys began to arrive at our hotel suite with hatboxes, bundles and parcels of various kinds. Again Margaret flew into a rage when she found the goods were sent COD. Again she bluffed and bullied apologetic merchants into charging the orders. Furs and nearly two dozen handsome watches were among the items she secured in Lucerne. But she didn't keep them all.

The fur dealer must have gotten suspicious. Or else he heard warnings from Paris and London. The day of our departure from the hotel, he made a dramatic and disastrous eleventh-hour descent. Little Ben and I were outside in the taxicab with Joe, the manservant, waiting to go to the station. Mrs. Paddleford was in the lobby at the cashier's desk, paying our bill. Suddenly, the fur dealer dashed up. I craned my neck to see and hear.

He advanced on Mrs. Paddleford, demanding payment for the furs she had bought. She tried to freeze him with a look. She blustered. She wheedled. She assured him she was only going for a short trip and would send him the money from Milan, where she expected a cable from America.

The fur dealer, however, was obdurate. He declared he would not allow her to leave Switzerland unless she paid the amount due him or gave him back the furs. Margaret was in despair. Our train was due to leave in thirty minutes. She had been all set for her "getaway" when this unexpected demand spoiled her pretty plans.

There was nothing to do but yield. With Margaret still protesting and fuming, the trunks were hauled off the taxicab and taken to a room in the hotel. They were opened. The fur man picked out his goods from among the fineries scattered about the place. He grinned. Doubtless he was chuckling over the surprise that was coming to other Lucerne merchants.

At last the ordeal was over. Margaret made her departure safely, but not as triumphantly or with as much dignity as she had planned. The rest of us were only too glad to leave without being popped into jail.

Milan, in northern Italy, was our next stop. We were there a week. It is one of the few pleasant memories I have of Europe. For it was in Milan where I renewed my musical studies. We looked up the friend of my former teacher in America—Madame Fabre, a famous prima donna who was once the chum of Adelina Patti. She agreed to take me for two hours every day. For a while, I was happy. I was even willing to believe Margaret's often-repeated assurances that a splendid role was waiting for me in America.

I would have liked to stay in Milan. But Margaret was restless. She wanted to be on the go. She had to be, I suppose. She was forever in fear of pursuit now. On the seventh night of our stay, she announced we would leave for Venice in the morning.

I will never forget our entry into the City of the Doges. Margaret had planned something a little elaborate. She had prospects, I presume, she wanted to impress—more friends' friends to whom she would present her letters of introduction. She had wired ahead for reservations at the Hotel d'Europe, and when she discovered we could make our trip to the hotel in one of the famous Venetian gondolas, she was charmed with the notion.

It would be a stately affair—the rich Mrs. Paddleford, American mil-

lionaire's wife, with her daughter and her son and her servant; the gon-
dola piled high with luggage; the gondolier guiding us swiftly along the
canal; the landing at the hotel quay; the bowing menials; the dignified
promenade from quay to lobby. If Venice didn't sit up and take notice, at
least she would write back to America about it.

From Venice we went on to Vienna, where she was back in form sufficiently to persuade one of the largest lace factories in the vicinity to credit
her with hundreds of dollars' worth of fine laces. In my next chapter, I
shall tell how fate, which Margaret Paddleford had been fleeing so long,
finally overtook her in the Austrian capital, and what my part was in
the dramatic exposure that sent her screaming and struggling to jail and
brought me back at last to America.

Chapter 10:

The Grand Tour, Vienna, 1922

*VIENNA, June 10—Genevieve Paddleford, who claims to be
the wife of a wealthy California oil trader, is under arrest in her
connection with a number of fraudulent operations in which
businessmen of Lucerne, Paris, and Vienna were the victims.*
—Reno Evening Gazette, *June 10, 1922*

Dear Reader,
The stock complaint of tourists returning from abroad with raw memories of sky-high hotel bills and restaurant checks is that all Europeans operate on the theory that all Americans are millionaires.

It is an old, old wail dating from prewar days. And it still holds good. Speaking from a limited though exciting experience as Mrs. Margaret Teal Paddleford's unwilling companion in her meteoric flight through Europe only a few months ago, I can confirm it.

Only I should like to point out that the millionaire delusion works two ways. If it means that many Americans are "stung," it may also mean that many Europeans find themselves disappointed and disgruntled. Certainly, it was to Mrs. Paddleford's advantage that Europe accept each visiting American as a Morgan or a Vanderbilt. And certainly this belief was not to the advantage of those who applied it to Mrs. Paddleford.

The millionaire delusion does exist—vividly and widely. In no other way can I account for the ease with which Mrs. Paddleford ingratiated herself into more than one high sector of European society, especially in Middle Europe.

There the war left its most ravaging results. There America poured in a flood of food and clothing. And there a legend has grown up among the peasantry that the United States is a country simply oozing gold, and that all Americans fairly drip dollars. I have had little children follow me along the streets of Vienna, begging for a krone, when I did not know myself where my next meal was coming from. They had spotted me as an American, and I might have turned my purse inside out a hundred times without shaking their conviction that I had kroner to burn.

The acquaintances Mrs. Paddleford sought in Vienna were far from the peasant class. They were widely traveled, cultured, intelligent people, yet I think that even they reflected the universal attitude and shared, in a measure, the universal opinion that any American who came to Europe must live in a mansion in New York and own a dozen motorcars.

When they were so ready to believe in American riches, it was no wonder it was little trouble for Mrs. Paddleford to gull them completely. When she spoke of her townhouse, her automobiles, her country estate, her multimillionaire husband, she spoke to the credulous.

Broadway is primed to say, "Blah!" to the poseur. Fifth Avenue consults Dun or Bradstreet or the Social Register before it believes fairy tales. But Ringstrasse of hungry, blighted, once-glorious Vienna, I believe, would swallow any story the visitor from the United States wanted to tell.

Believe me when I say I am not poking fun at the Viennese. Nothing is further from my intention than to scoff at these gracious, kindly, courtly men and women in the Austrian capital who received Mrs. Paddleford blindly without question. Nor am I implying that they were in any sense avaricious. If they had only been so, they would have investigated—and learned their jeweled guest was all but a pauper. As it was, they welcomed her to their homes without quibble or suspicion, as one would welcome any stranger who apparently "belongs."

There are surely times when foolish trust is in itself a virtue and simple credulity is the hallmark of breeding and gentility. When I think of Franz Lehar, the composer; Adolph Ungar, the millionaire Viennese department-store magnate; Mrs. Ungar, his beautiful wife; and other leaders of society and artistic circles who entertained Mrs. Paddleford, vouched for her, and suffered from her duplicity, I do not smile at them. I see them for what they were—honorables who looked only for honor where they extended their hospitality.

When we reached Vienna, we went at once to the Grand Hotel, where Mrs. Paddleford had installed our party in a suite deluxe. She immediately got in touch with people to whom she had letters of introduction, and one of these she persuaded to introduce me to Franz Lehar.

It was Franz Lehar who invited us to dine at his beautiful home and offered his services in any way we could make use of them while we were in Vienna. We accepted his invitation. We went with him to the opera. I have an unforgettable memory of that glittering night when we sat in a box with the famous composer and, during the entire act, were introduced to the wit and beauty of Viennese society.

Mrs. Paddleford prepared for the occasion as though she were going to be received at court. For three hours during the afternoon, she muddled and mauled over the shimmering assortment of gowns picked up in London, Paris, and other capitals. She was almost frantic with indecision when she finally made her selection. I remember she wore a wonderful creation of white satin embroidered with silver sequins, and about her neck and wrists and fingers blazed all the jewelry she had. She fussed over my own costume until I was almost exhausted.

"You must look your best, Marie!" she sputtered at me in anything but motherly tones. "We are going to meet the best people in Vienna society tonight, and that means the best people in any society anywhere!"

Her prediction was true enough. Vienna boasts no more popular figure than Franz Lehar. He is beloved of its people, and society has put him in a little niche all its own. Our little party was a target for opera glasses from every quarter of the audience, and we were swamped with visitors as soon as the house lights flared up after the first act. I cannot remember even their names—a confusion of "Herrs" and a sprinkling of titles—but Margaret did not miss one. She was busy cementing introductions into valuable alliances for her Vienna stay.

The opera was *Tosca*, and the star was Marie Jeritza—that same golden-voiced, golden-haired Jeritza who had captured New York on her first appearance last winter at the Metropolitan Opera House and who, back from the summer in her native country, was a greater idol than ever.

I will never forget the demonstration that swept the audience like a tidal wave as the curtain fell on the murdered Scarpia, the candles glowing at his head and feet. Jeritza was called before the curtain again and again. She was pelted with roses. Men and women were on their feet, crying "bravo" at the top of their voices. It thrilled me, for I could picture in my imagination the day when I, too, might be a great singer and inspire such scenes as this—if one's present troubles might be ended and I could again study the music I had learned to love.

"Oh, if I could only meet her!" I murmured to Franz Lehar.

"You shall, child." He smiled at me. "I will arrange a little dinner in your honor—and hers."

It is one of the great regrets of my girl's life that I never attended that dinner. The date was set, and M. Jeritza accepted. It was to take place on a Sunday night, two weeks from the night of *Tosca*. Then, at the last minute, I had to telephone my regrets. The dinner was held without me. At the hour that the guests sat down, I was in too much of a turn of mingled relief and bewilderment over Mrs. Paddleford's arrest to accept any invitations, let alone attend a formal dinner.

Her arrest did not come about until six weeks after we had arrived in Vienna. It was rendered on the complaint of merchants in London, Paris, Lucerne, Venice, and practically every city Mrs. Paddleford had touched in Europe. They had been seeking her from city to city. Her use of assumed names had thrown them off track. It was to this—and the vagaries that swung her from one goal to another—that she owed her Vienna breathing spell.

She made good use of it. I believe she actually hoped she had put them permanently off the track. Her contacts in Vienna were so pleasant that they inspired a feeling of self-confidence. She must have known detection was creeping closer and closer as long as she stayed there, but so assured was she of her knack to wriggle out of any scrape that she announced that she would settle down for a long stay. She even arranged for me to continue my music under a leading Viennese instructor.

One of the new friends she had made was Adolph Ungar, owner of one of the biggest and most expensive shops in Vienna. Believing she was the wife of a rich American, he had extended her almost unlimited credit, and Mrs. Paddleford had made the most of it. She bought three or four evening gowns at a time—each of a different shade, though the same model. There must have been between thirty and forty of these hanging in the closets of our suite, along with quantities of dainty lingerie, fur coats, and suits. Mr. Ungar was without suspicion that Mrs. Paddleford wasn't able to pay cash for the least of them.

I only wish I had been able to think as he did. But the extravagant purchases that so delighted Margaret's soul were a growing horror to me. I saw, duplicated among these people, who had been so courteous and gracious to us, the humiliation of our experiences in Paris and London. I could see this reckless buying ending only in another flight—or worse.

If I have described the night of *Tosca* and our other Viennese nights as gay, let not you, the reader, think that this period of our continental tour differed in any degree from the nightmare rest of it. For every swagger-shopping revelry of Margaret's, there was a storm of protest and anger in our rooms. For every sally into society in jewels and evening gowns, there was a sordid, bitter quarrel at home. Gloom was a thick as fog in our suite when Margaret was not there, for little Ben, Joe, and I could see the handwriting on the wall.

When Mrs. Paddleford, in Vienna, borrowed Joe's savings—$400— we all had a premonition that she couldn't keep up the pace much longer. Through all this desperate dragging of us from Paris to London, and from London to Brussels, and from Brussels all over southern and central Europe, we had maintained a sort of uncanny belief in Mrs. Paddleford's own frequent assertion that she was "too clever for any of them."

But I was having a mental transformation. For two weeks, I had not spoken to Margaret except in public and when she asked me a direct question I could not avoid answering. But I was doing some pretty straight thinking for a seventeen-year-old girl. I saw myself bound to this woman for life, forced to wink at her shady enterprises, finally driven—unless I took a stand of my own—into fraud as bad as she practiced. I saw little Ben growing up in this unhealthy, polluted atmosphere. Hitherto, I had been helpless to resist her. I was only a child. But now I was budding into womanhood. I owed it to myself, I owed it to this little boy, and I owed it to the sake of simple decency to rebel.

And so I rebelled. Suddenly I made up my mind to it on the afternoon, after my return from my music lesson when Margaret said to me, "Marie, if anyone asks for me, I'm not home. Do you hear? Anyone! I'm out—no matter what they want."

She expected trouble. Silently I made up my mind that, if trouble came, I would not help her to dodge it any longer. It was better to face whatever was to happen than to go on like this.

About four o'clock, there was a knock at the door. I answered it while Margaret hid behind a screen. Two strange men stood there with the hotel manager.

"Is your mother here?" the manager asked me.

"She's hiding behind there." I pointed to the screen. And right there was the beginning of the end of Mrs. Paddleford.

Little Ben and Joe were in the room. I stood alone by the door, trembling, aghast, yet glad at what I had done, fearing I didn't know what but aware that some disaster was about to happen, while the manager crossed the room and looked behind the screen. When Mrs. Paddleford confronted him, he bowed low before her amazed and outraged face. The manager spoke to me.

"Little girl," he said, "we must ask you to leave the room."

I didn't want to go, but he showed me instantly into Jack's room. There I crouched, listening to the sounds I could hear beyond the door— a low, steady murmur of men's voices; Margaret's angry protests; finally the slamming of trunks and a torrent of abuse from Margaret, punctuated with little shrieks of anger. Finally the door opened. I saw the two strange men standing before the open trunks in a room strewn with furs, gown, laces, lingerie—apparently half of Margaret's possessions. Margaret herself, white with rage and anxiety, was dressed for the street.

"I must go to police headquarters and clear up this outrage," she said in a strangled voice. "It's just the customs. They think I've smuggled something."

But it wasn't the customs. I suspected then, what I learned later, that Margaret's chickens had come home to roost. The police of Paris and London and Lucerne and Venice had caught up with her trail at last. At headquarters were a dozen telegrams asking that she be held. One of these, from London, resulted in a charge against her, additional to the swindling accusation.

It was nearly midnight when Margaret finally returned. Two guards were with her. They stationed themselves in the outer room while she retired to bed. Little Ben and I huddled in a corner, watching them, too dismayed to sleep.

"It's only the customs," was Margaret's good-night message to us. "It will all be arranged tomorrow."

But we didn't believe her. I shall tell, in my next installment, how truly our suspicions were justified in the events of the week that followed; how disaster piled on top of disaster until our Vienna visit, which opened so gloriously, appeared likely to end in a grand smash.

Chapter 11:

The Grand Tour—Rescued

Dear Reader,

On a midsummer morning, when a sense of freedom sparkled in every cloud and sun-streaked tree, I walked into the Vienna city prison to cut the last link in the chain of riches and wretchedness that for ten years had bound me to Mrs. Margaret Teal Paddleford. It was to be good-bye. I was going to America. I believed I would never see her again. Life for me, at seventeen, was starting over again.

As I write this now, seated in my new guardian's cozy New York apartment, it is hard for me to realize that only a few months have elapsed since I told Margaret, with a wave of pity at the last, that I was going home—and she answered me with a curse. It is hard for me to realize that Mrs. Paddleford, according to a letter I received from Dr. Paddleford this morning, is still in jail, and has been during all this time.

So much has happened to me since then—so much that is illuminating, encouraging, inspiring. I have learned the truth about my parentage. I know who my real mother was. I have discovered that there are other things in the world than society, schemes, money, blackmail, floggings, and selfishness. No thousand-dollar fur coat from Mrs. Paddleford ever gave me the thrill of a cheap little hat bought with money honestly earned by my own hand. In brief, I have found myself. The events of last July in Vienna are like something that happened in a previous incarnation.

And yet, looking back, I can see now, as I could not then, the extraordinary drama of that scene in the prison, when I waited in a stuffy little office, my faculties blunted by suffering, for the woman who shuffled through a grated door between two Austrian policemen. If that hour marked a beginning for me, it marked an ending for her.

I did not know Margaret Paddleford in that long-ago girlhood when she was little Eleanor McKinney, being courted in the days of hoop skirts and balloon sleeves and buggy rides. I did not know her when she married William Charles Toomey, rich secretary to a railroad king, or when he divorced her and she came to New York and won Ben Teal's heart in the apex of his glory and Broadway's czar producer.

But I have seen pictures of Eleanor McKinney and of Margie Teal, with her coal-black hair piled high in pompadour fashion, with her lips parted in that characteristic scornful smile, with dark blue eyes sparkling in the perfect oval of her face and ropes of pearls sparkling across the perfect sheen of her shoulders.

I was captivated by the beauty of her in the photographs, and the thought comes to me now of what an amazing career that beauty gave her; what a patchwork of triumphs and downfalls and marriages and millions and frauds she made out of her life; what a mean and sordid fate had claimed her at the end of her pyrotechnic path—arrested for petty swindling, accused of flimflamming shopkeepers, charged with shoplifting a few yards of lace!

Was she thinking, I wonder, as she brooded in the prison thousands of miles from Broadway, of the days when Ben Teal adored her? There was a man who had bankrupted his purse and broken his health to save her from just such a situation as this; now she could not find a friend to go her bail. Or did she remember Hollywood, the million-dollar Paddleford villa on Laurel Avenue, her society teas and musicales, her servants, her motors, her descent on New York, the Ritz, the Plaza, the shops of Fifth Avenue?

My own vicissitudes, strange though they were—an orphan skyrocketed from poverty to luxury and then dragged over half the world as a rebellious cat's paw in a maze of riches, cruelty, kindness, social intrigues, marriage plots, and divorce scandals—pale, after all, beside the drama that reached its last chapter that morning in the Vienna jail.

Margaret Paddleford's instinct must have told her that to submit to imprisonment in Vienna was to write "finis" to her fortunes, for it took three days of cajolery, argument, coaxing, and, finally, a threat to carry her on a stretcher to get her from hotel to prison.

I told in the last chapter of these confessions how, in our third week in Vienna, after a brilliant introduction to society as the American friends of the famous Franz Lehar, the police of Paris, London, Lucerne, and Vienna located Margaret Paddleford at the Grand Hotel.

I told how they accused her of swindling and how detectives descended on our suite, unceremoniously went through her baggage, confiscated the gorgeous furs and gowns and lingerie she had bought but not paid for in other European capitals, and added a shoplifting charge to the swindling count when a Lucerne saleswoman declared she had not sold Mrs. Paddleford the laces from her shop found among the other Paddleford possessions.

I told how Mrs. Paddleford, striving to keep these disastrous developments secret from me and from little Ben Teal, her son, disclosed to us that the investigation was only a matter of "the customs." How she returned from a conference with the police one night and retired, still insisting everything would be "all right," though two guards were stationed outside our rooms.

For three days she stayed in bed, pleading illness. The American consul, whom she sent for, made an inquiry and declared he could do nothing. The police were getting restive. They sent officer after officer to demand Mrs. Paddleford's arrest and arraignment. I was distracted by their bulldozing on one side and Mrs. Paddleford's moanings on the other. She had me send for a Vienna diamond broker with whom she had some dealings. She asked his advice. He told her to give herself up.

"What! Go to jail voluntarily?" shrieked Margaret.

"Do you want them to take you out on a stretcher?" asked the man. "That's what they say they will do. Do you want to be photographed that way? Do you want those pictures to be published in America?"

Margaret yielded. Throwing an old black frock over her lavender silk nightgown and covering this with an expensive silk mantle, she told me to order a taxicab. We walked with her downstairs, I on one side and our broker friend on the other, the guards trailing behind.

Mrs. Paddleford sat up straight and stiff, her face carved in hard lines, as we bumped through the broad streets. But I began to cry. Half hysterically, I offered to go to prison in her place. Margaret jumped at the suggestion, but the broker ridiculed it. "The police," he declared, "would never allow it."

My heart quivered with sorrow—for Margaret, for myself, for little Ben, for all of us and for the whole desperate situation—when the policemen hustled her through a huge, barred gate and I heard the iron clang behind her. The broker turned to me. All the way to the prison, he had been encouraging Margaret with the assurance that she would be released in a day or two. But now he said simply, "I think that is the last you will ever see of her, my dear!"

And it was—almost. I returned to the hotel. The manager knocked a few minutes later. He announced he must have our rooms. I was frantic at our helplessness—a seventeen-year-old girl, a little boy, and a bewildered valet with not a handful of kroner between them.

"Oh, can't you put us somewhere just for the night?" I begged.

The manager frowned. He was losing enough money, anyway. But it would have taken a Nero or a Caligula to have put our pathetic party on the streets. He consented to give us a small room in a remote wing of the hotel. There, in a space not much larger than a good-sized closet, the three of us huddled and cried through the night.

In the morning, we straggled to a little park near the hotel and took stock of our plight. We had no money. We were not sure we had any friends. We had no idea what to do. We had nothing. I went to the American consulate. Again, there was shrugging of shoulders and shaking of heads. All the consulate could do in the case of little Ben and me was to give us new passports. Joe was luckier. As a servant, he could secure his passage home, advanced by the American government. But Joe—the brick!—refused it. He said he would stick to us.

Hopeless, we wandered back toward the hotel. A man was outside, talking to the manager. He stared at us with an angry frown and pointed with an angry gesture. I recognized him. He was Adolph Ungar, the wealthy merchant at whose shop Mrs. Paddleford had bought thousands of dollars' worth of goods. I might say here, parentheses, that the Vienna charges of swindling against Mrs. Paddleford were later dropped when the goods were returned. But at that time, Mrs. Ungar was bitter.

We had met Mr. and Mrs. Ungar socially. Suddenly, I made a resolve. I turned to Ben and Joe. "I am going to see Mrs. Ungar," I said.

I did. I explained to her that we were stranded, penniless, with no choice except to starve to death—or worse. Behold—she kissed me!

Nothing I can write here will do justice to the gratitude I have for this motherly, understanding Austrian woman who came to our rescue in our darkest hour. She talked to her husband. She made him yield to her wishes. And for two weeks, we were guests in her home. It was a golden deed of kindness.

Through the Ungars, we were placed in touch with Franz Lehar. For a second time, I learned just what generosity and goodness there is in the world. Mr. Lehar declared his belief in Margaret's innocence. He still thought all her stories of her American millions were true. I could not let him help us under that delusion. I told him the truth. I told him we were all imposters. I asked him to go away and forget us.

And Franz Lehar—bless him!—sent us to his country estate for as long as we wished to stay and advanced us $1,000, a fortune in Austria, so that Mrs. Paddleford might have some comforts in prison. And, as a crowning touch, gave me the money with which to go back to America.

"You are young, Cynthia," he told me. "You can make your life what you want it to be. I am not rich enough to send you all home, but with your voice you can make enough money to send for them. You have talent. You have training. You will be a star someday."

Then and there, I resolved that Franz Lehar's faith in me should be justified. I have resumed my music. I am studying hard. Before many more days, I hope, as he predicted, that my voice will bring little Ben and Joe back home again.

Before I left Vienna, I went to see Margaret Paddleford. I could not go without telling her good-bye. Though she had beaten me, though she had been cruel, though she had all but wrecked my girlhood with an ill-starred marriage, though I could lay at her door all of our misfortunes and miseries, I no longer hated her. For the sake of simple humanity, I could not pass out of her life without one word of comfort.

For a month, I had not seen her. Yet that was not a long time. On the day she left the hotel, harassed and ill though she was, she still kept her appearance. If she was not as beautiful as Margie Teal and Eleanor McKinney, she was still a very handsome woman.

Nothing had prepared me for the creature that shuffled out of the dark corridor into the sunlit office. Gone were her fine clothes and jewels. She was dressed in a rough prison smock. Gone were paint and powder and a marcelled coiffure. Her black hair was slicked straight back from her face and tied in an ugly knot atop her head. And her face! Lined, sunken, yellow—she seemed to have aged twenty years!

"Margaret!" I cried, and stopped, engulfed in a wave of blinding pity.

"Well?" she demanded, and the dark eyes suddenly smoldered. "So you have come to see me at last?"

"Yes," I answered. "I am going away. I am going back to America. Mr. Lehar has advanced the money. It was Mr. Lehar who gave the money to make you comfortable here. He has been wonderful!"

Of a sudden, Mrs. Paddleford's face twisted with rage. She lifted one arm and shook her fist at me.

"Ingrate! Puppy! Guttersnipe!" she shrieked. "You are going to leave me! You are going to desert me—after all I have done for you! You ..."

She broke into a stream of curses. She scrambled from her chair. One of the guards sprang forward and seized her as she seemed about to attack me. Mrs. Paddleford sank back. I was overcome with varied emotions. I began to cry. I sobbed to her. There was nothing else to do.

Then the guard made a gesture. The interview was terminated. I stood staring at an empty chair where a minute before had been the poor woman who once had known unlimited luxury and now faced indefinite imprisonment in an alien country.

A week later, I was on the ocean, America bound.

If there are any of my readers disposed to criticize me for leaving Mrs. Paddleford in that situation, I think they will change their minds on reviewing the facts. Without even considering the torture my life had been with her, let them remember that it would have availed her nothing for me to stay in Vienna. And any duty I owed, I felt I owed it first to little Ben Teal. In Austria I could be nothing but an object of charity; in America I might win success and earn the money to bring Ben back home. And I owed a duty to myself. As Mrs. Paddleford's companion, I was assured a future that led straight to destruction. So I believed. As Cynthia Teal, "on her own," I could work out my own salvation. And that, after all, is what all of us must do in the end.

Will Mrs. Paddleford ever make a "comeback"? Will she refute or settle the charges against her in Europe and return, as she says she will, to fight Dr. Paddleford's divorce suit and wrest riches from the world again? I do not know. I can only present what evidence I have:

First, a cablegram from a Lucerne correspondent to a New York inquirer, bearing an October date: "Mrs. Paddleford, after weeks in prison here, has been transferred to the hospital. Her condition is not serious, but her illness probably will be prolonged. The swindling charge against her will be taken up after her recovery. Sums involved in Lucerne are said to amount to nearly $7,000, partly covered by returned goods. Charges in Vienna have been dropped."

Second, a letter from Dr. Paddleford to my present guardian stating that he has sent Mrs. Paddleford a copy of his divorce petition, that he has written the American consul what facts he knows about Mrs. Paddleford, and that he has refused her attorney's suggestion that he, Dr. Paddleford, furnish her passage home to the United States in the event her troubles are settled.

Third, I quote from a letter Mrs. Paddleford wrote to a friend in New York: "I will come back and have a great deal more than I ever had. I will come back and marry again with money. Two weeks ago I did not expect to live. I have had two bad spells that nearly took me on the long journey from which there is no return. But, remember, I am coming back!"

Will she? It rests with fate.

Chapter 12:

Hope in New York, 1922

Dear Reader,

Two weeks before my eighteenth birthday, I walked down the gang-plank of a transatlantic liner into New York City with exactly $32 in my purse, no clothing except the barest skimmings of a wardrobe once worth thousands, my only possession a battered trunk stacked with letters and unpaid bills of Mrs. Margaret Teal Paddleford, and the single idea ruling me that somewhere, somehow, I must make not only my own living in the world but a success of my life.

How well equipped I was to begin this battle, I will leave to the reader's judgment by confessing that, in my anxiety to be economical, I picked an uptown hotel famous, I have since learned, for catering mostly to millionaire patrons. I went there simply because I had heard it was more economical than the Plaza or the Ritz. I should have sought a room in a $10-a-week boardinghouse, but I am quite honest when I say I did not think respectable people lived in boardinghouses. I know better now.

"Eight dollars a day," said the clerk, when I asked him for the cheapest room. He didn't startle me: I was too unworldly to be startled. I took the room gratefully because, though my entire girlhood was spent in worldly atmospheres, I was so coddled and sheltered from humdrum, workaday folk that I actually didn't know there were hotels with $4-a-day rooms!

That was part of my heritage from Mrs. Paddleford—ignorance of life. I inventoried the rest of my inheritance that night when, in my "cheap" little room, I delved into the contents of my trunk. First, however,

I sat down in a chair facing the window that looked out over the gleaming lights of Manhattan and inventoried myself.

I was free. Back there in Vienna, three thousand miles away, I had left the only person I feared on Earth. My life as Mrs. Paddleford's adopted daughter was over—never, I vowed, to be taken up again.

It was just ten years before that she took me from an orphan asylum. In those years, I had been lifted into luxury and taught to live like a hothouse flower one moment and a girl Oliver Twist the next. I was, first, the despised playmate of a little boy; second, the helpless victim of a woman's rages; third, the tongue-tied witness of her trick to marry a rich husband; fourth, the protesting beauty bait of her scheme to gouge money out of millionaire society; and, last, the bewildered and rebellious companion of her final flight through Europe.

Ten years! And how had they benefited me? I emerged from them at seventeen with a smattering of French, music, china painting, and other "light arts," and not even a grammar school education; with a cultured voice and not the faintest idea of how to capitalize it; with a taste for champagne and caviar and not even an applesauce income; with a list of acquaintances that included millionaires, society leaders, Broadway "rounders," underworld crooks, and stage and opera stars—and with not a friend in the world!

And yet I was free. I was responsible to no one but myself. I had but one obligation to fill. If, back there in Vienna, I left one person I feared, I also left there the one person I loved. If my life as Mrs. Paddleford's daughter was over, my life as sister to her son was not. Little Ben Teal Jr. had no one to look to but me for his next meal. In some way, I must wrest from this New York I thought I knew so well, and now dreaded, the wherewithal to keep him from hunger and hardship and finally bring him back to his own country. It was distinctly "up to me" to make good!

A job was imperative. I believed my voice would get me one, or my playing. But how did one go after positions as a singer or a pianist? I hadn't the remotest notion. In my predicament, I turned to the trunk. It contained, I knew, Mrs. Paddleford's list of addresses and telephone numbers of people she knew in New York. Among them I hoped to find one or more who would help me.

Never will I forget the shock to my optimism an hour's browsing through the trunk gave me. I opened envelope after envelope—nothing but bills, duns, snubs, and threats of lawsuits. I read figures until I was sick. And out of the pile of paper popped bills and yet more bills. Was there anyone whose trust she had not violated?

I had made a little list of names as I went along. Suddenly I stopped. Each name on that list represented, if not someone from whom she had borrowed money or whom she had angered with her use of their letters of introduction, then someone who would know of her debts and her imprisonment abroad.

The futility of what I was doing overwhelmed me. I knew with fatal assurance, sitting there in that heap of fraud, that I was chasing a will-o'-the-wisp when I thought of any goodwill from any of these ex-friends.

I was about to burst into tears, when my eye, wandering over a sheaf of papers, stopped at a name. It was signed to a telegram addressed to Mrs. Paddleford at Los Angeles, informing her that one of her New York creditors was willing to settle for a certain amount. The name was that of a representative of a large collection agency. The owner of the name was as familiar to me as the name itself. For three years, he had pursued Mrs. Paddleford with letters and in person from coast to coast. During our stay at the Plaza and the Ritz, he called at least twice a week. To us children, Ben and me, he had always been kind. We had told him our troubles. He had sympathized with us. This obscure collector, with efforts to make Mrs. Paddleford pay up, was almost like "one of the family."

My heart warmed when I thought of him now, as it did not at the memory of any other faces. He, as no other, I told myself, would know the truth of my story. He would know I was never Mrs. Paddleford's accomplice but always her victim. And, knowing that, he would help me, though everybody else was suspicious.

So it came about that I, Cynthia Teal, with a room at a swagger hotel and the acquaintance of millionaires and blue bookers, got my only "lift" when I was in trouble from a bill collector who had dogged my foster mother's trail for years.

Oh, I tried some of the others first. Those who would even speak to me on the telephone were so frosty that words stuck in my throat. Would they call? Really, they were so busy now! Then mightn't I come by to see them about something very important? They were "so sorry, but they didn't know when they could give me an appointment"!

And that was that. It was the bill collector who, when I got him on the wire next day, came promptly to the hotel, and—walking up and down Park Avenue with me, and listening to my woeful account of Europe and my present, desperate plight and my need for a job of some kind, no matter how humble—it was this man who laid his hand on my shoulder and said, "Poor kid! You've had a tough time. I'll speak to my wife tonight and see if we can't find room for you at home. You'll break yourself in a week where you're stopping now. And, in the meantime, I'll see what I can do about a job. I think I know a place I can get you on as a telephone operator."

Telephone operator! Zip went my dreams of Broadway stardom, of opera, of fame! To live at the most expensive hotel in New York and look for a job as a telephone operator! It was incongruous; it was humiliating. But— it was a job. If he could get me that, or anything, I would take it, I told him.

Back in my room at the hotel, I had a reaction. What wages would a telephone operator get? Fifty dollars a week, or a hundred? I didn't know, but I had a sickening intuition that it would be less than either of these sums. I was beginning to learn. One day alone in New York had disillusioned me more than ten years with Mrs. Paddleford. I shook my head. As a telephone operator, I couldn't earn enough to support myself, let alone support little Ben and bring him home again.

I decided to try Mrs. Paddleford's private telephone directory again. The disheartening experience of the previous night repeated itself. But at last I struck a cordial answer. The woman had been one of my foster mother's closest friends. I had been taught to call her Auntie. And the warmth of her greeting was fairly thrilling after so many rebuffs.

Over the telephone, I bubbled out an outline of my story. When she learned that Margaret was in prison in Europe and I was practically stranded in New York, she told me she would call that afternoon.

I will touch as briefly as I can on the sinister experience that followed.

Auntie called. She asked me questions, she learned I was accountable to no one; she invited me to come and stay with her. She ended with a hint that she had many rich friends she wanted me to meet.

When she left, overjoyed that I wasn't going to be a telephone operator but could live with Auntie until I found something better to do, I rushed out to walk exuberantly along Madison Avenue. And there chance intervened to save me from . . . well, I don't like to think what.

I met my friend the bill collector. I told him my good news. For a moment, he stared at me in amazement. Then he repeated sharply the name I had spoken: Auntie.

"Don't you know," he demanded, "that that woman is not a respectable woman and her place is one of the most notorious in New York?"

Chill revelation—horror—swept over me. I saw it all—her questions about my clothes and my age and my marriage. She wanted to establish that I was a responsible, married woman. Auntie, whom I had thought so kind, wanted me only for one unspeakable purpose.

Thirty minutes later, in my $8 room, I huddled on the bed, sobbing my heart out. The bill collector had told me telephone girls' jobs were scarce. I couldn't go to Auntie's; that was unthinkable! For a moment, there swirled before me only one solution: suicide. Why not kill myself then and there and get it all over with? I had neither pistol nor poison, but I was a guest in one of the tallest buildings in New York. In two minutes, I could be on the roof. I saw myself trembling on the brink of that steel-and-concrete precipice, with the city below me a maze of rooftops and twinkling lights. One step, and I could plunge out of my misery into dark forgetfulness! I rose from my chair, giddy with a great temptation.

At that moment, the telephone rang. I answered it dully—to learn that Miss Blank was calling. I shall not give the name of this woman. I can say only that she had been particularly kind to my foster mother before we sailed to Europe. It was she who gave us letters of introduction to Lord Northcliffe, to the French woman surgeon, to other prominent people. I knew she must have heard of her violated trust, but I felt that if I could only tell her my story face-to-face, she would help me. I had telephoned her the night before, but she was out. I had left a message that I would like to see her. I knew little about her, save that she was young—not many years older than I—and worked for a living, and was as quick to understand as she was loyal. I told the office to show her up at once.

When I shook hands, I noticed restraint in her manner, but when she had seated herself and listened for fifteen minutes to my confession of suffering and heartache, her steady gaze softened. I ended with my last and most bitter disillusion and a desperate admission that there seemed nothing left for me but to put myself out of the way. She leaned forward, fixing me with an earnest gaze.

"Listen, my dear," she said. "I am eight years older than you and I have learned a lot in those eight years. One thing is never to give up the ship. Let me tell you something. It wasn't so very long ago that I, too, was broke and jobless and, I thought, without a friend in the world. I, too, was living in a swagger hotel then, though I didn't have the money to buy my next meal. I reached the same black, desperate decision you have reached. Only I went a step farther—I actually tried to finish it. It almost finished me, but not quite. And then, when I was getting well and still as blue and bitter as ever, a man came to me. He wasn't one of the fine friends I used to know who had turned me down—to the last one of them—when I most needed a little word of help. He was a total stranger. But he gave me a chance—to work and to make good. I took it and I made good. Why did he give it to me? That's beside the mark. Perhaps he was down and out once, and somebody gave him a chance. He was paying his debt to fate that way. I've never paid mine. But I'm going to pay it now. I'm going to give you your chance. Will you take it?"

There is not much for me to add to this story, except that I am taking my chance—the one a woman I had no claim on Earth upon was willing to give me, because she, too, knew what it meant to grope in darkness with none to flash a kindly light or say, "Here is the way."

She has given me a home, enough money to send a small allowance regularly to little Ben, and the opportunity to develop my voice and "find myself." She has become my guardian; I am legally, as well as morally, bound no longer to Mrs. Margaret Teal Paddleford. For the first time in my life, I think, I am happy.

It would be idle for me to write words of gratitude here to this woman. My money debt to her, I shall pay. The greater debt I owe—my chance—I cannot pay in coin. But someday, perhaps, when I have made good, when I am successful, when I have faced life and bested it honestly and squarely, there may come to me a girl, penniless, lonely, desperate, without, she thinks, a friend on Earth.

And will I give her a chance? I'll say I will!

Aunt Eleanor's Genealogy

James and Clara McKinney: Albert McKinney's parents; Eleanor's paternal grandparents.

Albert McKinney or McKinnie: Eleanor's father; husband of Ida Gilman.
Genevieve Hastings: Eleanor's unwed mother in Ohio.
Ida Gilman McKinnie: wife of Albert McKinnie in Portland, Oregon.

Gilman McKinnie: Albert's son by Ida Gilman; Eleanor's half brother.
Florence McKinnie Elsner: wife of Gilman in Chinook, Montana.

Kenneth, Evelyn, Laura, and Ben McKinnie: children of Gilman andFlorence McKinnie in Chinook, Montana.

Author: son of Laura McKinnie Palm; grandson of Gilman McKinnie; grandnephew of Eleanor.

Laura McKinnie: Albert's daughter by Ida Gilman; sister of Gilman; half sister of Eleanor (died, age seven, in Portland, Oregon).

Rudolph McKinney: Albert's brother in Ohio.
Clara McKinney: Albert's sister in Ohio.

James Madison Gilman and Laura Frances Graves of Portland: Ida Gilman's parents; grandparents of Gilman McKinnie and Laura McKinnie.

Aunt Eleanor McKinney: aka Christina McIntire, Eleanor McKinnie Gilman Toomey, Margaret Busby, Margaret "Maggie" Teal, Genevieve Thompson, Genevieve Paddleford, Mrs. Grace Potter, Mrs. Lois Millicent Wilson, Mrs. Heath Wilson Roberts, Mrs. John Fawcett, Millicent Paddleford Fawcett, and Helen Fawcett Thompson (name on death certificate).

William Charles Toomey: Eleanor's first husband.

Ben Teal: Eleanor's second husband.
    Ben Teal Jr.: Eleanor's son by Ben Teal; later known as Jack Paddleford.
    Cynthia Marie Teal: adopted daughter of Aunt Eleanor and Ben Teal.

George Edgar Paddleford: Aunt Eleanor's third husband.

John Chauncey Fawcett: Aunt Eleanor's fourth husband.

J. R. Hall Thompson: Aunt Eleanor's fifth husband (undocumented).

Notes and Sources

S ome sources are listed as Background Sources. These unnumbered sources reference and corroborate the background narration.

BOOK ONE
Chapter 1

1. "Mr. A. McKinnie," Business Notices, *Morning Oregonian*, July 22, 1980.

2. "Wedding Bells," *Daily Oregonian*, June 27, 1882.

3. "Hastings," Schedule 5—Persons who Died during the Year Ending May 31, 1980, Madison Township, Fayette County, Ohio. P.1, Supervisors Dist. No. 5, Enumeration Dist. No. 56.

4. Piecing together the movements of the McKinney family in Ohio rides on census and directory documents cited by Ancestry.com. These documents are enumerated as follows:

   James F. McKinney: Connecticut Town Marriage Records, pre-1870 (Barbour Collection); US Federal Census, 1860, 1870, 1880.

   Rudolph McKinney: Cook County Marriage Index, 1855.

   Albert McKinney: United States Federal Census, 1870; US City Directories, 1872, 1876, 1877, 1778.

   Eleanor McKinney: Massachusetts Marriage Records, 1840–1915, as per Ben Teal; US City Directories for Portland, 1886–91.

   Genevieve Hastings: US Census Mortality Schedules, 1880–85.

5. How did Eleanor arrive in Portland?

Before 1883, travel to Portland from the East would have employed both river steamship and passenger trains.

The Northern Pacific completed its isolated Pacific Division traversing Washington Territory between Puget Sound at New Tacoma and the Columbia River at Kalama. Scheduled service began on January 5, 1874, and included runs between Portland and Kalama, provided by steamboats on the Willamette and Columbia Rivers.

Portland was linked to the national railroad network when Northern Pacific (NP) complete the nation's third transcontinental route by using the line of the Oregon Railway & Navigation Co. (OR&N). The first transcontinental train arrived in Portland on September 11, 1883. Tacoma, Washington, was the NP's official western terminus, but Portland was the largest and most important city in the Pacific Northwest and remained so for the rest of the nineteenth century. The OR&N and NP began operating a joint passenger train between Portland and St. Paul, the eastbound *Atlantic Express* and the westbound *Pacific Express*; the transfer between the two roads took place at Wallula Junction, Washington (http://www.sps700.org/gallery/essays/portlandrailroadhistory.shtml).

6. "Gilman, (Capt.) James M.," "Early Oregon Wills, 5, Multnomah Co., Oregon," July 27, 1891.

7. "Married in St. Mary's," *St. Paul Globe*, Thursday, April 20, 1899.

Chapter 2

1. "Death of Captain Gilman," *Oregonian*, July 13, 1891.

"Captain James M. Gilman," *History of the Pacific Northwest, Volume I* (Portland, OR: North Pacific History Co., 1889).

Hines, Rev. H. K., "James M. Gilman," in *An Illustrated History of the State of Oregon* (Chicago: Lewis Publishing Company, 1893).

2. "Early Oregon Wills."

3. "Death of Mrs. McKinnie," *Oregonian*, December 3, 1893.

4. "Died Destitute Though Rich," *San Francisco Call*, November 21, 1896.

5. "Death of W. W. Spaulding," *Morning Oregonian*, October 19, 1904.

Chapter 3

1. Heffern, Horace, "The Jade of Diamonds," *International Detective Cases* (listed on cover as *True Crime Cases* and *Actual World-Wide Mysteries*) (UK: William Cecil Merrett Limited, 1941), p. 64.

2. "Married in St. Mary's," *St. Paul Globe*, April 20, 1899.
   "William Charles Toomey to Eleanor McKinnie Gilman," certified copy of marriage record, Marriage License Book No. 23, District Court, Second Judicial District, Ramsey County, Minnesota, April 19, 1899, p. 154.

3. "James J. Hill Letters," in the *James J. Hill Papers* (St. Paul, MN: James J. Hill Reference Library). (Note: Copies from William Toomey file: one letter from James J. Hill to Mr. R. Joyce, National Surety Company, New York, NY, October 2, 1906; one letter from William Toomey to Mr. Hill, March 11, 1907.)

4. "J. J. Toomey, Former Hill Secretary, Dies," *St. Paul Dispatch*, January 28, 1942.

5. "William Charles Toomey, Plaintiff, vs. Eleanor McKinnie Toomey, Defendant," transcript of divorce decree, District Court, Second Judicial District, Ramsey County, Minnesota, #90024, September 30, 1904.

6. "Mrs. Toomey Loses," *Minneapolis Journal*, June 28, 1905.

7. Heffern, "The Jade of Diamonds."

8. Laudon, Robert Tallant, "Gertrude Sans-Souci (1873–1913) and Her
9. Ibid.

10. "William C. Toomey," banner ad, *Chicago Daily Tribune*, November 2, 1915.
    "4 Stock Aides Held in $9,000,000 Fraud," *New York Times*, July 18, 1936.
    "52 Indicted Here in $4,5000,000 Fraud," *New York Times*, November 8, 1935.
    "Garland and Twelve Associates Found Guilty," *New York Times*, March 19, 1937.

Portland Background Sources:
"History of Portland, Oregon,"
Wikipedia,https://en.wikipedia.org/wiki/history_Portland_Oregon

"Portland History," PdxHistory.com
Finn, J. D. John, *Wicked Portland, The Wild and Lusty Underworld of a Frontier Seaport Town*, History Press, Charleston, SC 29403, 2012.

James J. Hill Background Sources:
Malone, Michael P., *James J. Hill, Empire Builder of the Northwest* (Norman, OK: University of Oklahoma Press, 1996).

Dr. Bettingen Background Sources:
"Mrs. Toomey Is Growing Younger," *Minneapolis Journal*, June 23, 1905.
"Only Four Witnesses," *Minneapolis Journal*, June 24, 1995.
"Her Life Story," *Duluth Evening Herold*, June 24, 1905.
"Mrs. Toomey Blushes," *Minneapolis Journal*, June 26, 1905.
"Wanted Woes Published," *Minneapolis Journal*, June 27, 1905.

Chapter 4
1. Anthony Bianco, *The Ghosts of 42nd Street* (New York: Harper Perennial, 2004), p. 18.
2. Ibid., p. 50
3. Ibid., p. 42
4. Bates, W. M., "Ben Teal," clipping from *New York Dramatic News*, Billy Rose Theater Collection, Lincoln Center, NY. (Note: "The *New York Dramatic News* was one of the numerous theatrical papers that sprang up in New York City during the last few decades of the nineteenth century. Although it never attained the status of the New York Clipper, or the Dramatic Mirror, it is useful for research in popular entertainment."—Pratt, Judith, in "The Publishing History of the New York Dramatic News and Dramatic Times, *Theatre Survey* 23, no. 2 (2010): pp. 240–43.)
5. Ibid.
6. "Mrs. Ben Teal Is Gracious Hostess," *Minneapolis Tribune*, February 3, 1907.
7. Shelton, Lewis E., "Mr. Ben Teal: America's Abusive Director," in *Ideas of the Theatre* (Washington, DC: Academica Press, 2005), p. 37.
8. Henderson, Mary C., *Theater in America* (New York: Harry N Abrams, 1991).

9. Shelton, *Ideas of the Theatre*, p. 23.

10. O'Brien, Mique, "Ben Teal Who Must Be Obeyed," *Sunday Telegraph*, November 1, 1903.

11. Clipping, May 20, 1910, Billy Rose Theater Collection.

Background Sources

"Although frequently seen . . . ," clipping in *New York Star*, February 10, 1915, Billy Rose Theater Collection.

Shelton, Lewis E., "The Terrible Mr. Ben Teal and the Shubert Brothers," in *The Passing Show* 15, no. 1 (spring 1992).

"Bigger Is Better," in *The Cambridge History of American Theatre, Vol. 2: 1870–1945* (Cambridge, UK: Cambridge University Press, 1999).

Wilmeth, Don E., and Miller, Tice L., "Ben Teal," in *The Cambridge Guide to American Theatre* (Cambridge, UK: Cambridge University Press, 1996).

Grau, Robert, "Ben Teal," in *The Business Man in the Amusement World* (New York: Broadway Publishing Co., 1910).

Chapter 5

1. "Mrs. Teal's Trial for Perjury Begins," *New York Times*, February 24, 1909.

2. Ibid.

3. "Gould Prisoners Held in $5,000 Bail," *New York Times*, February 22, 1908.

4. Ibid.

5. "Gould Plot Witness Confesses Her Part," *New York Times*, July 26, 1908.

Background Sources

"Three Arrests in Gould Plot," *Los Angeles Times*, July 22, 1908.

"Ben Teal Says There Is a Plot," *Los Angeles Times*, July 23, 1908

"Find New Witness in the Gould Plot," *New York Times*, July 23, 1908.

"Frank Gould to Testify," *New York Times*, July 24, 1908.

"Gould Is Witness," *Los Angeles Times*, July 25, 1908.

"Girl a Cool Witness in the Gould Hearing," *New York Times*, July 25, 1908.

"Gould Plot Witness Confesses Her Part," *New York Times*, July 26, 1908.

"Further Confessions in Gould Conspiracy," *Los Angeles Times*, July 28, 1908.

"Frank Gould Admits He Knows Actress," *New York Times*, July 29, 1908.

"Skeleton Is Barred," *Los Angeles Times*, July 29, 1908.

"Gould Perjury Charge Holds," *Los Angeles Times*, August 14, 1908.

"Gould Witness Accused," *Los Angeles Times*, February 24, 1909.

"Lock Up Mrs. Teal's Jury for the Night," *The New York Times*, February 26, 1909.

"Gould Paid for Bessie's Flat," *Los Angeles Times*, February 26, 1909.

"Mrs. Teal Sentenced to a Year In Jail," *New York Times*, February 27, 1909.

"Mrs. Teal, Doomed to Prison," *Trenton Evening News*, February 27, 1909.

"All Mother-in-Law, Says Frank Gould," *New York Times*, May 11, 1907.

"Frank Gould Will Not Talk," *New York Times*, March 10, 1910.

"Divorced Wife Sues Frank Gould," *New York Times*, April 24, 1920.

Columbia, David Patrick, "Upon Visiting Lyndhurst," *New York Social Diary*, www.newyorksocialdiary.com/socialdiary/2005.

Lagumina, Salvatore J., "At the Creation of the Century," in *New York At Mid-Century: The Impellitteri Years* (Westport, CT: Praeger, 1992), p. 1.

Micheletti, Ellen, "All About Romance," in *The Gilded Age*, www.likes-books.com/gildedage.html.

"Frank Jay Gould," *Wikipedia*, https://en.wikipedia.org/wiki/Frank_Jay_Gould.

"Jay Gould," *Wikipedia*, https://en.wikipedia.org/wiki/Jay_Gould.

Chapter 6

1. "Lock Up Mrs. Teal's Jury for the Night," *New York Times*, February 26, 1909.

2. Ibid.

3. "Mrs. Teal Sentenced to a Year in Jail," *New York Times*, February 27, 1909.

4. "Blackwell Island a Prison Terrible," *New York Times*, March 27, 1914.

Background Sources

"Gould Prisoners Held in $5,000 Bail," *New York Times*, February 22, 1908.

"Three Arrests in Gould Plot," *Los Angeles Times*, July 22, 1908.

"Ben Teal Says There Is a Plot," *Los Angeles Times*, July 23, 1908.

"Find New Witness in the Gould Plot," *New York Times*, July 23, 1908.

"Frank Gould to Testify," *New York Times*, July 24, 1908.

"Girl a Cool Witness in the Gould Hearing," *New York Times*, July 25, 1908.

"Gould Is Witness," *Los Angeles Times*, July 25, 1908.

"Gould Plot Witness Confesses Her Part," *New York Times*, July 26, 1908.

"Further Confessions In Gould Conspiracy," *Los Angeles Times*, July 28, 1908.

"Frank Gould Admits He Knows Actress," *New York Times*, July 29, 1908.

"Skeleton Is Barred," *Los Angeles Times*, July 29, 1908.

"Gould Witness Accused," *Los Angeles Times*, February 24, 1909.

"Mrs. Teal's Trial for Perjury Begins," *New York Times*, February 24, 1909.

"Lock Up Mrs. Teal's Jury for the Night," *New York Times*, February 26,1909.

"Gould Paid For Bessie's Flat," *Los Angeles Times*, February 26, 1909.

"Year in Prison for Mrs. Teal," *San Francisco Chronicle*, February 27, 1909.

"Mrs. Teal, Doomed to Prison" *Trenton Evening News*, February 27, 1909.

"Frank Gould Will Not Talk," *New York Times*, March 10, 1910.

"Divorced Wife Sues Frank Gould," *New York Times*, April 24, 1920.

"Better Prisons For City Urged," *New York Times*, September 6, 1914.

"Blackwell's Island Name," *New York Times*, May 1, 1921.

"Topics: A Backward Glance at Welfare Island," *New York Times*, June 11, 1966.

"Welfare Island Little More Than a Name," *New York Times,* February 11, 1934.

Edward Marshall, "New York's First Prison," *New York Times*, January 1914.

"The Tombs," *Wikipedia*, https://en.wikipedia.org/wiki/The_Tombs.

"A Tale of the Tombs," *Correction History*, http://www.correctionhistory.org/html/chronicl/nycdoc/html/histry3a.html

"Blackwell's Island Part 1," *Correction History*, http://www.correction-history.org/html/chronicl/nycdoc/html/blakwel1.html.

"Frank Jay Gould," *Wikipedia*, https://en.wikipedia.org/wiki/Frank_Jay_Gould.

Chapter 7

1. Charles Samuels, "Queen of the Gold Diggers," *True* magazine, November 1939.

2. Shelton, *Ideas of the Theatre*.

    "Ben Teal and the Authoritarian Perspective of Directing," *Toledo Blade*, May 8, 1915.

3. "Mrs. Ben Teal Is Gracious Hostess," *Minneapolis Tribune*, January 3, 1907.

4. "A History of the Ansonia," 2008, http://www.ansoniarealty.com/history.

5. "Once Jailed Here," *New York Times,* June 11, 1922.

6. "Gossip," *New York Star,* December 21, 1910.

7. "Gossip," *New York Star,* February 10, 1915.

8. "How Society's Reformed Girl Thief Went Back to Her Past," *Indianapolis Star,* December 19, 1926.

9. Ibid.

10. "Stock Company Planned for Dainty Musical Comedies," *New York Times,* July 18, 1915.

Background Sources

"Gould Prisoners Held in $5,000 Bail," *New York Times,* July 22, 1908.

"Find New Witness in the Gould Plot," *New York Times,* July 23, 1908.

"Stock Company Planned for Dainty Musical Comedies," *New York Times,* July 18, 1915.

"Who Owes, Miss Munro or Mrs. Carter-Payne?" *New York Times,* August 23, 1906.

"'Iole' has Wit, Color, Charm, and Vivacity," *New York Times,* December 30, 1913.

"Matinee Trials New Authors," *New York Times,* September 16, 1915.

"Gossip," *New York Star,* January 22, 1907.

"Gossip," *New York Star,* May 18, 1910.

"Gossip," *New York Star,* October 28, 1906.

Shelton, Lewis E., *The Passing Show.*

Shelton, Lewis E., "Mr. Ben Teal, America's Abusive Director," *Journal of American Drama and Theatre* 2 (spring 1990): pp. 55–79.

Chapter 8

1. "Ben Teal Bankrupt," *New York Sun,* April 7, 1909.

2. "Wealthy Man's Bride Is Exposed," *Chicago Herald and Examiner,* January 17, 1932.

3. "Mourn for Montgomery," *New York Times,* April 24, 1917.

Background Sources

"Stage Celebrities Die on Same Day," *New York Times*, April 21, 1917.

"Ben Teal Sues Waiter," *Washington Post*, March 28, 1917.

"Cynthia's Slippery Mama Was Finally Caught," *Denver Post*, January 15, 1928.

"Ben Teal Sues a Head Waiter," *New York Times*, March 27, 1917.

"Mrs. Paddleford Once Jailed Here," *New York Times*, June 11, 1922.

Obituary, *Variety*, April 27, 1917.

Shelton, *Ideas of the Theatre*.

Chapter 9

1. Heffern, "The Jade of Diamonds," p. 55.
2. "Boiler Avenue, Spindle Top, 1903," Paleontological Research Institute, Ithaca, NY.
3. "Sunshine Special," *Union Pacific*, http://www.up.com/cs/groups/public/documents/up_pdf_nativedocs/omhq17a129812002902.pdf.

Background Sources

"Sunshine Special," *Wikipedia*, http://en.wikipedia.org/wiki/Sunshine_Special.

"Dining Cars," *Wikipedia*, http://en.wikipedia.org/wiki/Dining_car.

"The Hurricane of 1900," *Wikipedia*, http://en.wikipedia.org/wiki/Hurricane_of_1900.

Chapter 10

Background Sources

"Hotel Galvez," *Wikipedia*, http://en.wikipedia.org/wiki/Hotel_Galvez.

"Hotel Galvez," *Historic Hotels*, http://www.historichotels.org/hotels-resorts/hotel-galvez-and-spa-a-wyndham-hotel/?uri=hotel-g alvez-a-wyndham-historic-hotel/.

"How Pretty Cynthia's Slippery Mama Was Finally Caught," *Zanesville Signal*.

Cynthia Teal, *Amazing Confessions of Fascinating Cynthia Teal*, *Indianapolis Star*, October 15, 1922.

Chapter 11
Background Sources

"A Happy Day for Little Children," *New York Times*, October 12, 1894.

"Cardinal Recalls State Aid of 1870," *New York Times*, October 14, 1949.

"In The Foundling Asylum," *New York Times*, March, 1878.

"New Foundling Home," *New York Times*, October 4, 1889.

"Waif's Name and Church Chosen by Fixed System," *New York Times*, March 8, 1925.

Chapter 12

1. Swope, Kevin, *Descendants of Benjamin Almon Paddleford Family Tree*, 1835–1961.
2. "Medicos Banqueted," *Los Angeles Times*, June 15, 1904.
3. "Stetson-Paddleford," Events in Society, *Los Angeles Times*, August 3, 1904.
4. "San Luis Potosi," *Wikipedia*, http://en.wikipedia.org/wiki/San_Luis_Potos%C3%ADhttp://www.archive.org/stream/cu31924004686022#page/n0/mode/2.
5. Mexican Petroleum Company of Delaware, *MexPet Record* 1, no.1 (May 1916): p. 5.
6. Archer, W. J., *Mexican Petroleum* (New York: Pan American Petroleum & Transport Co., 1922), p. 50.
7. Miller, Robert Ryal, *Mexico: A History* (Norman, OK: University of Oklahoma Press, 1985), p. 283. (Note: "*Diccionario Porrua* (1991) puts the decline in absolute numbers at 300,000 (15,000,000 to 14,700,000) between 1910 and 1920. Given the high birth rate during that period, the loss of population because of war, disease, hunger, and emigration was in the millions, with at least 1,000,000 killed in war.")
8. "Refugees from Tampico Tell Story," *Los Angeles Evening News*, May 1, 1914.
9. "Americans Stand to Fight," *Los Angeles Times*, March 30, 1915.
10. "Edna Stetson," Obituaries, *Los Angeles Times*, October 27, 1915.

Background Sources

Brenner, Anita, *The Wind That Swept Mexico* (Austin, TX: University of Texas Press, 1971).

Davis, Margaret Leslie, *Dark Side of Fortune, Triumph, and Scandal in the Life of Oil Tycoon Edward Doheny* (Berkeley, CA: University of California Press, 1998).

Eisenhower, John S. D., *Intervention! The United States and the Mexican Revolution, 1913–1917* (New York: W. W Norton & Co., 1993).

Gilly, Adolfo, *The Mexican Revolution* (New York: The New Press, 2005).

Gonzales, Michael J., *The Mexican Revolution 1910–1940* (Albuquerque, NM: University of New Mexico Press, 2002).

Miller, Robert Ryal, *Mexico: A History* (Norman, OK: University of Oklahoma Press, 1985), pp. 283–323.

Shorris, Earl, *The Life and Times of Mexico* (New York: W. W. Norton & Co., 2004), pp. 215–74.

Chapter 13

1. Davis, *Dark Side of Fortune*, pp. 105–9.

2. Eisenhower, *Intervention!*, p. 117.

3. Davis, *Dark Side of Fortune*, p. 116.

4. "Our Best Asset-Men," *MexPet Record* 1, no. 4 (May 1916): p. 3.

5. Davis, *Dark Side of Fortune*, p. 115.

Background Sources

Gilly, *The Mexican Revolution*.

Gonzales, *The Mexican Revolution 1910–1940*.

MexPet Record 1, no.1, May 1916.

Frank McLynn, *Villa and Zapata* (New York: Carroll & Graf Publishers, 2000).

Welsome, Eileen, *The General and the Jaguar* (Lincoln, NB: University of Nebraska Press, 2006).

Bowman, Lynn, *Los Angeles: Epic of a City* (Berkeley: CA: Howell-North Books, 1974).

Davis, *Dark Side of Fortune*.

Eisenhower, *Intervention!*.

Gonzales, *The Mexican Revolution*.

Chapter 14

1. Dirks, Tim, *Filmsite*, AMC Networks, Inc., May 1996.
2. "Charges Wife Trapped Men," *Los Angeles Times*, March 18, 1923.

Chapter 15

1. "Tampico Gets Improvements," *Los Angeles Times*, August 10, 1919.
2. Brown, Jonathon C., *Oil and Revolution In Mexico* (Berkeley, CA: University of California Press, 1993), p. 311.
3. "Millions Spent on Oil Fields," *Los Angeles Times*, March 21, 1921.

Background Sources

Lee, Supply, "Most American Foreign City," *Los Angeles Times*, 1920.
"Doheny Reports Mexican Oil Boom," *New York Times*, November 25, 1920.

Chapter 16

1. Brown, *Oil and Revolution in Mexico*, pp. 373–74.
2. "Cynthia Teal Now Known as Marie Paddleford, Concert Star," *Indianapolis Star*, March 12, 1922.
3. Lin, James, *The Lincoln Highway*, http://lincolnhighway.jameslin.name/history/part3.html.
4. Davis, *Dark Side of Fortune*, p. xiii.
5. Brown, *Oil and Revolution in Mexico*.

Chapter 17

1. "Cynthia Teal, Now Known as Marie Paddleford, Concert Star," *Indianapolis Star*, March 12, 1922.
2. "Amazing Confessions of Fascinating Cynthia Teal Trained to Swindle Millionaire Society," *Indianapolis Star*, November 19, 1922.
3. "Reveals Past Life of Wife," *Los Angeles Times*, January 14, 1922.
4. "Naughton-Paddleford," *New York Times*, November 16, 1921.
5. "Oil Man, Wife Are Separated," *Los Angeles Times*, January 11, 1922.
6. Ibid.

Chapter 18

1. *Paddleford vs. Paddleford Divorce*, D17520, Superior Court Los Angeles County, July 25, 1923.

2. Ibid.
3. Ibid.
4. Ibid.
5. Ibid.
6. "To Play Mrs. Stillman," *Los Angeles Times*, February 1, 1923.

Chapter 19
1. "Six Days to London," banner ad, *New York Times*, March 27, 1922.
2. "SS *Paris*," *Wikipedia*, https://en.wikipedia.org/wiki/ss_paris_(1916).
3. Samuels, Charles, "Queen of Gold Diggers," *True* magazine, November 1940.
4. "California Oil Man's Wife Held in Vienna on Charges of Swindling Business Men," *San Francisco Chronicle*, June 11, 1922.
5. "Paddleford Repudiates Jailed Wife," *Los Angeles Times*, June 11, 1922.
6. Ibid.
7. "Is Facing Trial as Swindler," *Los Angeles Times*, June 19, 1922.
8. "Paddleford Children Stranded in Vienna," *Los Angeles Times*, June 29, 1922.
9. Ibid.
10. "Suit Reveals Past of Wife," *Los Angeles Times*, September 27, 1922.
11. "Paddleford Case Dropped by Swiss," *Minneapolis Tribune*, December 12, 1922.
12. "The Jail Hotel," *Lucerne Hotel Group*.
13. "Los Angeles Woman Free," *Los Angeles Times*, December 13, 1922.

Background Sources
"Angeleno's Wife Held in Vienna," *Los Angeles Times*, June 10, 1922.
"Former St. Paul Woman Is Arrested in Vienna for Duping Wealthy Europeans," *Minneapolis Tribune*, June 10, 1922.
"Local Woman Brings Worry to Officers," *Los Angeles Times*, June 21, 1922.
"Noted Beauty Ill in Prison, Asks for Aid," *San Francisco Chronicle*, July 6, 1922.
"Husband Deserts Mrs. Paddleford," *Evening World*, August 31, 1922.
"Will Let Wife Stay in Prison," *Los Angeles Times*, August 31, 1922.
"California Woman Freed by Swiss Jury," *Oakland Tribune*, December 12, 1922.

Chapter 20
1. "To Play Mrs. Stillman," p. I11.
2. Ibid.
3. Ibid.
4. Ibid.
5. "Creditors Raid Elegant Home," *Los Angeles Times*, March 11, 1923.
6. "Morton, Jelly Roll (Ferdinand Joseph Lamothe)," *Encyclopedia of Jazz Musicians*, http://www.jazz.com/encyclopedia/morton-jelly-roll-ferdinand-joseph-lamothe.
7. "The tracks were treating me very dirty these days . . . ," Library of Congress recording, in Lomax, Alan, *Recorded Life of Jelly Roll Morton*, p. 74.
8. Tenenholtz, David, "Jelly Roll Morton," *Encyclopedia of Jazz Musicians*, http://www.jazz.com/encyclopedia/morton-jelly-roll-ferdinand-joseph-lamothe.
9. Hanley, Peter, "Jelly Roll Morton: An Essay in Genealogy," http://www.doctorjazz.co.uk/genealogy.html#genjelly.

Background Sources
"Jelly Roll Morton," http://www.jazz.com/encyclopedia/morton-jelly-roll-ferdinand-joseph-lamothe.
"Jelly Roll Morton," *Wikipedia*, https://en.wikipedia.org/wiki/Jelly_Roll_Morton.
"Jelly Roll Morton is one of the most colourful of characters in jazz . . . ," http://www.jazzscript.co.uk/life/mortonlife.htm.

Chapter 21
1. "Wife's Lawyer in Paddleford Case Drops Out," *Los Angeles Times*, March 14, 1923.
2. "Mrs. Paddleford Is Jailed," *Los Angeles Times*, March 23, 1923.
3. Ibid.
4. "Mrs. Paddleford Sought," *Associated Press*, May 19, 1923.
5. "Paddleford Writ Issued," *Los Angeles Times*, June 21, 1923.
6. "Paddleford Given Decree," *Los Angeles Times*, June 20, 1923.
7. "Charges Wife Trapped Men," *Los Angeles Times*, March 18, 1923.
8. "Divorce Plaintiff Tables Turned," *Los Angeles Times*, May 4, 1923.

9. "Paddleford Given Decree," *Los Angeles Times*, June 20, 1923.
10. Ibid.
11. Ibid.
12. Ibid.

Background Sources
"Paddleford Divorce Hearing Postponed," *Oakland Tribune*, January 6, 1923.
"Continue Paddleford Suit," *Los Angeles Times*, January 6, 1923.
"Hectic Woman Faces Charge of Stealing Gowns," *Modesto Evening News*, March 16, 1923.
"Bill Flood Produced in Fraud Case," *Los Angeles Times*, March 28, 1923.
"Paddleford Writ Issued," *Los Angeles Times*, June 21, 1923.
"Suit Reveals Past of Wife," *Los Angeles Times*, September 27, 1922.
"International Love Pirate Being Sought by L.A. Police," *Modesto Evening News*, May 19, 1923.
"Mrs. Paddleford Sought," *Associated Press*, May 19, 1923.

Chapter 22

1. "Divorcee Is in Trouble Once More," *Los Angeles Times*, April 2, 1924.
2. "Ex-Wife of Paddleford Again Taken," *Los Angeles Times*, November 21, 1924.
3. Ibid.
4. Ibid.
5. "Long Missing Girl, Thought Found, Again Disappears," *Washington Post*, April 6, 1924.
6. "List of United States Citizens for the Immigration Authorities," New York, Passenger Lists, 1820–1957, Cynthia Teal, Ship *Caledonia*, Ancestry.
7. "Mrs. Paddleford Arrested Abroad," *New York Times*, May 29, 1926.
8. "Los Angeles Club Woman Put in Jail," *Los Angeles Times*, May 29, 1926.
9. Ibid.
10. "Mrs. Paddleford Arrested Abroad," *New York Times*, May 29, 1926.
11. "Lost Passports Story," *London Times*, July 17, 1926.
12. "List of United States Citizens for the Immigration Authorities," New York, Passenger Lists, 1820–1957, Genevieve Paddleford, Ship *Letitia*, Ancestry.
13. "Mrs. Paddleford Tried," *Los Angeles Times*, November 24, 1927.

Chapter 23

1. "Prison Is New Home of Woman Who Had Palace on the Nile," *Washington Post*, November 29, 1927.
2. "Defense Aide in Paddleford Case Passes," *Los Angeles Times*, November 24, 1927.
3. "Man Dies in Court Battle," *Oakland Tribune*, November 24, 1927.
4. "Mrs. Paddleford Goes to Prison in Ambulance," *Minneapolis Tribune*, November 29, 1927.
5. "Paddleford Name Given for Number," *Los Angeles Times*, November 30, 1927.
6. "Fifth Husband Awaits Convict at End of Term," *Oakland Tribune*, January 26, 1928.
7. "Cupid Can't Even Get in San Quentin," *Los Angeles Times*, February 24, 1928.
8. "Angeleno Plans Club in Mexico," *Los Angeles Times*, May 27, 1922.
9. Ibid.
10. "Fiancé Wants Convict Freed," *Los Angeles Times*, January 28, 1928.
11. "Why the Swindling Society Mama Is Back in Jail," *Ogden Standard Examiner*, June 16, 1929.
12. "Adventuress Wins Reversal of Conviction," *Los Angeles Times*, May 19, 1928.
13. "F. L. R. Silvey in U.S. City Directories 1821–1989," *Ancestry*.

Background Sources

Winter, Yves, "San Quentin: The Everyday Prison," in *Carceral Notebooks 6* (2010): pp. 53–66.

"Castle Owner in Salinas Jail," *Los Angeles Times*, October 28, 1927.

"Mrs. Paddleford Tried," *New York Times*, November 24, 1927.

"World Adventuress Goes to Penitentiary," *New York Times*, November 29, 1927.

"Adventuress Sent to Prison," *Los Angeles Times*, November 29, 1927.

"Paddleford Appeal Filed," *Los Angeles Times*, December 2, 1927.

"Mrs. Paddleford Seeking Liberty," *Los Angeles Times*, February 7, 1928.

Chapter 24

1. "Why the Swindling Society Mama Is Back in Jail," *Ogden Standard Examiner*, June 16, 1929.
2. "The People of the State of California vs. Eleanor M. Paddleford," in Statement of the Defendant and Proceedings Upon Pronouncement of Judgement, Superior Court of the County of Santa Barbara, State of California, April 9, 1929.
3. "Why the Swindling Society Mama Is Back in Jail," *Ogden Standard Examiner*, June 16, 1929.
4. Ibid.
5. Ibid.
6. "Mrs. Paddleford Guilty," *Los Angeles Times,* April 7, 1929.
7. Ibid.

Background Sources

"Former Beauty to Be Set Free at San Quentin," *Oakland Tribune*, October 16, 1930.

Chapter 25

1. "Why the Swindling Society Mama Is Back in Jail," *Ogden Standard Examiner*, June 16, 1929.
2. "Eleanor McKinney Paddleford, Alias Grace Potter," California State Prison. Reg. No. 4688, California State Archives, Sacramento, CA.
3. Ibid.
4. "Former Beauty to Be Set Free at San Quentin," *Oakland Tribune*, October 16, 1930.
5. "Hunt Made for Female Ex-Convict," *Los Angeles Times*, February 10, 1931.
6. "Eleanor McKinney Paddleford, Alias Grace Potter," California State Prison. Reg. No. 4688, California State Archives, Sacramento, CA.

Background Sources

"Erratic Woman in Hard Luck," *Los Angeles Times*, February 7, 1930.
"Law Seeks Woman at Prison Door," *Los Angeles Times*, October 15, 1930.
"Woman to Win Parole Chance," *Los Angeles Times*, November 17, 1930.
"Mrs. Paddleford Nearer Freedom," *Los Angeles Times*, October 16, 1930.

Chapter 26

1. "Dear Otto," letter to the Honorable Otto G. Foelker from Lewis L. Fawcett, Supreme Court of the State of New York, case file: Eleanor McKinney Paddleford, SQ no. 46888, California State Archives, Sacramento, California, March 6, 1932.
2. "John C. Fawcett," New York Passenger Lists, 1820–1957, *Ancestry.*
3. "History: Graycliff," www.graycliff.com/graycliff/history.
4. "John C. Fawcett Married to Mrs. Heath Wilson Roberts at Nassau in Bahamas," *Brooklyn Daily Eagle*, January 30, 1931.
5. "John C. Fawcett in the New York Passenger Lists," *Vulcania*, New York, NY, 1931, *Ancestry.*
6. Samuels, "Queen of the Gold Diggers."
7. "Mr. and Mrs. John C. Fawcett Entertain at Small Dinner," *Brooklyn Daily Eagle*, February 19, 1931.
8. "Much Arrested Wife Divorced," *Los Angeles Times*, Dec. 20, 1931.
9. "J. C. Fawcett Gets Secret Annulment," *New York Times*, December 20, 1931.
10. Fawcett, "Dear Otto" letter.
11. "American Woman Held in Carlsbad for Fraud," *New York Times*, May 23, 1931.
12. Warden, San Quentin Penitentiary, W. S. Whitman, William J. Burns International Detective Agency, Inc., New York, NY, November 10, 1932.
13. "Paddleford Case Brings New Order," *Los Angeles Times*, December 20, 1931.
14. "Samuels, "Queen of the Gold Diggers."
15. "Holidays to Be Spent in Pasadena," *Los Angeles Times*, December 20, 1931.
16. "Paddleford Given Decree," *Los Angeles Times*, July 20, 1923.
17. Fawcett, "Dear Otto" letter.
18. Ibid.

Background Sources

"Earl Warren," *Wikipedia*, http://en.wikipedia.org/wiki/Earl_Warren.
"John C. Fawcett," *New York Times*, March 1, 1943.

Chapter 27

1. Heffern, "The Jade of Diamonds."
2. "Mrs. Fawcett Says She Speaks Russian, French, Italian, German, and English," *Seattle Times*, 1936.
3. Fawcett, "Dear Otto" letter.
4. Ibid.
5. "Dear Mr. Whyte," J. E. Lewis, Deputy Parole Officer, refer file no. 46888, State Board of Prison Directors.
6. "Summary Report of Investigation," Tom Pendergast, State Parole Officer, State Board of Prison Directors, San Francisco, California, Prisoner 46888, Paddleford, November 9, 1932.
7. Lewis "Dear Mr. Whyte," letter.
8. Letter to Warden, San Quentin Penitentiary, W. S. Whitman, William Burns International Detective Agency, #16592, October 17, 1933.

Chapter 28

1. Henckaerts, Jean-Marie, *Mass Expulsion in Modern International Law and Practice* (New York: Springer, 1995), p. 5.
   Forsythe and Lawson, *Encyclopedia of Human Rights* (Oxford, UK: Oxford University Press, 1996), pp. 53–54.
2. "The FBI and the American Gangster 1924–1938," in *The FBI: A Centennial History, 1908-2008* (Washington, DC: Federal Bureau of Investigation, 2008).
3. "Paddleford Woman to Be Trailed," *Los Angeles Times*, November 6, 1932.
4. "French Hold Genevieve Paddleford, Adventuress," *Oakland Tribune*, May 3, 1934.

Background Sources

Daley, Suzanne, "Expose of Brutal Prison Jolts France's Self-Image," *New York Times*, January 28, 2000.

"Chambéry," *Wikipedia*, https://en.wikipedia.org/wiki/Chamb%C3%A9ry.

"Neuchâtel, Switzerland," *Wikipedia*, https://en.wikipedia.org/wiki/Neuch%C3%A2t.

"Seek Mrs. Paddleford in Los Angeles Fraud," *New York Times*, November 7, 1932.

"Mrs. Paddleford to Appeal Conviction," *Santa Ana Register*, April 30, 1934.

"Mrs. Paddleford to Fight on Sentence," *San Bernardino County Sun*, May 4, 1934.

"Mrs. Paddleford Put in Jail Again," *Oakland Tribune*, June 14, 1935.

"Mrs. Paddleford in Trouble in France," *San Mateo Times*, June 19, 1935.

"American Jailed on Bad Check Charges," *Santa Ana Register*, June 20, 1935.

"Former Marion Fawcett Passes Worthless Checks," *News-Herald*, June 20, 1935.

"France Jails Visitor," *Salt Lake Tribune*, June 21, 1935.

Chapter 29

1. Heffern, "The Jade of Diamonds."

Background Sources

We Had Everything but Money (Greendale, WI: Reminisce Books, 1992).

"Ex–St. Paul Adventuress Dies in Western Prison," *St. Paul Tribune*, September 22, 1941.

Thompson, Mrs. J. R., Aliases: Fawcett, Helen; Williams, Ella; Potter, Grace, Washington State Penitentiary Commitment Record, #16701, October 2, 1936.

"Gentlemen," letter from California Parole Officer Ed Whyte to W. S. Whitman, William J. Burns International Detective Agency, Inc., San Francisco, CA, June 22, 1936.

"Dear Sir," E. W. Yoris, Chief of Detectives, City of Seattle, WA, California State Parole Office, July 17, 1936.

Forest Williams, "Grim Reaper Halts Fantastic Career," *Seattle Post*, October 12, 1941.

Chapter 30

1. "Felon, on Trial as Killer, Suicide," *Los Angeles Times*, December 12, 1938.

2. "Posse Fails in Hunt for Man's Body," *Los Angeles Times*, November 28, 1929.

3. "Gas Killer Suspect Caught in Oakland," *Berkeley Daily Gazette*, September 14, 1928.

4. "Mother Tells of Murders," *Los Angeles Times*, May 6, 1938.

5. Ibid.

6. "Convicts Threaten Confession Getter," *News-Review*, August 19, 1938.

7. Forest Williams, "Grim Reaper Halts Fantastic Career," *Seattle Post*, October 12, 1941.

8. Ibid.

9. "Convicts Threaten Confession Getter," *News-Review*, August 19, 1938.

10. "Mother and Son Blamed in Death," *San Bernardino County Sun*, May 13, 1938.

11. "Lifer Admits Bassett Death," *Los Angeles Times*, May 8, 1938.

12. "Mother and Son Go on Trial for Slaying," *Reno Evening Gazette*, November 28, 1938.

13. "Confession of Mrs. Smith Read to Jury," *Daily Capital Journal*, December 8, 1938.

14. "Felon, on Trial as Killer, Suicide," *Los Angeles Times*, December 12, 1938.

15. "Mother Names Son in Four Murders—Shocking Tale of Slaying of Bassett," *Daily Mail*, May 5, 1938.

16. John Cahill, "The Old Hag's 'Perfect Crime' That Took Ten Years to Solve," *Port Arthur News*, January 22, 1939.

17. "Aged Confessed Murderess Gets Prison Release," *News-Review*, March 13, 1953.

Chapter 31

1. "Memo to the Governor," Board of Prison Terms and Paroles, John W. Schaefer, Secretary, re: Helen Millicent Fawcett, #16701, November 22, 1940.

2. "Dear Madam," letter from P. E. Maloney, Acting Superintendent, Washington State Penitentiary, to Florence McKinney Elsner, November 24, 1941.

Background Sources

"Aged Confessed Murderess Gets Prison Release," *News Review*, March 13, 1953.

Helen Fawcett Thompson, Vital Statistics, File 265, Register No. 374, Census No. 16701. Washington State Prison, Walla Walla, Washington, September 24, 1970.

Samuels, "Queen of the Gold Diggers."

"Mrs. Paddleford, Famed for Adventures, Dies," *Los Angeles Times,* September 23, 1941.

BOOK TWO
Chapter 1
Cynthia Teal, *The Amazing Confessions of Cynthia Teal, Indianapolis Star,* October 1, 1922.

Chapter 2
Ibid., October 15, 1922.

Chapter 3
Ibid., October 22, 1922.

Chapter 4
Ibid.

Chapter 5
Ibid., October 29, 1922.

Chapter 6
Ibid., November 19, 1922.

Chapter 7
Ibid., November 26, 1922.
Chapter 8
Ibid., December 3, 1922.

Chapter 9
Ibid., December 10, 1922.

Chapter 10
Ibid., December 17, 1922.

Chapter 11
Ibid., December 24, 1922.

Chapter 12
Ibid., December 31, 1922.

Photo Credits

Front cover

Genevieve Paddleford, 1927, Corbis Photo Collection, History & Genealogy Dept., Los Angeles Public Library.

Back cover

Sunshine Special near Forney, Texas, 1929, University of North Texas Libraries, the Portal to Texas History, texashistory.unt.edu, courtesy Museum of the American Railroad.

Chapter 1

Ida Gilman McKinnie, 1882, author's collection.

Chapter 2

Chinook, Montana street, 1899, in Chinook Centennial 89ers, *Chinook: The First 100 Years* (Great Falls, Montana: VisYuill Enterprises, 1989), courtesy Blaine County Museum.

O'Hanlon Store, Morris photo, *Chinook: The First 100 Years*, courtesy University of Montana.

Gilman McKinnie, 1904, Palm family collection.

Florence McKinnie, 1904, author's collection

Chapter 4

Ben Teal, circa 1891, Ben Teal file, Billy Rose Theater Collection, New York Public Library for the Performing Arts, Lincoln Center.

Ben Teal, circa 1900, Ben Teal file.

Chapter 5

Lyndhurst Castle, Tarrytown, NY, copyright 2017 National Trust for Historic Preservation.

Lower East Side, Edwards Photos, Flickr, in ablac, "New York in Black and White," http://wirednewyork.com.

Chapter 7

The Ansonia, New York, 1905, Detroit Publishing Company Collection, Library of Congress Prints & Photographs, Division LC-D4-17421, http:// commons.wikimedia.org.

Chapter 8

Ben Teal, 1917, Ben Teal file.

Chapter 9

Sunshine Special near Forney, Texas.

Chapter 10

Hotel Galvez, 1911, H. H. Morris, Galveston, Texas.

Chapter 11

Cynthia Marie Teal, 1913, *Indianapolis Star*, October 1, 1922.

Chapter 12

George Edgar Paddleford, 1904, Marilyn Paddleford private family collection.

Chapter 14

La Santa Fe Station, Los Angeles, http://framework.latimes.com/2015/02 /04/santa-fe-railroads-la-grande-station/#/0.

Chapter 15

1. Tampico Cathedral, https://goo.gl/images/YdbPwK.

Chapter 16

Plaza Hotel, before 1923, author unknown, New York Public Library Digital Gallery, https://commons.wikimedia.org/wiki/File:Plaza_Hotel_NYC.jpg.

Chapter 19

SS *Paris* leaving New York, http://cruiselinehistory.com/wp-content/uploads/2008/06/cce00001.jpg.

Chapter 20

Ferdinand "Jelly Roll" Morton, Red Hot Jazz Archive, http://www.redhotjazz.com/ferdmorton.jpg.

Chapter 21

Ben "Jack" Teal, *New York Times*, July 20, 1923.

Chapter 23

Genevieve Teal, 1907, Corbis Photo Collection, History & Genealogy Dept., Los Angeles Public Library

Chapter 26

George S. Paddleford and Jack Teal, Huasteca Forest, 1927, Marilyn Paddleford home file.

Acknowledgments

I would like to acknowledge my wife, Joyce, who gave me the encouragement and latitude to research and write this story. I am especially grateful to the professional contacts I made at Warner Coaching, Inc.—in particular my very skillful editor, Annie Tucker, whose enthusiasm for and attention to the development of this story kept it from becoming a bulky family document left to gather dust.

Along the way, I have met many helpful professional researchers and librarians. I met the dedicated volunteers who work at the Billy Rose Theater Division of the New York Public Library for the Performing Arts, at 40 Lincoln Center Plaza. I visited the James J. Hill Center in downtown St. Paul, Minnesota. Its historic architecture is stunning, and the librarian who greeted me was exceptionally hospitable. Equally helpful were the reference librarians at the Oregon Historical Society Library in downtown Portland, and Christina Rice, the reference librarian at the Los Angeles Public Library. The attendant at the Central Civil Operations Administration of the Los Angeles Superior Court at the Stanley Mosk Courthouse was very courteous and helpful, as was the archivist at the California State Archives, Sacramento, California. The Internet has been an indispensable resource. I wish to acknowledge the librarians at Lafayette College for helping me to access historical newspapers on Proquest. com, and Ancestry.com has been an integral anchor as well.

Of particular note is the generosity of Marilyn Paddleford, who willingly shared some of her family photos and documents. I want to acknowledge my sister-in-law, Miriam, who has long shared an interest in this story. Finally, I would be remiss not to mention the boys around the coffee table at the Chinook Motor Inn for their prodding and patience.

About the Author

V. E. Palm is a retired New Jersey public school teacher. He taught fourth, fifth, and sixth grades, and completed his career as an adjunct professor at Felician University. He resides with his wife, Joyce, near Easton, Pennsylvania, and spends summers in Montana.

84131384R00207

Made in the USA
San Bernardino, CA
05 August 2018